Houghton Mifflin
Reading

Teacher's Edition
Grade 1

Let's Be Friends

Back to School

Theme 1 **All Together Now**

Theme 2 **Surprise!**

▶ **Theme 3** **Let's Look Around!**

Theme 4 **Family and Friends**

Theme 5 **Home Sweet Home**
Focus on **Poetry**

Theme 6 **Animal Adventures**

Theme 7 **We Can Work It Out**
Focus on **Plays**

Theme 8 **Our Earth**

Theme 9 **Special Friends**
Focus on **Folktales**

Theme 10 **We Can Do It!**

Senior Authors J. David Cooper, John J. Pikulski

Authors David J. Chard, Gilbert G. Garcia, Claude N. Goldenberg,
Phyllis C. Hunter, Marjorie Y. Lipson, Shane Templeton,
Sheila W. Valencia, MaryEllen Vogt

Consultants Linda H. Butler, Linnea C. Ehri, Carla B. Ford

HOUGHTON MIFFLIN   BOSTON

Let's Look Around!

OBJECTIVES

Phonemic Awareness blending and segmenting phonemes

Phonics double final consonants; blending more short *a* words; plurals with -*s;* verb endings -*s, -ed, -ing;* blending more short *i* words; possessives with *'s;* clusters with *r;* contractions with *'s*

Reading Strategies phonics/decoding; evaluate; predict/infer; question

Comprehension topic, main idea, details/summarizing; making predictions; categorize and classify

High-Frequency Words recognize high-frequency words

Fluency build reading fluency

Grammar what is a sentence; naming part of a sentence; action part of a sentence

Writing a class description; writing about favorite seasons; a persuasive letter; writing about favorite foods; a class story; writing about trips; writing a story

Spelling short *a* sound; short *i* sound; clusters with *r*

Vocabulary seasons of the year; months of the year; possessives; size words; color words; words that show position

Listening/Speaking/Viewing gathering information; fact or opinion; nonverbal cues; retelling a story; main idea and details; listening to gather information

Information and Study Skills using the library; alphabetical order

Let's Look Around !

CONTENTS

Leveled Bibliography **T6**
Theme Skills Overview **T8**
Management Routines **T10**
Instructional Routines **T11**
Cross-Curricular Activities **T12**
Planning for Assessment **T14**
Launching the Theme **T16**
Teacher Read Aloud: *Belling the Cat* **T18**

Week 1

Nonfiction

Lesson Overview **T20**
Daily Lesson Plans **T24**
Managing Flexible Groups **T26**
Ready-Made Small Group Activities **T28**
Daily Routines. See Daily Lesson Plans.

Sharing the Big Book: *Counting on the Woods*
  by George Ella Lyon **T32**
Phonics Library: *Cabs, Cabs, Cabs* by Wayne Mazzola **T39**
Get Set Story: **Animals in the Cold** by Sam Wallis **T48**

Main Story: **Seasons** by Ashley Wolff **T56**
Language Arts Link: **Ha! Ha! Ha!** **T74**
Phonics Library: *Pam Can Pack* by Ruth Kwan **T83**

Skill Lessons. See Daily Lesson Plans.
Leveled Readers Lessons, Leveled Practice **T88**

Vocabulary Reader

Nonfiction

Nonfiction

Realistic Fiction

Below Level *On Level* *Above Level* *Language Support*

Leveled Readers

T3

Week 2

Fiction

Lesson Overview **T92**
Daily Lesson Plans **T96**
Managing Flexible Groups **T98**
Ready-Made Small Group Activities **T100**
Daily Routines. See Daily Lesson Plans.

Sharing the Big Book: *: Pearl's First Prize Plant*
   by A. Delaney **T104**
Phonics Library: *Lots of Picking* by Kelly Teele **T111**
Get Set Story: **Ham and Eggs** by Kathryn Mitter **T120**
Main Story: Miss Jill's Ice Cream Shop
   by Nancy Shaw **T128**
Science Link: **Making Ice Cream** **T146**
Phonics Library: *Tim's Cat* by Virginia Houston **T155**

Skill Lessons. See Daily Lesson Plans.
Leveled Readers Lessons, Leveled Practice **T160**

Nonfiction

Fantasy

Nonfiction

Below Level

On Level

Above Level

Tim's Pig Eats

Language Support

Leveled Readers

Week 3

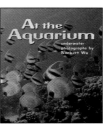

Fantasy

Lesson Overview **T164**
Daily Lesson Plans **T168**
Managing Flexible Groups **T170**
Ready-Made Small Group Activities **T172**
Daily Routines. See Daily Lesson Plans.

Sharing the Big Book: *Hilda Hen's Scary Night*
   by Mary Wormell **T176**
Phonics Library: *Let's Trim the Track!* by Rafael Lopez **T183**
Get Set Story: **The Trip** by Lynne Chapman **T192**

Main Story: At the Aquarium

Underwater Photographs by Norbert Wu **T200**
Drama Link: **Why Sun and Moon Live in the Sky** **T218**
Phonics Library: *Fran Pig's Brick Hut* by Mark Dempsey **T227**

Skill Lessons. See Daily Lesson Plans.
Leveled Readers Lessons, Leveled Practice **T232**

Nonfiction

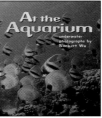

Nonfiction

Play

Below Level

On Level

Above Level

Language Support

Leveled Readers

Leveled Theme Paperbacks

Resources **R1**
   Lesson Plans for Leveled Theme Paperbacks • Skill
   Reteaching Lessons • Challenge/Extension Activities
   • Information and Study Skills Lesson • Word Wall Cards
   • Activity Masters • Music • Word Lists • Technology
   Resources • Pronunciation Guide

Acknowledgments **G1**
Index **I1**

Leveled Bibliography

BOOKS FOR INDEPENDENT READING AND FLUENCY BUILDING

 To build vocabulary and fluency, choose books from this list for children to read outside of class. Suggest that they read for at least twenty minutes a day, either independently or with an adult who provides modeling and guidance.

Key

 Science

 Social Studies

 Multicultural

 Music

 Math

 Classic

 Art

 Career

Classroom Bookshelf

WELL BELOW LEVEL

Sunshine, Moonshine
by Jennifer Armstrong
Random 2003 (32p) paper
The sun and moon shine down on a boy as he spends a day by the sea.

City Dog*
by Karla Kuskin
Clarion 1994 (32p)
A city dog explores the countryside for the first time.

 Swan Harbor: A Nature Counting Book
by Laura Rankin
Dial 2003 (32p)
From one robin to twenty swans, all kinds of animals, in every season, can be found around a coastal town.

 City Signs
by Zoran Milich
Kids Can 2002 (32p)
City photos reveal environmental print everywhere, including on signs and in parks.

Good Morning, Good Night
by Michael Grejniec
North-South 1997 (32p)
also paper
A boy and girl act out a series of opposites. **Available in Spanish as** **Bueños días, bueños noches.**

BELOW LEVEL

The Best Fall of All
by Laura Godwin
McElderry 2002 (32p)
Happy the dog and Honey the cat enjoy playing outside on a fall day.

Look Down Low
by Dana Meachen Rau
Compass Point 2002 (24p)
A boy looks at lots of interesting things on the ground with his magnifying glass.

 Rosie's Walk
by Pat Hutchins
Simon 1968 (32p) also paper
Out for a walk, Rosie the hen unwittingly leads the fox following her into one disaster after another.

In the Tall, Tall Grass
by Denise Fleming
Holt 1991 (32p)
A caterpillar sees all kinds of creatures as it crawls through the tall grass.

ON LEVEL

 All Kinds of Kids
by C. M. Gardeski
Children's Press 2002 (32p)
also paper
Kids like to do many different things, but they all share wonderful smiles.

Raccoon Tune
by Nancy Shaw
Holt 2003 (32p)
A family of raccoons makes a ruckus in the neighborhood as they search for supper.

City Cats, Country Cats
by Barbara Shook Hazen
Random 2003 (32p)
Rhyming text tells about things city and country cats like to do.

 A Tree for Me
by Nancy Van Laan
Knopf 2000 (32p) also paper
A child climbs five trees and finds them occupied by animals from one owl to five spiders.

ABOVE LEVEL

 Lots and Lots of Zebra Stripes
by Stephen R. Swinburne
Boyds Mills 1998 (32p)
Dazzling photos reveal the many patterns found in nature.

Everybody Works
by Shelley Rotner and Ken Kreisler
Millbrook 2003 (32p)
Photos and brief text describe some of the many ways in which people accomplish their work.

No One Saw
by Bob Raczka
Millbrook 2002 (32p)
Rhyming text and paintings by modern artists highlight how artists see the world in their own way.

Minerva Louise and the Red Truck
by Janet Morgan Stoeke
Dutton 2003 (32p)

Daffy hen Minerva Louise sees all kinds of interesting things when she unexpectedly goes for a ride in a farm truck.

Parts
by Shelley Rotner
Walker 2001 (32p)
Rhyming text and close-up photos provide clues to identify larger, everyday objects.

---

*Included in Classroom Bookshelf, Level 1

Armadillo's Orange
by Jim Arnosky
Putnam 2003 (32p)
Lost in an orange grove, Armadillo relies on his neighbors to help him get home.

 A Year for Kiko∗
by Ferida Wolff
Houghton 1997 (32p)
From catching snowflakes in January to chasing fireflies in July, Kiko enjoys the seasons.

BOOKS FOR TEACHER READ ALOUD

Possum and the Peeper
by Anne Hunter
Houghton 1998 (32p)
Possum sets out to discover who's making the peeping noise that wakes him from his winter nap.

 Red Is a Dragon
By Roseanne Thong
Chronicle 2001 (32p)
A girl describes all of the colors she sees around her.

Whales Passing
By Eve Bunting
Scholastic 2003 (32p)

A boy and his father watch a pod of whales as they surface and breach.

An Ant's Day Off
By Bonny Becker
Simon 2003 (32p)
An ant takes a break from his busy schedule to see what's going on in the big, wide world.

Caps for Sale
by Esphyr Slobodkina
Harper 1947 (48p)
A band of mischief-making monkeys steals a napping peddler's colorful caps. **Available in Spanish as Se venden gorras.**

A Tree Is Nice
by Janice May Udry
Harper 1956 (32p) also paper
Poetic text reveals the reasons why trees are so nice. **Available in Spanish as Un árbol es hermoso.**

Black All Around
By Patricia Hubbell
Lee and Low 2003 (32p)
A girl celebrates things around her that are black, from shoes and licorice to dogs and the night sky.

Technology

Computer Software Resources

- **Curious George® Learns Phonics**
  Provides interactive phonics practice. Houghton Mifflin Company
- **Curious George® Learns to Spell**
  Provides interactive spelling practice. Houghton Mifflin Company

Video Cassettes

- **In the Tall, Tall Grass** *by Denise Fleming. Spoken Arts*
- **How to Hide a Butterfly and Other Insects** *by Ruth Heller. Weston Woods*
- **Owl Moon** *by Jane Yolen. Weston Woods*
- **Caps for Sale** *by Esphyr Slobodkina. Weston Woods*
- **Frog, Where Are You?** *by Mercer Mayer. Weston Woods.*

Audio

- **Henry and Mudge in the Green Time** *by Cynthia Rylant. Live Oak*
- **Hide-and-Seek** *by Alvin Tresselt. Spoken Arts*
- **Henny Penny** *by Paul Galdone. Spoken Arts*
- **A Tree Is Nice** *by Janice May Udry. Weston Woods.*

Technology Resources addresses are on page R65.

Education Place®

www.eduplace.com *Log on to Education Place® for more activities relating to* Let's Look Around!, *including vocabulary support—*
  e • **Glossary**
  e • **WordGame**

Book Adventure®

www.bookadventure.org *This Internet reading incentive program provides thousands of titles for children to read.*

Accelerated Reader® Universal CD-ROM

This popular CD-ROM provides practice quizzes for Anthology selections and for many popular children's books.

Theme Skills Overview

	Week 1
	Seasons Nonfiction pp. T20–T91 

Pacing
Approximately 3 weeks

Combination Classrooms

See the **Combination Classroom Planning Guide** for lesson planning and management support.

Learning to Read **Phonemic Awareness** **Phonics**	⏱ **Blending and Segmenting Phonemes** ⏱ **Double Final Consonants** T ⏱ **Blending More Short *a* Words** T ⏱ **Plurals with -*s*** T **Phonics Review: Words with Short *u***
Comprehension	**Guiding Comprehension** ⏱ **Topic, Main Idea, Details/Summarizing** T ⏱ **Evaluate**
Fluency	⏱ **Decodable Text** *Cabs, Cabs, Cabs; Fall Naps; Pam Can Park* **Language Arts Link** How to Read Jokes and Lyrics
Vocabulary Readers **Leveled Readers** • Fluency Practice • Independent Reading	**Vocabulary Reader** ······························ **Leveled Readers** *A Summer Day* *Fun in the Snow* *Fall Leaves* *Summer* Lessons and Leveled Practice
Word Work **Vocabulary** **High-Frequency Words** **Spelling**	⏱ **Seasons of the Year** ⏱ **Months of the Year** ⏱ **High-Frequency Words:** *animal, bird,* T *cold, fall, flower, full, look, of, see* The Short *a* Sound T
Writing and Oral Language **Writing** **Grammar** **Listening/Speaking/Viewing**	✏ **A Class Description** **Writing About Favorite Seasons** **Writing a Story** **What Is a Sentence?** T Gathering Information Responding: Retell the Story Fact or Opinion
Cross-Curricular Activities	Classroom Management Activities

T Skill tested on Integrated Theme Test and/or Weekly or Theme Skills Test

Target Skills

| Phonemic Awareness |
| Phonics |
| Comprehension |
| Vocabulary |
| Fluency |

Nonfiction

Week 2	Week 3
Miss Jill's Ice Cream Shop Fantasy pp. T92–T163 	**At the Aquarium** Nonfiction pp. T164–T235 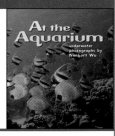
◉ **Blending and Segmenting Phonemes**	◉ **Blending and Segmenting Phonemes**
◉ **Verb Endings -s, -ed, -ing** T	◉ **Clusters with r** T
◉ **Blending More Short i Words** T	◉ **Contractions with 's** T
◉ **Possessives with 's** T	**Phonics Review: Short i; Verbs Ending with -s, -ed, -ing; Possessives with 's**
Phonics Review: Double Final Consonants; Plurals with -s; Final Consonants ck, s as /z/; Short a	**Guiding Comprehension**
Guiding Comprehension	◉ **Categorize and Classify** T
◉ **Making Predictions** T	◉ **Question** T
◉ **Predict/Infer** T	◉ **Decodable Text** Let's Trim the Track!; Brad's Quick Rag Tricks; Fran Pig's Brick Hut
◉ **Decodable Text** Lots of Picking; Bill Bird; Tim's Cat	**Drama Link** How to Read a Play
Social Studies Link How to Read a Social Studies Article	
Vocabulary Reader	**Vocabulary Reader**
Leveled Readers 	**Leveled Readers**
Tim's Pig Mama and Kit Go Away Lazy Fox Tim's Pig Eats	Let's Grab It! Looking for Birds On the Beach Grab It!
Lessons and Leveled Practice	Lessons and Leveled Practice
◉ **Possessives** ◉ **Words That Describe Size**	◉ **Color Words** ◉ **Words That Show Position**
◉ **High-Frequency Words: all, call, eat, every, first, never, paper, shall, why** T	◉ **High-Frequency Words: also, blue, brown, color, funny, green, like, many, some** T
The Short i Sound	Consonant Clusters with r
✎ **A Persuasive Letter** **Writing About Favorite Foods** **Writing a Story**	✎ **A Class Story** **Writing About Trips** **Writing a Story**
Naming Part of a Sentence T	**Action Part of a Sentence** T
Nonverbal Cues Responding: Retell the Story Retelling a Story	Main Idea and Details Responding: Retell the Story To Gather Information
Classroom Management Activities	Classroom Management Activities

Additional Theme Resources

- Lesson Plans for Leveled Theme Paperbacks
- Reteaching Lessons
- Challenge/Extension Activities
- Information and Study Skills Lesson
- Word Wall Cards/Activity Masters
- Music
- Word Lists
- Technology Resources
- Pronunciation Guide

Technology

Education Place®
www.eduplace.com

Log on to Education Place® for more activities relating to *Let's Look Around!*

Lesson Planner CD-ROM
Customize your planning for *Let's Look Around!* with the Lesson Planner CD-ROM.

Management Routines

Assigning Partners

When assigning partners, it is important to think about the nature of the task, as well as children's reading levels, learning styles, and abilities.

- Assign partners of similar ability when children are practicing a skill that is new to both of them. This works particularly well in an activity such as practicing spelling words.

- Assign partners of different abilities when a mentor can be helpful to a struggling learner. This works particularly well in an activity such as buddy reading, where a more proficient reader can help a struggling child to read and understand more difficult texts. It also works well when matching children who share interests. Remember, however, that it is not ideal for students to be repeatedly placed in the role of mentor.

Partners can work on spelling by using the Take-Home Word Lists in *My Handbook* at the back of their **Practice Book**.

- On Day 1 of each week, partners quiz each other on the week's spelling words.

- Children circle the words they need to practice.

- Children take home the word lists and practice spelling the circled words.

Practice Book page 227

Week 3
Comprehension Check *The Surprise Family*

Name _____

Alike and Different

What was so surprising about the hen's family? Write and draw your answer. Sample answer is provided.

The hen had a family of ducklings, not chicks. She had a boy, too. **(6 points)**

(2)

Book Boxes

Book boxes are a good way to organize and store reading books for individual or group use. You can make book boxes by covering old cartons or commercial magazine organizers with adhesive paper. Use the boxes to store familiar stories, books chosen by children, and magazines or other materials children can read on their own for practice.

Jackie

Instructional Routines

Previewing the Text

Previewing a selection builds background (key vocabulary and story concepts) and provides context. Use the illustrations to guide children through the preview.

To conduct a guided preview

- display an Anthology, and provide a focus by directing children's attention to the illustrations,
- encourage discussion that includes key vocabulary,
- ask questions that build background and provide a focus for reading,
- encourage children to make predictions.

Specific ideas for previewing the text can be found at the beginning of each Main Story. (See page T57.)

Extra Support/Intervention

Preview the Selection

pages 22–25 What do animals do in the spring? What happens to plants in the spring?

pages 26–29 What do animals do in the summer? What happens to plants in the summer?

pages 30–33 What do animals do in the fall? What happens to plants in the fall?

pages 34–39 Point to the big animal on page 37 and explain that it is a woodchuck. What do animals do in the winter? What happens to plants in the winter?

Word Sorting/Matching

Materials	Teacher's Resource Blackline Masters 9, 13

Playing a word-matching memory game is a good way for children to practice high-frequency words and phonics skills. Copy and cut out the cards on **Teacher's Resource Blackline Master** 9 and use them to model the procedure.

- Players arrange the cards face-down in rows, then take turns revealing and reading two cards at a time.
- If a player finds two cards that match, the cards are removed and the child is awarded a point; otherwise the cards are put back in place.
- Play continues until all cards are matched.

Use **Teacher's Resource Blackline Master** 13 to create a new set of cards for a game in which children match beginning sounds. Additional word cards are provided on **Teacher's Resource Blackline Masters** 51 (words with clusters with *r*) and 71 (contractions). You can also make word cards for other phonics skills children learn throughout the year.

Cross-Curricular Activities

Independent Activities

Assign these activities at any time during the theme while you work with small groups.

Additional Independent Activities

- Challenge/Extension Activities, Resources, pp. R15, R17, R19, R21, R23, R25, R27, R29, R31, R33, R35, R37, R39, R41

- **Classroom Management Handbook,** pp. 50–73

- **Challenge Handbook,** Activity Masters CH3-1–CH3-12

- Ready-Made Small Group Activities, pp. T28–T29, T100–T101, T172–T173

Math Center

Counting Fish

👥 Groups	🕐 20 minutes
Objective	Draw, count, and compare groups.
Materials	Number cube, **Teacher's Resource Blackline Master 44**

Make copies of **Teacher's Resource Blackline Master 44.**

Tell children the rules of the game.

- Roll the number cube and draw that number of fish.

- Count to verify the total. Write that number.

- Compare the total of your fish with the other totals in the group.

- Place the fish drawings in order from least to most.

- Have the group determine if any numbers are missing.

Science Center

Healthy Foods We Like

👥 Groups	🕐 30 minutes
Objective	Make a healthy foods chart.
Materials	Chart paper, magazines, supermarket flyers, scissors, paste

Write the words *Healthy Foods We Like* in the center of the paper.

- Have children find pictures of healthy foods they like in magazines and supermarket flyers.

- Tell them to cut out the pictures and paste them onto the chart.

- Ask children to label their pictures.

- Display and discuss the poster.

Consider copying and laminating these activities for use in centers.

Art Center

Leaf Rubbings

👤 Singles	🕐 30 minutes
Objective	Make a leaf rubbing collage.
Materials	Newspaper, drawing paper, leaves, crayons

Demonstrate how to make a leaf rubbing.

- Select a leaf and cover it with drawing paper.
- Rub the side of a crayon on the paper over the leaf.
- Continue the process with other leaves to make a collage.
- Display children's leaf rubbing collages.

Social Studies Center

My Favorite Place

👤 Singles	🕐 30 minutes
Objective	Draw and write about a favorite place.
Materials	Drawing paper, crayons, pencils

- As a class, discuss children's favorite places. Have them tell about vacation places, a place where a family member lives, or a special place in your town or neighborhood.
- Ask children to draw a picture of a favorite place.
- Have them write a caption that tells about their favorite place.
- Make the pictures into a class book and share it at group time.

Phonics Center

Glowing Word Stars

👥 Pairs	🕐 30 minutes
Objective	Sort short *a* and short *i* words; make word stars.
Materials	Plastic bags, word cards, cardboard, string, black crayons, yellow paint

In advance, prepare plastic bags each with five short *a* and five short *i* word cards. Cut out five-pointed stars. Punch a hole in one point of each and attach a piece of string.

- First, pairs sort the word cards.
- One child makes a short *a* word star and the other makes a short *i* word star.
- Using black crayons, children write one word near each point of the star. Then children paint their stars yellow.
- Hang the word stars for children to read!

Planning for Assessment

During instruction in Theme 3 . . .

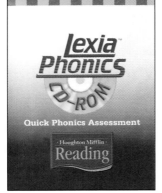

1 SCREENING AND DIAGNOSIS

Screening
- Baseline Group Test
- Emerging Literacy Survey

Diagnosis
- Leveled Reading Passages Assessment Kit
- Lexia Quick Phonics Assessment CD-ROM

2 MONITORING PROGRESS

ONGOING INFORMAL ASSESSMENT
- Guiding Comprehension questions
- Story Retellings
- Comprehension Checks
- Oral Reading/Fluency Checks
- Skill lesson applications
- Monitoring Student Progress boxes
- Writing Samples
- Observation Checklists
- Children's Self-Assessments

END-OF-THEME REVIEW
Assessing Student Progress
- provides suggestions for administering formal assessments, information and recommendations for Fluency Assessment, and program resources for differentiating instruction.

FORMAL ASSESSMENT
- End-of-Week Skills Checks or Alternative Assessments
- Theme 3 Weekly Skills Tests
- Theme 3 Integrated Theme Tests
- Theme 3 Theme Skills Tests
- Fluency Assessment

3 MANAGING AND REPORTING

HOUGHTON MIFFLIN **Assessment System**

Create tests and practice online, get instant results online or by scan-and-score, report performance on your state standards, and run prescriptions to differentiate instruction.

National Test Correlation
Documenting Adequate Yearly Progress

SKILLS for *Let's Look Around!*	ITBS	Terra Nova (CTBS)	CAT	SAT	MAT
Phonemic Awareness					
• Blending Phonemes*					
Phonics					
• Short *a, i*	O	O	O		O
• Final Consonants	O	O	O	O	O
• Initial Consonant Substitution*				O	
• Double Final Consonants	O	O	O		O
• Plurals with *-s*	O	O			
• Verb Endings *-s, -ed, -ing*	O	O			
• Possessives with *'s*	O				
• Clusters with *r*	O	O			
• Contractions with *'s*	O	O			
High-Frequency Words					
• High-Frequency Words		O	O		
Comprehension Strategies and Skills					
• Strategies: Question, Evaluate*, Predict/Infer*		O	O		O
• Skills: Topic, Main Idea, Details/Summarizing, Making Predictions, Categorize and Classify	O	O	O	O	O
Vocabulary					
• Vocabulary*	O	O	O	O	O
Spelling					
• Short Vowels *a, i*	O	O			O
Grammar					
• What is a Sentence?	O	O	O		
• Naming Part of a Sentence	O	O	O		
• Action Part of a Sentence	O	O	O		
Listening/Speaking/Viewing					
• Main Idea and Details*	O	O		O	O

*These skills are taught, but not tested, in this theme.

KEY

ITBS Iowa Tests of Basic Skills

Terra Nova (CTBS) Comprehensive Tests of Basic Skills

CAT California Achievement Tests

SAT Stanford Achievement Tests

MAT Metropolitan Achievement Tests

Launching the Theme

Theme **3**

Let's Look Around !

Read Together

Sleeping Outdoors

Under the dark is a star,
Under the star is a tree,
Under the tree is a blanket,
And under the blanket is me.

by Marchette Chute

10   11

Introducing the Theme: Discussion Options

Combination Classroom

See the **Combination Classroom Planning Guide** for lesson planning and management support.

Read aloud the theme title on Anthology page 11. Ask children to look at the picture and tell how the picture fits with the theme title. (Sample answer: The picture fits with the theme title because the girl is looking around.)

Read aloud the poem "Sleeping Outdoors" by Marchette Chute. Ask these questions:

1 What things in the poem are outdoors?
(the dark, a star, a tree, a blanket, and a person)

2 Would you like to sleep outdoors? Why or why not?
(Answers will vary.)

Ask children to describe things they see during the day and night. Then ask what kinds of stories children might read in *Let's Look Around!* (Sample answer: stories about interesting things that might happen in the world around us)

Using the Read Aloud

Read aloud *Belling the Cat*. Fold your Teacher's Edition so that children can see page T19 as you read. After reading the story on page T18, use the following questions to discuss how the story relates to the theme *Let's Look Around!*

1 Why do the mice have to look around carefully?
(The cat might be nearby and gobble them up.)

2 What was Baby Mouse's idea?
(to put a bell around the cat's neck)

3 Do you think anyone volunteered to put the bell on the cat? Why?
(Sample answer: No. It would be too dangerous.)

Read aloud for oral language and vocabulary development. Read aloud other stories to help develop children's oral comprehension, vocabulary, and listening skills. You may want to choose books to read aloud from the Leveled Bibliography on pages T6–T7.

 Home Connection

Send home the theme letter for *Let's Look Around!* to introduce the theme and suggest home activities. (See **Teacher's Resource Blackline Masters**.)

For other suggestions relating to *Let's Look Around!,* see **Home/ Community Connections**.

Classroom Management

At any time during the theme, you can assign the independent cross-curricular activities on Teacher's Edition pages T12–T13 while you give differentiated instruction to small groups.

For additional independent activity centers related to specific selections, see the pages listed below.

- Week 1: pages T28–T29
- Week 2: pages T100–T101
- Week 3: pages T172–T173

Monitoring Student Progress

Monitoring Progress

Throughout the theme, monitor your children's progress by using the following program features in the Teacher's Edition:

- Guiding comprehension questions
- Literature discussion groups
- Skill lesson applications
- Monitoring Student Progress boxes
- Theme Wrap-Up, pages T236–T238

Belling the Cat

There once was a family of mice who were always being chased by a big cat. Whenever they left the safety of their nest, they would have to look carefully around to be sure the cat wasn't lurking nearby, ready to pounce on them and gobble them up.

"The problem with the cat," said Father Mouse, "is that he walks so softly that you never hear him coming. You have to keep your eyes open all the time to be sure the cat isn't sneaking up on you."

"If only the cat walked more loudly, we could hear it approaching," sighed Mother Mouse.

"I know what we can do!" squeaked Baby Mouse excitedly. "We can put a bell around the cat's neck! Then we'll always be able to hear the cat when he's nearby."

"What a clever little mouse you are!" exclaimed proud Father Mouse.

"Just think, all we need is a bell," said Mother Mouse.

"Ah, but who will put the bell around the cat's neck?" asked Grandfather Mouse.

Do you think anyone volunteered?

Lesson Overview

Literature

Seasons

written and illustrated by
Ashley Wolff

Selection Summary

As the seasons change, so do the animals we see.

❶ Big Book

• *Counting on the Woods*

❷ Decodable Text

Phonics Library

• *Cabs, Cabs, Cabs*
• *Fall Naps*
• *Pam Can Pack*

❸ Get Set Story

❹ Main Story

Seasons
Genre: Nonfiction

Vocabulary Reader

Nonfiction

❺ Language Arts Link

Instructional Support

Planning and Practice

Teacher's Edition

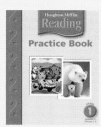

Practice Book

Teacher's Resources

Transparencies

Decodable Text

Differentiated Instruction

Intervention Strategies
for Extra Support

Instructional Activities
for Challenge

Instructional Strategies for
English Language Learners

Ready-Made Centers

**Building Vocabulary
Flip Chart**
- center activities
- word skills practice

**Reading in Science and
Social Studies Flip Chart**
- books and center activities
- support for state
  content standards

**Hands-On Literacy Centers
for Week 1**
- activities
- manipulatives
- routines

Technology

Audio Selections
*Animals in the Cold
Seasons*

www.eduplace.com
- over 1,000 Online Leveled Books

Accelerated Reader®

Leveled Books for Reaching All Learners

Fluency

Increase children's reading fluency using these activities.

● BELOW LEVEL
Model fluent reading of sentences. Display sentences on the board, pointing out punctuation and key words. Have children choral read.

▲ ON LEVEL
Have partners read a page in unison with the audio CD.

■ ABOVE LEVEL
Have pairs take turns reading a page or two aloud to each other. Have partners provide feedback to each other.

◆ LANGUAGE SUPPORT
Model blending using key vocabulary. Have children repeat key words. Model fluent reading of key words by using them in sentences and have children echo read.

Skills Practice

- Topic, comprehension strategy, and vocabulary linked to main selection
- Lessons in Teacher's Edition, pages T88–T91

● BELOW LEVEL

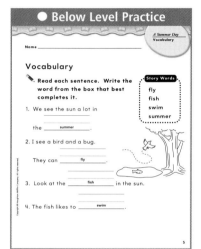

▲ ON LEVEL

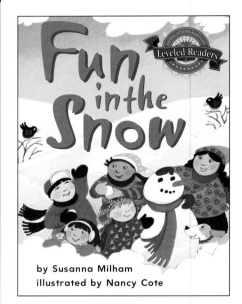

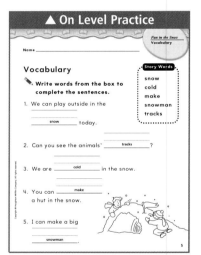

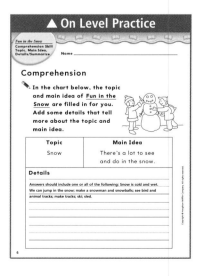

■ ABOVE LEVEL

Fall Leaves
by Joanna Solins

■ Above Level Practice

Fall Leaves
Vocabulary

Name _____

Vocabulary

✎ Use the words from the box to finish the sentences. They will tell about fall leaves.

Story Words
maple
change
points
bright
leaves
syrup

1. You can look for _____ leaves _____

2. Trees _____ change _____ colors.

3. Maple tree leaves turn _____ bright _____ red.

4. A maple leaf has three big _____ points _____

5. We get something sweet from _____ maple _____ trees.

6. Maple _____ syrup _____ is made from maple sap.

5

■ Above Level Practice

Fall Leaves
Comprehension
Topic, Main Idea,
Details/Summarize

Name _____

Comprehension

✎ Read the topic and main idea for **Fall Leaves**. Then write two details.

Topic: Fall leaves

Main Idea: Leaves change color in the fall

Detail:
Answers will vary but may include: Oak leaves turn dark red; birch leaves have a zigzag edge.

Detail:
_____

✎ Draw a picture to help you retell the book.

Answers may vary but should include pictures of some or all of the following: People walking through a woods, trees and fall leaves, acorns.

6

◆ LANGUAGE SUPPORT

Summer
written by Leslie Kwok
illustrated by
Janet Montecalvo

◆ Language Support Practice

Summer
Build Background

Name _____

Build Background

✎ Draw a circle around the pictures that show things you can do in the summer. Then draw a picture of something you like to do in the summer.

5

◆ Language Support Practice

Summer
Story Words

Name _____

✎ Use the story words to complete the sentences. You may use a word more than once.

Story Words
fly
likes to
swim

Jose _____ likes to _____ play ball in the summer.

He _____ likes to _____ play in the park.

Liz likes to _____ swim _____ in the summer.

I like to watch the birds

_____ fly _____. I see them from my window every morning.

6

Leveled Theme Paperbacks

- Extended independent reading in theme-related paperbacks

- Lessons in Teacher's Edition, pages R2–R5

Mack
by James M. Pare
illustrated by Terry Sloot

Houghton Mifflin

Barnyard Tracks
by Dee Dee Duffy
illustrated by Janet Marshall

Reading

● **BELOW LEVEL**   ▲ **ON LEVEL**

Reading

Counting
on the
Woods

a poem by
George Ella Lyon

photographs by
Ann W. Olson

■ **ABOVE LEVEL**

Technology

HOUGHTON MIFFLIN
Online Leveled Books
www.eduplace.com

- over 1,000 Online Leveled Books

Leveled Readers
Audio available

Daily Lesson Plans

Technology
Lesson Planner CD-ROM allows you to customize the chart below to develop your own lesson plans.

T Skill tested on Integrated Theme Test and/or Weekly or Theme Skills Test

80–90 minutes

Learning to Read

Phonemic Awareness
Phonics
Comprehension

Vocabulary Reader

Leveled Readers
- Fluency Practice
- Independent Reading

20–30 minutes

Word Work

Spelling
High-Frequency Words
Vocabulary

20–30 minutes

Writing and Oral Language

Writing
Grammar
Listening/Speaking/Viewing

DAY 1

Daily Routines, T30–T31
Phonics, High-Frequency Words,
🕐 Phonemic Awareness,
Independent Reading, Writing

Sharing the Big Book, T32–T35
🕐 **Comprehension Strategy,** T32
Evaluate

🕐 **Comprehension Skill,** T33
Topic, Main Idea, Details/Summarizing **T**

🕐 **Phonics,** T36–T38
Double Final Consonants **T**
Blending More Short *a* Words **T**
Plurals with *-s* **T**

🕐 **Reading Decodable Text,** T39–T41
Cabs, Cabs, Cabs

Leveled Readers
A Summer Day
Fun in the Snow
Fall Leaves
Summer

Lessons and Leveled Practice, T88–T91

Spelling, T42
The Short *a* Sound
🕐 **Vocabulary,** T42
Spelling Patterns *-ack, -ap*

Daily Language Practice
1. Does jim have a cat?
   (Does Jim have a cat?)

✏ **Shared Writing,** T43
A Class Description

Viewing, T43
Gathering Information

DAY 2

Daily Routines, T44–T45
Phonics, High-Frequency Words,
🕐 Phonemic Awareness,
Independent Reading, Writing

🕐 **High-Frequency Words,** T46–T47
animal, bird, cold, fall, flower, full, look, of, see **T**

Reading the Get Set Story, T48–T51
Building Background, T48

🕐 **Vocabulary:** *animals, birds, cold, fall, flowers, full, look, of, see, buds, is, lots, pick, pups, will*

🕐 **Comprehension Skills,** T50
Topic, Main Idea, Details/Summarizing **T**

Leveled Readers
A Summer Day
Fun in the Snow
Fall Leaves
Summer

Lessons and Leveled Practice, T88–T91

Spelling, T52
The Short *a* Sound
🕐 **Vocabulary,** T52
High-Frequency Words

Daily Language Practice
2. I have ann ox.
   (I have an ox.)

✏ **Interactive Writing,** T53
A Class Description

WEEK 1   **DAILY LESSON PLANS**

Target Skills of the Week

Phonemic Awareness	Blending and Segmenting Phonemes
Phonics	Double Final Consonants; Short *a*; Plurals with *-s*
Comprehension	Topic, Main Idea, Details/Summarizing
Vocabulary	Spelling Patterns; High-Frequency Words; Seasons of the Year; Months of the Year
Fluency	Decodable Text: Phonics Library; Leveled Readers

DAY 3

Daily Routines, T54–T55

Phonics, High-Frequency Words,

🎯 Phonemic Awareness,

Independent Reading, Writing

Vocabulary Reader

Reading the Main Story, T56–T66

🎯 **Comprehension Strategy,** T57
Evaluate

🎯 **Comprehension Skill,** T57, T68–T69
Topic, Main Idea, Details/Summarizing **T**

Responding, T67

Leveled Readers

A Summer Day
Fun in the Snow
Fall Leaves
Summer

Lessons and Leveled Practice, T88–T91

Spelling, T70
The Short *a* Sound

🎯 **Vocabulary,** T70
Seasons of the Year

Daily Language Practice
3. Cann you see the hen.
(**Can** you see the hen?)

✏️ **Writing:** Responding, T67
Write a Sentence

Grammar, T71
What Is a Sentence?

Speaking, T67
Retelling

DAY 4

Daily Routines, T72–T73

Phonics, High-Frequency Words,

🎯 Phonemic Awareness,

Independent Reading, Writing

Reading the Language Arts Link, T74–T75

Comprehension:
How to Read Jokes and Lyrics

🎯 **Phonics Review,** T76–T77
Reading Short *u* Words

Vocabulary Reader

Leveled Readers

A Summer Day
Fun in the Snow
Fall Leaves
Summer

Lessons and Leveled Practice, T88–T91

Spelling, T78
The Short *a* Sound

🎯 **Vocabulary,** T78
Months of the Year

Daily Language Practice
4. the mman is my dad.
(**The man** is my dad.)

✏️ **Independent Writing,** T79
Writing About Favorite Seasons

DAY 5

Daily Routines, T80–T81

Phonics,

High-Frequency Words,

🎯 Phonemic Awareness,

Independent Reading, Writing

🎯 **Comprehension: Rereading for Understanding**
(Topic, Main Idea, Details/Summarizing **T**) T82

🎯 **Rereading for Fluency,** T82

🎯 **Reading Decodable Text,**
T83–T85
Pam Can Pack
End-of-the-Week Skills Check

Vocabulary Reader

Leveled Readers

A Summer Day
Fun in the Snow
Fall Leaves
Summer

Lessons and Leveled Practice, T88–T91

Spelling, T86
The Short *a* Sound

🎯 **Vocabulary,** T86
Review: High-Frequency Words

Daily Language Practice
5. We hadd to go
(We **had** to go.)

✏️ **Independent Writing,** T87
Writing a Story

Grammar, T87
Review: What Is a Sentence?

Listening and Speaking, T87
Fact or Opinion?

Managing Flexible Groups

Leveled Instruction and Leveled Practice

	DAY 1	DAY 2
WHOLE CLASS	• Daily Routines (TE pp. T30–T31) • Read Aloud the Big Book *Counting on the Woods.* (TE pp. T32–T35) • Phonics lesson (TE pp. T36–T38)	• Daily Routines (TE pp. T44–T45) • High-Frequency Words lesson (TE pp. T46–T47) • Building Background, Vocabulary (TE p. T48)
SMALL GROUPS		
Extra Support	**TEACHER-LED** • Preview vocabulary; support reading with Vocabulary Reader. • Read Phonics Library: *Cabs, Cabs, Cabs.* (TE pp. T39–T41) • Read Books 23–27, I Love Reading Books.	**TEACHER-LED** • Read Anthology: Get Set Story. (TE pp. T48–T51) • Read Phonics Library: *Fall Naps.* (TE p. T47) **Partner or Individual Reading** • **Fluency Practice** Reread Phonics Library: *Cabs, Cabs, Cabs.* (TE pp. T39–T41)
On Level	**TEACHER-LED** • Read Phonics Library: *Cabs, Cabs, Cabs.* (TE pp. T39–T41) • Begin Leveled Theme Paperback: On Level. (TE p. R3)	**Partner or Individual Reading** • Read Anthology: Get Set Story. (TE pp. T48–T51) • Read Phonics Library: *Cabs, Cabs, Cabs* (TE p. T47) AND Leveled Theme Paperback: On Level. (TE p. R3) • **Fluency Practice** Reread Phonics Library: *Tam Cat* (TE pp. T39–T41) AND read Books 23–27, I Love Reading Books.
Challenge	**Partner or Individual Reading** • Read Phonics Library: *Cabs, Cabs, Cabs.* (TE pp. T39–T41) • Read Leveled Theme Paperback: On Level. (TE p. R3)	**TEACHER-LED** • Read silently, Anthology: Get Set Story. • Reread aloud to answer Guiding Comprehension. (TE p. T51) • Read Little Big Book *Counting on the Woods.* (TE pp. R4–R5) • **Fluency Practice** Read Phonics Library: *Fall Naps.* (TE p. T47) ✔
English Language Learners	**TEACHER-LED** • Preview vocabulary; support reading with Vocabulary Reader. • Together, read Phonics Library: *Cabs, Cabs, Cabs.* (TE pp. T39–T41) • Together, read Books 23–27, I Love Reading Books.	**TEACHER-LED** • Reread Phonics Library: *Cabs, Cabs, Cabs.* (TE pp. T39–T41) • Read Phonics Library: *Fall Naps.* (TE p. T47) **Partner or Individual Reading** • Read with audio CD of Anthology: Get Set Story.

Independent Activities

• Complete, review **Practice Book** pages (123–137) and **Leveled Readers Practice Blackline Masters** (TE pp. T88–T89).
• Reread familiar selections.
• Read trade book from Leveled Bibliography (TE pp. T6–T7).

✔ Opportunity to informally assess oral reading rate.

DAY 3	**DAY 4**	**DAY 5**
• Daily Routines (TE pp. T54–T55) • Vocabulary, Purpose Setting, Comprehension Strategy and Skill (TE pp. T56–T57) *After Reading at Small Group Time* • Responding (TE p. 67) • Comprehension lesson (TE pp. T68–T69)	• Daily Routines (TE pp. T72–T73) • Science Link (TE pp. T74–T75) • Phonics Review (TE pp. T76–T77)	• Daily Routines (TE pp. T80–T81) • Rereading (TE p. T82)

FLEXIBLE GROUPS — **WEEK 1**

DAY 3

TEACHER-LED
- Read Anthology: Main Story. (TE pp. T56–T66)
- **Fluency Practice** Reread Get Set Story (TE pp. T48–T51) AND Phonics Library: *Fall Naps.* (TE p. T47) ✔

TEACHER-LED
- Read silently, Anthology: Main Story.
- Reread aloud to answer Guiding Comprehension. (TE pp. 51, T56–T66)
- **Fluency Practice** Reread Phonics Library: *Fall Naps* (TE p. T47) ✔ OR begin Leveled Reader: On Level. (TE p. T89)

Partner or Individual Reading
- Read Anthology: Main Story. (TE pp. T56–T66)
- **Fluency Practice** Reread Anthology: Main Story OR read Leveled Reader: Above Level. (TE p. T90)

TEACHER-LED
- Reread Phonics Library: *Fall Naps.* (TE p. T47)
- Together, reread Anthology: Get Set Story. (TE pp. T48–T51)

Partner or Individual Reading
- Read with audio CD of Anthology: Main Story.

DAY 4

TEACHER-LED
- Read the On My Way Practice Reader. (TE p. R2)
- **Fluency Practice** Reread Books 23–27, I Love Reading Books. ✔

Partner Reading
- **Fluency Practice** Reread Anthology: Main Story (TE pp. T56–T66) OR complete Leveled Reader: On Level. (TE p. T89)

TEACHER-LED
- Reread silently, Anthology: Link.
- Reread aloud to answer Guiding Comprehension. (TE pp. T56–T66, T74–T75)
- **Fluency Practice** Reread Little Big Book *Counting on the Woods.* (TE pp. R4–R5) ✔

TEACHER-LED
- Together, reread Anthology: Main Story. (TE pp. T56–T66)
- Begin Leveled Reader: Language Support (TE p. T91) OR On My Way Practice Reader. (TE p. R2)

Individual Reading
- **Fluency Practice** Read with audio CD of Anthology: Get Set Story, Main Story.

DAY 5

TEACHER-LED
- Read Phonics Library: *Pam Can Pack.* (TE pp. T83–T85)
- Read Leveled Reader: Below Level. (TE p. T88)
- **Fluency Practice** Reread the On My Way Practice Reader (TE p. R2) OR Books 23–27, I Love Reading Books. ✔

TEACHER-LED
- Reread Anthology: Link. (TE pp. T74–T75)
- Read Phonics Library: *Pam Can Pack.* (TE pp. T83–T85)
- Respond to Leveled Theme Paperback: On Level. (TE p. R3)
- **Fluency Practice** Reread week's Phonics Library books OR Leveled Reader: On Level. (TE p. T89) ✔

Individual Reading
- **Fluency Practice** Reread Anthology: Main Story and Link (TE pp. T56–T66, T74–T75) OR Leveled Reader: Above Level. (TE p. T90)
- Read Phonics Library: *Pam Can Pack.* (TE pp. T83–T85)

TEACHER-LED
- Read Phonics Library: *Pam Can Pack.* (TE pp. T83–T85)
- Complete Leveled Reader: Language Support (TE p. T91) OR On My Way Practice Reader. (TE p. R2)
- **Fluency Practice** Reread Books 23–27, I Love Reading Books. ✔

Turn the page for more independent activities.

Ready-Made Small Group Activities

 Word Work

Cross Curricular

Building Vocabulary Center Activity 7
● ▲ ■ *Home Sweet Home*

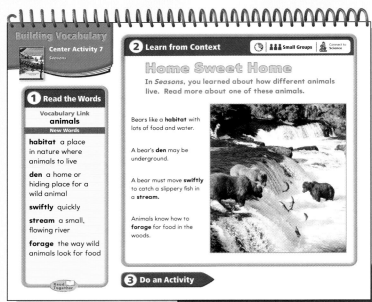

Leveled Activities on side 2

Game Board 2
● ▲ ■ *Toy Store*

Key Vocabulary Cards 30–37

insects

Spelling Word Cards 1–6

him

Reading in Science Independent Book
▲ *Measuring Weather*

Reading in Science Center Activity 7
● ▲ ■ *What's the Weather?*

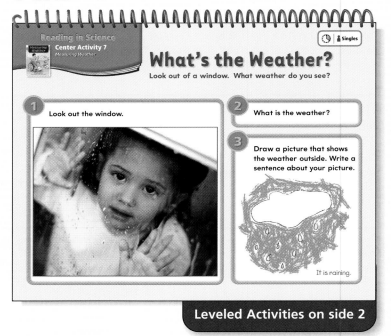

Leveled Activities on side 2

Leveled for ● Below Level, ▲ On Level, ■ Above Level

Reading

Routine Card 2
● ▲ ■ *Buddy Reading*

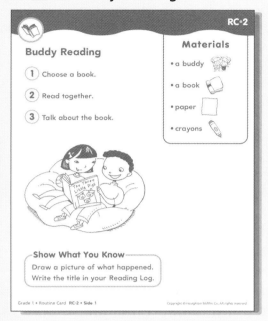

RC•2

Buddy Reading
1. Choose a book.
2. Read together.
3. Talk about the book.

Materials
- a buddy
- a book
- paper
- crayons

Show What You Know
Draw a picture of what happened.
Write the title in your Reading Log.

Grade 1 • Routine Card RC-2 • Side 1   Copyright © Houghton Mifflin Co. All rights reserved

Routine Card 5
● ▲ ■ *Read about a Topic*

RC•5

Read about a Topic
1. Read a book.
2. Draw one main idea in the big circle.
3. Draw details about the main idea in the boxes.
4. Write about the pictures.

Materials
- a nonfiction book
- pencil

Show What You Know
Read your paper to a friend. Put your paper in your Work Folder.

Grade 1 • Routine Card RC-5 • Side 1   Copyright © Houghton Mifflin Co. All rights reserved

Writing

Routine Card 6
● ▲ ■ *Write in Your Journal*

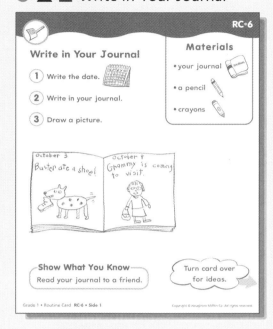

RC•6

Write in Your Journal
1. Write the date.
2. Write in your journal.
3. Draw a picture.

Materials
- your journal
- a pencil
- crayons

Show What You Know
Read your journal to a friend.

Turn card over for ideas.

Grade 1 • Routine Card RC-6 • Side 1   Copyright © Houghton Mifflin Co. All rights reserved

Challenge Card 3–1
■ *Barnyard Tracks*

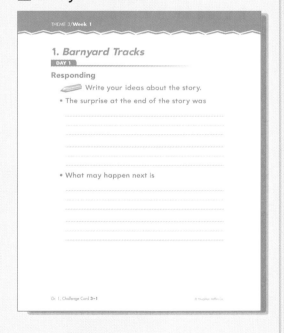

THEME 3/**Week 1**

1. Barnyard Tracks
DAY 1

Responding
Write your ideas about the story.
- The surprise at the end of the story was

_____

_____

- What may happen next is

_____

_____

Gr. 1, Challenge Card 3–1   © Houghton Mifflin Co.

Multiple Tiers of Intervention

Core Program Intervention

- research-based
- systematic
- assessment-driven
- extra support
- English learner support
- reteaching

Small Group Intervention
Daily lessons and activities for differentiated instruction

Intervention Strategies for Extra Support, pages 76–87

Instructional Activities for Challenge, pages 80–91

Instructional Strategies for English Learners, pages 28–33

Intensive Intervention
Proven efficacy for struggling readers

Reading Intervention for Early Success

For these materials and more, see **Small Group Independent Activities Kit.**

Day at a Glance
pages T30–T43

Learning to Read

Sharing the Big Book

Phonics Instruction
Double Final Consonants
Blending More Short *a* Words
Plurals with *-s*

Reading Decodable Text
Cabs, Cabs, Cabs

• • • • • • • • • • • • • • • • • • • •

Leveled Readers, T88–T91

● *A Summer Day*
▲ *Fun in the Snow*
■ *Fall Leaves*
◆ *Summer*

Word Work

Spelling: The Short *a* Sound
Vocabulary: Spelling Patterns
-ack, -ap

Writing & Oral Language

Shared Writing
Viewing

Daily Routines

Daily Message

Review high-frequency words and language skills. Tell children that today they will read about things in the woods. Read the message aloud, pointing to each word as it is read. Call on individuals to answer each question.

Hello, Boys and Girls!
   Have you ever gone for a walk in the woods? What did you see there?

Model concepts of print. Display word cards *for, have, what,* and *you*. Ask all children to find each matching word in the message. Then call on children to point to each word. Ask why the words *have* and *what* begin with capital letters in the message. (The words are used to begin sentences.)

Word Wall

KINDERGARTEN REVIEW **High-Frequency Words** Briefly review the words *see, is, the, here, for, and, go,* and *are*. Remind children that they learned these words in kindergarten. Have children chant the spelling of each: *s-e-e* spells *see, i-s* spells *is, t-h-e* spells *the, h-e-r-e* spells *here, f-o-r* spells *for, a-n-d* spells *and, g-o* spells *go, a-r-e* spells *are*. Have children point to and read the words. Tell them they will read these words this week in new stories.

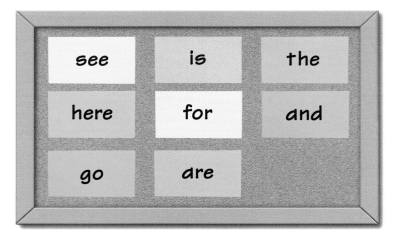

see	is	the
here	for	and
go	are	

Blackline Masters for these word cards appear in Theme 1 on pp. R39–R41.

🎯 Daily Phonemic Awareness

Blending and Segmenting Phonemes: Name the Picture

Distribute **Picture Cards** *bed, bug, cat, cot, dig, dog, fan, hat, hop, hug, jam, jug, kiss, lamp, lip, map, mug, nut, pan, rug, sad, tag,* and *tub* to children.

- Tell children that you will say some sounds. Explain that they should blend the sounds together to name a picture that one of them is holding. The child holding the correct card should then display it and say its name.

- Model with this example. Say, *The sounds in this word are /k/ /ŭ/ /p/. Listen: /k/ /ŭ/ /p/, cup. That's cup!* Display the **Picture Card** *cup*.

- Continue with the **Picture Cards** listed above.

- Now have children work in pairs. One child can segment the sounds in a picture card name, and a partner can blend them to name the picture.

Daily Language Practice

Grammar Skill: Capitalizing Names

Have children correct the following sentence:

Does jim have a cat?

(Does Jim have a cat?)

✏️ Daily Writing Prompt

Ask children to write about something interesting they have seen while out walking, or have them write about self-selected topics. Encourage them to use what they know about letters and sounds to record their ideas.

An Activity Master for this writing activity appears on R48.

We found a bird's nest.

Daily Independent Reading

Daily independent exploration and reading of books will increase children's reading fluency. Have children read from the following.

- Leveled Bibliography, pages T6–T7

Choose books from this list for children to read, outside class, for at least twenty minutes a day.

- Little Big Book *Counting on the Woods*

Sharing the Big Book

Building Background

Read aloud the title. Then display pages 8–9. Have children tell what they see. Then ask children to name other things they might see in the woods.

Fluency Modeling

Tell children you will read a selection about the woods. Explain that you will model how to read with expression.

COMPREHENSION STRATEGY

Evaluate

Teacher Modeling Read aloud the Strategy Focus on Big Book page 5. Model how to use the Evaluate strategy.

Think Aloud *I think I am going to read about the woods in this story. As I read, I'll think about what I am learning, and whether the author did a good job keeping me interested.*

Meet the Author
When George Ella Lyon was young, she wanted to be a tightrope walker or a singer. Everything changed when she started writing poetry in the second grade. She has been a poet ever since.

Meet the Photographer
Ann W. Olson took the photographs for this book near her home in Kentucky. She lives there near her friend, George Ella Lyon. She loves walking in the woods on a sunny day. Maybe after seeing her photographs, you will, too.

Counting on the Woods

a poem by George Ella Lyon

photographs by Ann W. Olson

Strategy Focus
During the story, think about what you are learning.

4   5

to the waterfall given for all

6   7

One path, a stick for a staff.

8   9

Two birds, daybreak's words.

Mourning doves perched in a black walnut tree

10   11

Hercules beetle, stag beetle, and spotted grape beetle

Three bugs in the moss rug.

12

13

12   **13**

Rye

Four worms,
how the earth turns.

14

15

14   **15**

Five nests
where new
ones rest.

Bald-faced hornet nest

Acadian flycatcher and nest

16

*top, Broad-winged hawk nest
above, Tent caterpillar nest
left, Eastern bluebird and nest*

17

16   **17**

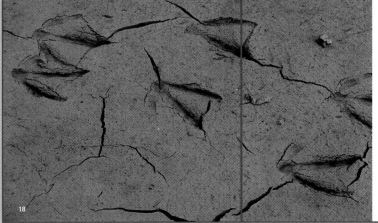

Six tracks.

18

19

18   **19**

TARGET SKILL

COMPREHENSION SKILL

Topic, Main Idea, Details/ Summarizing

Tell children that the topic of a book is what the book is about. Remind them of the title and the pictures on pages 8–9. Ask children what they think this book is about.

Oral Language and Fluency

Read Aloud: Big Book

Read the selection aloud. Emphasize the rhyming pattern and the number words *one* to *ten*. Explain that a *staff* (page 9) is a walking stick, *innumerable* (page 29) means "too many to count," *daybreak's words* (page 10) means that the birds sing in the morning, and *how the earth turns* (page 15) means that the worms dig tunnels and mix up the dirt underground.

Concepts of Print Point out the captions that accompany the photos. Tell children that the author used these captions to tell more information about the woods. Page through the book again and read each caption.

Oral Language: Discussion Options

Retelling Begin a chart with the numerals and number words *one* to *ten* in one column. As you page through the story, have children name the woodland item that goes with each number. Record the names on the chart. You may want to use rebus pictures also.

Have children take turns retelling the story, using the chart to help them remember the story sequence.

Literature Discussion Circle Quickly review the speaking and listening etiquette in these Discussion Tips:

- Think about what you want to say.
- Raise your hand before talking, and wait your turn.
- Listen politely when other people are talking.

Then discuss the following questions as a class:

- In this book, what was your favorite thing to see in the woods?
- What new thing did you learn from the book?
- Why do you think the author wrote about the woods?

THEME 3: Let's Look Around!

Canada geese

20

Who's coming back?

21

20

21

22

Seven stones,
the little creek's home.

23

22

23

*Two crested dwarf irises with
a star chickweed*

Three great trillium

24

Eight
flowers
fed on dirt
and
showers.

Two pink lady's slippers

25

24

25

Nine vines,
earth to sky
they climb.

Grape vines

26

27

26

27

Ten trees whose innumerable leaves clean the air for everything that breathes.

Sycamore tree

28   29

28   **29**

30   31

30   **31**

REACHING ALL LEARNERS

Challenge

Make a Counting Book

Write the numbers 1 to 10 on a paper, and have children look through the story for more woodland items. Have children write the name of one thing beside each number to make their own woods counting story.

English Language Learners

Develop Vocabulary

Display pictures of woods. Have children call out the names of any plants or animals they know. Help children identify those animals they do not know.

OBJECTIVES

- Blend and segment phonemes.
- Recognize double final consonants and the sounds they represent.

Target Skill Trace

Preteach, Teach	p. T36
Reteach	p. R14
Review	p. T148–T149
See	*Handbook for English Language Learners*, pp. 83, 89; *Extra Support Handbook*, pp. 78, 84.

Materials

- **Large Sound/ Spelling Card** *duck*
- **Practice Book** punchout trays and letter cards *c, f, f, g, g, k, l, l, s, s, t, t*

PHONICS: Double Final Consonants

❶ Teach Phonics

Connect sounds to letters. Explain that some words have two of the same consonants at the end. Write *gas* and *bass* on the board.

- Read the words. Underline *s* in *gas* and *ss* in *bass*. Explain that *s* and *ss* are spellings for /s/. Repeat for /l/: *pal, pull*; /t/: *mat, mitt*; /f/: *if, stuff*; /n/: *in, Ann*; /g/: *big, egg*.

- Point to -*ck* on **Large Sound/Spelling Card** *duck*. Write *duck*. Say that the letters *ck* together stand for /k/ at the end of *duck*.

❷ Guided Practice

Check understanding. Write *ck, ff, ll, ss, tt* on the board. Call on children to point to the letters that stand for the last sound in *will*. Continue with *grass, call, huff, back, muff, pick, mitt, hiss, quick, mess*.

Connect sounds to spelling and writing. Distribute the punchout letters. Say *pass*. Have children hold up side by side the two letters that stand for the last sound in *pass*. Continue with *luck, back, pill, mitt, puff, mill, kick, doll, egg*.

❸ Apply

Have children complete **Practice Book** pages 123–124.

Practice Book page 123

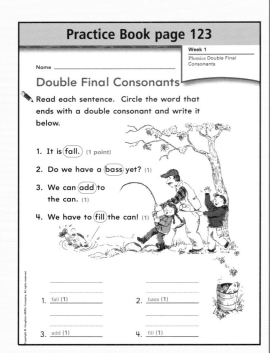

Name _____

Week 1
Phonics Double Final Consonants

Double Final Consonants

Read each sentence. Circle the word that ends with a double consonant and write it below.

1. It is (fall.) (1 point)

2. Do we have a (bass) yet? (1)

3. We can (add) to the can. (1)

4. We have to (fill) the can! (1)

1. fall (1)   2. bass (1)

3. add (1)   4. fill (1)

Monitoring Student Progress

If . . .	Then . . .
children score 8 or below on **Practice Book** pages 123 and 124,	use the Reteaching lesson on **Teacher's Edition** page R14.
children have met the lesson objectives,	use the Challenge/ Extension activities on **Teacher's Edition** page R15.

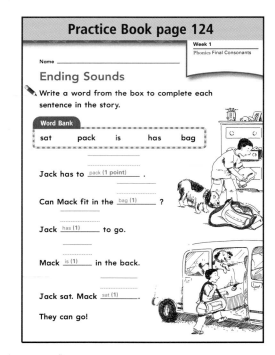

Practice Book page 124

Name _____

Week 1
Phonics Final Consonants

Ending Sounds

Write a word from the box to complete each sentence in the story.

Word Bank

| sat | pack | is | has | bag |

Jack has to ___pack (1 point)___ .

Can Mack fit in the ___bag (1)___ ?

Jack ___has (1)___ to go.

Mack ___is (1)___ in the back.

Jack sat. Mack ___sat (1)___ .

They can go!

Practice Book page 125

Name _____

Week 1
Phonics Short *a*

Words with Short *a*

Name each picture. Write *a* if the picture name has the short *a* sound.

1. a (1 point)	2. a (1)	3.	4. a (1)
5.	6. a (1)	7. a (1)	8. a (1)
9.	10. a (1)	11.	12.
13. a (1)	14. a (1)	15.	16.

PHONICS: Blending More Short *a* Words

❶ Phonemic Awareness

Model how to blend and segment phonemes.

- Have children repeat after you: /s/ /ă/ /k/, *sack*. Have them repeat these sounds and blend to say each word: /p/ /ă/ /k/ (*pack*), /w/ /ă/ /ks/ (*wax*), /s/ /t/ /ă/ /f/ (*staff*), /m/ /ă/ /t/ (*Matt*).

- Have children repeat after you: *wag*, /w/ /ă/ /g/. Have them repeat these words and say the sounds: *lass* (/l/ /ă/ /s/), *Mack* (/m/ /ă/ /k/), *pads* (/p/ /ă/ /d/ /z/), *racks* (/r/ /ă/ /k/ /s/).

❷ Teach Phonics

Connect sounds to letters: *a* /ă/. Display **Large Sound/Spelling Card** *apple*. Remind children that *a* is a vowel that stands for the /ă/ sound at the beginning of *apple* and in the middle of *bat*.

Model how to blend short *a* words. Using **Large Letter Cards** and **Blending Routine 1,** model how to blend *pass*. See instructional Routines, p. T11. Repeat with *Matt* and *lack*.

Extend. Have children blend *nest* and *pond*.

❸ Guided Practice–Word Building

Check understanding. Write *bass*. Have children blend *bass* as you point to the letters. Repeat for *quack, mass, tack, jazz, back* and the sentence *Max and Matt pack the sack*.

Connect sounds to spelling and writing. Say *rack*. Have children repeat it, say its sounds, and build it with punchout letters. Write the word and have children check their work. Repeat with *wag, wax, lass, Mack, tax, jazz, Zack*.

Extend. Have children build *nest* and *pond*.

❹ Apply

Have children complete **Practice Book** pages 125–126.

OBJECTIVES

- Blend and segment phonemes.
- Blend and read words with short *a* and double final consonants.

Target Skill Trace

Preteach, Teach	p. T37
Reteach	p. R16
Review	p. T148

Materials

- **Large Sound/Spelling Card** *apple*
- **Large Letter Cards** *a, c, d, e, k, l, M, n, o, p, s, s, t, t*
- **Blending Routines Card 1**
- **Practice Book** punchout trays and letter cards *a, c, d, e, g, j, k, l, M, n, o, p, r, s, s, t, w, x, Z, z, z*

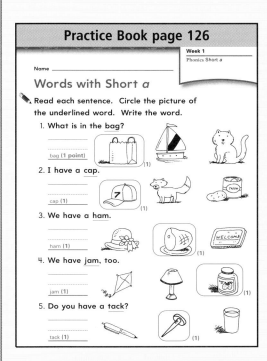

Practice Book page 126

Week 1
Phonics Short *a*

Name _____

Words with Short *a*

🖉 Read each sentence. Circle the picture of the underlined word. Write the word.

1. What is in the bag?

   bag (1 point) _____ (1)

2. I have a cap.

   cap (1) _____ (1)

3. We have a ham.

   ham (1) _____ (1)

4. We have jam, too.

   jam (1) _____ (1)

5. Do you have a tack?

   tack (1) _____ (1)

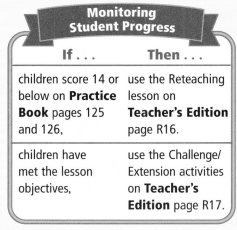

Monitoring Student Progress

If . . .	Then . . .
children score 14 or below on **Practice Book** pages 125 and 126,	use the Reteaching lesson on **Teacher's Edition** page R16.
children have met the lesson objectives,	use the Challenge/Extension activities on **Teacher's Edition** page R17.

OBJECTIVES

● Blend and read words with the plural ending *-s*.

Target Skill Trace

Preteach, Teach	p. T38
Reteach	p. R18
Review	p. T149
See	*Handbook for English Language Learners,* p. 87; *Extra Support Handbook,* pp. 79, 85.

Materials

● **Large Sound/Spelling Cards** *seal, zebra*
● **Practice Book** punchout trays and letter cards *a, b, c, e, f, g, g, h, i, j, k, l, n, s, s, t, u*

Practice Book page 127

Name _____

Week 1
Phonics Plurals with *-s*

More Than One

✏ Read each sentence. Circle the picture of the underlined word.

1. Where are the <u>animals</u>?

(1 point)

2. Ben has <u>cats</u>.

(1)

3. Nan has <u>hens</u>.

(1)

4. Kit has a <u>pig</u>.

(1)

Monitoring Student Progress

If . . .	Then . . .
children score 2 or below on **Practice Book** page 127,	use the Reteaching lesson on **Teacher's Edition** page R18.
children have met the lesson objectives,	use the Challenge/ Extension activities on **Teacher's Edition** page R19.

INSTRUCTION

 PHONICS: Plurals with *-s*

❶ Teach Phonics

Connect sounds to letters. Write *cat* and *cats,* and read the words.

● Explain that an *s* at the end of a word can mean more than one.

● Remind children that *s* can stand for /s/ or /z/. To review these sounds, use **Large Sound/ Spelling Cards** *seal* and *zebra.*

Model how to blend words with plural *-s*. Write these word pairs on the board: *rag, rags; back, backs; nap, naps; cab, cabs; ham, hams.*

● Tell children that when *s* is added to the end of a word, they must add the sound /s/ or /z/ to the end as they are blending.

● Using **Blending Routine 1,** model with the first pair of words: /r/ /ă/ /g/, *rag;* /r/ /ă/ /g/ /z/, *rags.*

● Call on individuals to blend and read the remaining words and tell what sound the *s* stands for.

Extend. Have children blend *twigs.*

❷ Guided Practice–Word Building

Check understanding. Write *bags, cabs, hat, tag, ax, tacks, rags, pans, sack, pads, caps.* Call on a child to read each word. Tell children to raise their hands if the word names more than one.

Connect sounds to spelling and writing. Distribute the punchout trays and letter cards.

● Say *bats* and have children repeat it.

● Have children spell the word with letter cards sound by sound. Write *bats* on the board and have children check their work.

● Repeat with *eggs, bugs, jets, huts, legs, sacks, cans, kits, fans.*

Extend. Have children build *twigs.*

❸ Practice/Apply

Have children complete **Practice Book** page 127.

HOUGHTON MIFFLIN
Reading
Phonics Library

Decodable Text

Let's Look Around!

Cabs, Cabs, Cabs
by Wayne Mazzola
illustrated by Robert de Michiell

Mack has a big tan cab.

5

PHONICS LIBRARY

Reading Decodable Text

Have children preview *Cabs, Cabs, Cabs* Ask them to tell what the man is doing on page 5.

Model the Phonics/Decoding Strategy. Read the steps of the strategy on **Poster B** and use the strategy to read the story title.

Think Aloud *I see three words. They are all the same. I see the letters C, a, b, s. I think about the sounds for the letters and blend the sounds: /k//ă//b/, /z/, Cabs. That's a word. When I look at the picture on the cover, I think that Cabs makes sense.*

Apply the Phonics/Decoding Strategy. Have children read *Cabs, Cabs, Cabs*. If they have difficulty, remind them to look at each letter and sound out the word. If necessary, use prompts such as these:

• *What sound does each letter stand for? Say each sound.*

• *Now say each sound and hold it until you say the next sound. What is the word?*

• *Is that a word you know? Does it make sense in the story?*

OBJECTIVES

• Apply the Phonics/Decoding Strategy to decode double final consonants; short *a* words; plurals with *-s*.

• Reread to build fluency.

Word Key

Decodable words with double final consonants; short *a*; plurals with *-s* ———

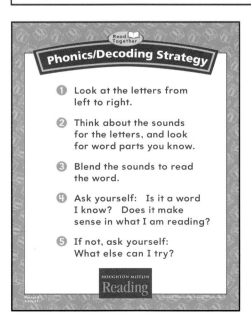

Read Together
Phonics/Decoding Strategy

1 Look at the letters from left to right.

2 Think about the sounds for the letters, and look for word parts you know.

3 Blend the sounds to read the word.

4 Ask yourself: Is it a word I know? Does it make sense in what I am reading?

5 If not, ask yourself: What else can I try?

HOUGHTON MIFFLIN
Reading

Reading Decodable Text T39

Mack <u>can</u> <u>pass</u> two big <u>cabs</u>.

6

The big tan cab hit a big <u>tack</u>.

7

Oral Language

Discuss these questions with children. Have them speak in complete sentences.

- What did Mack have to do after his cab got a flat tire? (Mack had to quit.)

- How do you think Mack feels at the end of the story? How do you know? (Sample answer: Mack is sad at the end of the story. He has a sad look on his face.)

Mack has to quit.

8

Build Fluency

Model fluent reading.

- Read aloud pages 7 and 8. Then have children read the pages aloud.

- Have children reread the same pages several times until each child can read them aloud effortlessly.

Home Connection

Hand out the take-home version of *Cabs, Cabs, Cabs*. Ask children to reread the story with their families. (See the **Phonics Library Blackline Masters**.)

OBJECTIVES

- Identify the sound and letter for short *a* in VC and CVC words.
- Spell words with spelling patterns *-ack*, *-ap*.

Materials

- teacher-made word cards *pack, cap*

SPELLING WORDS

Basic

an*	man
had	can*
at*	cat

Challenge

catch	add

Forms of these words appear in the literature.

Practice Book page 227

Take-Home Word List	Take-Home Word List
Miss Jill's Ice Cream Shop	Seasons
The Short *i* sound	**The Short *a* sound**
in	an
it	at
him	can
Spelling Words	**Spelling Words**
1. in	1. an
2. it	2. at
3. him	3. can
4. big	4. cat
5. sit	5. had
6. did	6. man
Challenge Words	**Challenge Words**
1. dish	1. catch
2. milk	2. add
My Study List Add your own spelling words on the back.	My Study List Add your own spelling words on the back.

Take-Home Word List

INSTRUCTION

SPELLING: The Short *a* Sound

❶ Teach the Principle

Pretest Say each underlined word, read the sentence, and repeat the word. Have children write only the underlined word.

Basic Words

1. Hal has **an** ax.
2. I am **at** the ranch.
3. My dad **can** clap.
4. The **cat** ran fast.
5. I **had** a plan.
6. That **man** has a hat.

Teach Write the Basic Words, and read them with children.

- Explain that in each word, the vowel *a* is followed by a consonant. Have children identify each final consonant.
- Say that in this vowel-consonant pattern, the short *a* sound, /ă/, is usually spelled *a*.

❷ Practice/Apply

Listen for Short *a* Write *can, sit, man, beg, had, not, cat, rug, an.* Have children read the words and tell which ones have the /ă/ sound.

Practice/Homework Assign **Practice Book** page 227, the Take-Home Word List.

Penmanship Ball-and-stick *and* continuous-stroke penmanship models are available in the **Practice Book** (pp. 216–223) and the **Teacher's Resource Blackline Masters** (pp. 143–194).

INSTRUCTION

VOCABULARY: Spelling Patterns *-ack*, *-ap*

Teach Post *pack* and *cap* on the Word Wall. Read the words and explain that these words will help children read and spell other words.

Practice/Apply Make a class chart of words that rhyme with *pack* and *cap*. (*pack, tack, back, hack, lack, rack, sack; cap, nap, gap, lap, tap, map, zap*) Have children read the words and identify the parts that are the same. (*-ack, -ap*)

SHARED WRITING:
A Class Description

Introduce the topic for a class description.

- Tell children that today they will write a description of their classroom.

Prompt children to contribute to the class description.

- Ask, *What do you see in our classroom?* Have children contribute sentences as you write them on chart paper.

- Explain that each sentence is a group of words that tells about something.

Display the class description.

- Read the description aloud. Children can illustrate different sentences in the description.

VIEWING:
Gathering Information

Model how to get information from a picture. Display photographs or pictures that show seasonal changes. Use prompts such as the following:

- *Do you see people? What does their clothing tell you about the weather?*

- *Are there animals in the picture? What are they doing?*

- *What does the sky look like? Can you tell what time of day it is? Can you tell what the weather is like?*

- *What kinds of plants do you see? What time of year do you think it is?*

Ask children to get information from a picture.

- Have small groups examine different pictures for clues and information.

- Invite each group to share its picture with the class and name three things they discovered.

OBJECTIVES

- Contribute ideas for a class description.
- Find at least three pieces of information from a visual source.

Materials

- chart paper
- photographs or pictures showing seasonal changes

English Language Learners

Develop Vocabulary

Before they answer questions about the seasons, English language learners will benefit from reviewing some common items in the pictures. Point to things such as a tree, a flower, a boy, a girl, and so on. Have children say the words. Help with vocabulary and pronunciation, as needed. Encourage children to use the articles *a* or *an* with each noun.

Day at a Glance
pages T44–T53

Learning to Read

High-Frequency Words
Reading the Get Set Story
Animals in the Cold
Reading Decodable Text
Fall Naps

• • • • • • • • • • • • • • • • • •

Leveled Readers, *T88–T91*

- ● *A Summer Day*
- ▲ *Fun in the Snow*
- ■ *Fall Leaves*
- ◆ *Summer*

Word Work

Spelling: The Short *a* Sound
Vocabulary: High-Frequency Words

Writing & Oral Language

Interactive Writing

Daily Routines

Daily Message

Review skills. Point to each word as you read the message aloud. Invite children to answer the question and complete the sentence. Then display word cards for *we, you, me,* and *where.* Have children look and match each card to a word in the message. If children have trouble matching the words, have them compare the letters one by one.

Good Morning, Class!

Yesterday we read about many animals. Can you tell me where some of the animals live? The birds live in a _____.

Model concepts of print. Call on children to find and circle a question mark.

Word Wall

KINDERGARTEN REVIEW **Pattern Words** Have children find the word *wet* on the Word Wall. Ask children to identify each letter and the sound it stands for. (/w//ĕ//t/) Model blending the sounds. Next, model blending the words *an, dig, hen, box, pot,* and *it.* Tell children they will work with words that rhyme with these words this week.

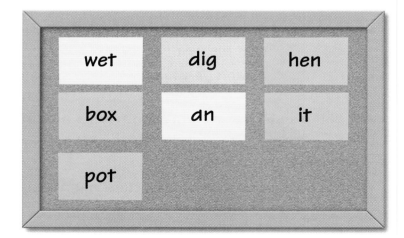

Blackline Masters for these word cards appear in Theme 1 on pp. R42–R44 and in Theme 2 on p.

# Daily Phonemic Awareness

Blending and Segmenting Phonemes: Simon Says Blend

Play "Simon Says" by giving instructions and calling out the sounds for one of the key words. Children blend to form the word and follow the instructions.

- Say these commands:

Simon says to /t//ă//p/ your toes. (tap)
Simon says to /s//l//ă//p/ your knees. (slap)
Simon says to /k//l//ă//p/ your hands. (clap)
Simon says to salute the /f//l//ă//g/. (flag)
Simon says to /f//l//ă//p/ your arms. (flap)
Simon says to /kw//ă//k/. (quack)
Simon says to step /b//ă//k/. (back)

- Challenge: *Simon says to /s//t//ă//m//p/ your feet.* (stamp)

- Next, have children form small groups. Members take turns playing Simon, segmenting commands for the others to blend.

Daily Language Practice

Grammar Skill: Beginning Sentences with Capital Letters

Spelling Skill: The Short *a* Sound

Have children correct the following sentence:

I have ann ox.

(I have **an** ox.)

Daily Writing Prompt

Provide old magazines and have children describe what they see in one of the photographs, or have them write on self-selected topics.

Daily Independent Reading

Daily independent exploration and reading of books will increase children's reading fluency. Ask children to read from the following.

- Leveled Bibliography, pages T6–T7

Choose books from this list for children to read, outside class, for at least twenty minutes a day.

- Reread Phonics Library story *Cabs, Cabs, Cabs.*

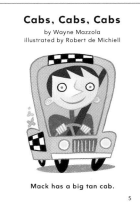

Cabs, Cabs, Cabs
by Wayne Mazzola
illustrated by Robert de Michiell

Mack has a big tan cab.

5

HIGH-FREQUENCY WORDS

OBJECTIVES
• Read and write *animal, bird, cold, fall flower, full, look, of, see.*

Target Skill Trace

Teach	pp. T46–T47
Reteach	pp. R30
Review	p. T86
See	*Handbook for English Language Learners,* pp. 85, 87; *Extra Support Handbook,* pp. 82–83.

Materials

• Word Wall Cards and **Practice Book** punchout word cards: *animal, bird, cold, fall, flower, full, look, of, see*

❶ Teach

Reintroduce and review the word *see*. Point to the word *see* in the Kindergarten Review section of the Word Wall.

- Remind children that they have read this word before, and have them read it aloud with you. Point out that the *s* has the /s/ sound, and *ee* stands for /ē/. Blend /s/ /ē/, *see.*
- Call on children to complete this sentence: *I see a _____.*
- Lead the class in a cheer to help children remember the word. Clap on each letter as you spell and say the word, *s-e-e, see!*

Introduce the new high-frequency words. Display Word Wall Card *bird.*

- Read the word aloud and have children repeat it after you.
- Call on a child to use *bird* in a sentence.
- Post *bird* in the New Words section of the Word Wall.
- Lead the class in a cheer to help children remember the word. Clap on each letter as you spell and say the word, *b-i-r-d, bird!*
- Repeat the procedure for the other high-frequency words.

Chart/Transparency 3–1

In the Fall

It is <u>fall</u>.

But it is not too <u>cold</u>.

<u>Look</u> here.

You can <u>see</u> an <u>animal</u>.

You can see a <u>bird</u> too.

Do you see the <u>flower</u> pot?

It does not have a flower in it.

But it is <u>full</u> <u>of</u> bugs!

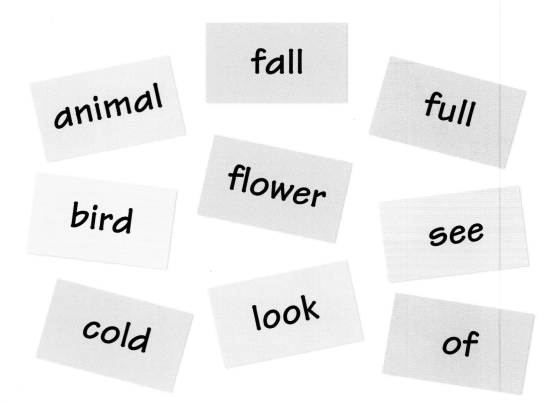

❷ Guided Practice

Have children read the words in context.

Display **Chart/Transparency 3–1.**

- Tell children to follow along as you read the title and the sentences. Point out that the sentences tell about the fall season.

- As you reread the sentences, have children read the underlined words with you.

- Tell children to read the sentences to themselves.

- Call on children to read the sentences aloud.

❸ Apply

- Have children complete **Practice Book** pages 128 and 129 independently, in pairs, or in small groups.

- Have small groups of children practice reading their punchout word cards *animal, bird, cold, fall, flower, full, look, of, see* to one another.

- Have children read the **Phonics Library** story *Fall Naps* independently, with partners, or in small groups.

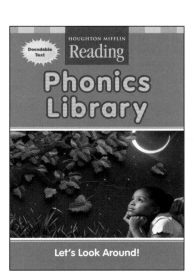

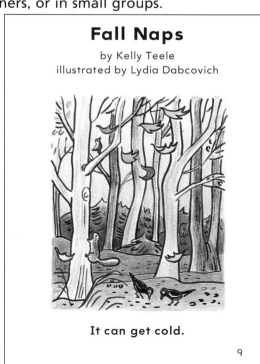

Fall Naps

by Kelly Teele
illustrated by Lydia Dabcovich

It can get cold.

9

Practice Book page 128

Week 1
High-Frequency Words

Name _____

Words to Know

✎ Write a word from the box to complete each sentence in the story.

Word Bank

| animal | full | see | flower |

It Is Cold

"Look!" said Zack.

_____

"I _see (2 points)_ a bird."

"Look!" said Jack.

_____

"I see an _animal (2)_ ."

It is _full (2)_ of nuts."

"Look!" said Pat.

"I have a fall _flower (2)_ here."

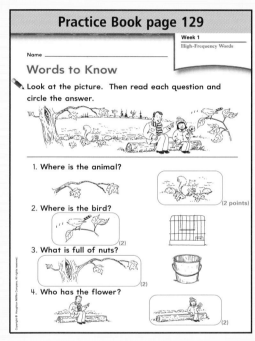

Practice Book page 129

Week 1
High-Frequency Words

Name _____

Words to Know

✎ Look at the picture. Then read each question and circle the answer.

1. Where is the animal?
(2 points)

2. Where is the bird?
(2)

3. What is full of nuts?
(2)

4. Who has the flower?
(2)

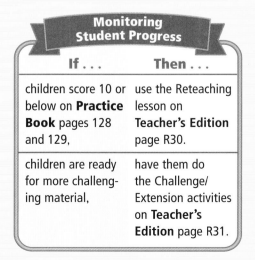

**Monitoring
Student Progress**

If . . .	Then . . .
children score 10 or below on **Practice Book** pages 128 and 129,	use the Reteaching lesson on **Teacher's Edition** page R30.
children are ready for more challenging material,	have them do the Challenge/ Extension activities on **Teacher's Edition** page R31.

High-Frequency Words   **T47**

For This Week

Stories to Read

❶ Get Set Story **❷ Main Story** **❸ Language Arts Link**

Nonfiction   Nonfiction   Nonfiction

Words to Know

animals	full	is
birds	look	lots
cold	of	pick
fall	see	pups
flowers	buds	will

12

Get Set Story

Animals in the Cold

by Sam Wallis

13

Get Set Story

Building Background: Weather and Seasons

Tell children that this week they will read stories about the weather in different places and seasons.

- Ask children to share what they know about the weather in fall, winter, spring, and summer.
- Have children describe the weather on Anthology pages 13–15.

Vocabulary

Have children look at Words to Know on Anthology page 12.

- Read the words with children. Point out that some of the words are on the Word Wall.
- Have children listen to the ending sounds in *buds, is, lots,* and *pups.* Point out that *s* can stand for the sound /s/ or /z/.
- Reread *will* and *pick.* Remind children that at the end of words, *ll* stands for the /l/ sound and *ck* stands for the /k/ sound.
- Have children read to a partner the title of the selection on Anthology page 13. Ask how they figured out how to say the words.

Words to Know

High-Frequency Words

animals	fall	look
birds	flowers	of
cold	full	see

Words with double final consonants; plurals with -s; short *a*

| buds | lots | pups |
| is | pick | will |

 English Language Learners

Winter Weather

Have children talk about what winter is like where you live. If necessary, explain that winter is a cold and snowy season in many places. Point out that in some parts of the world, the weather is wintery all year long. Ask, *Would you like living somewhere cold and snowy? Why or why not?*

THEME 3: Let's Look Around!
(Anthology pp. 12–13)

T48

It is cold here. It is not hot in the sun.

14

Lots of animals live here. They do not see buds and flowers.

15

READING STRATEGY
Phonics/Decoding

Plurals with -s

Teacher/Student Modeling Point out the *s* in *buds*. Have children say the sound /z/. Remind them that *s* at the end of a word often stands for /z/. Help them to blend *buds* sound by sound, /b/ /ŭ/ /d/ /z/, *buds*. Then have children read the second sentence on Anthology page 15.

Extra Support/Intervention

Phonics/Decoding Strategy

If children have trouble decoding, review sounds and letters for short *a*, plurals with *-s*, and double final consonants. Then help them use what they know to decode *buds*, *can*, *will*, and *pups*, using sound-by-sound blending.

Look! A big animal can dig a den. It can **pick** up its cub and go in.

16

Birds **fall** in and go for a dip. They **will** get wet.

17

COMPREHENSION SKILL

Topic, Main Idea, Details/Summarizing

Explain that selections that give readers facts and information usually have a topic, a main idea, and details. Tell children that the topic is what the selection is about: animals in the cold. Ask, *Do many different animals live in the cold?* Explain that the big, important idea in this selection is that many different animals live in cold places. Have children name some of the animals from the selection. (seal, caribou, polar bear, walrus, fox, puffin) Tell them that these are all details that tell more about the big idea.

A den is full of fox pups.

They are not cold in the den.

18

19

CRITICAL THINKING

Guiding Comprehension

1 **TOPIC, MAIN IDEA, DETAILS** What is the author's important idea about animals in the cold? (Sample answer: There are many different animals living in the cold.)

2 **SUMMARIZING** Think about the topic, main idea, and details. Use them to tell about the selection in a few sentences. (The selection is about animals in the cold. Many different animals live in the cold. Some of them are polar bears, foxes, and puffins.)

3 **FANTASY AND REALISM** How do you know whether this selection is about make-believe things or things that happen in real life? (It has photographs of real animals; it tells about real animals.)

REACHING ALL LEARNERS

Extra Support/Intervention

Topic, Main Idea, Details Chart

If children have trouble summarizing, make a chart of the topic, main idea, and details from the selection. Then have children use the chart as a guide and tell about the selection in a few sentences.

OBJECTIVES

- Spell the Basic Words.
- Use high-frequency words in sentences.

Materials

- **Practice Book** punchout trays and letters *a, c, d, h, m, n, t*

Challenge

Completing Sentences

Have children write a Challenge Word to complete each sentence.

1. Baseball players have to ___ a ball. (*catch*)

2. In math, we ___ to find "two plus three." (*add*)

SPELLING:
The Short *a* Sound

Review the Principle Remind children that *a* spells /ă/ at the beginning of *an* and in the middle of *cat*. Also remind them that /ă/ is a vowel sound called *short a*.

Practice/Apply Have children use punchout letters and trays to build words according to the following instructions. After children build each word, write the word and have children check their work.

- Build the word *at*. Then add *c* to build *cat*.
- Build the word *an*. Then add a letter to build *can*.
- Change one letter in *can* to build *man*.
- Build *had*. Which letter remained the same? (*a*)

Penmanship Ball-and-stick *and* continuous-stroke penmanship models are available in the **Practice Book** (pp. 216–223) and the **Teacher's Resource Blackline Masters** (pp. 143–194).

 # VOCABULARY:
High-Frequency Words

Review the Week's Words Together, read each word in the New Words section of the Word Wall and the Kindergarten Review word *see*. Model how to use one of the words in a sentence.

Practice/Apply Have children read the new words and use them in sentences.

- Point to one of the new words. Have a child read it and use it in a sentence.
- That child can choose another word and ask a classmate to read it and use it in a sentence.
- Repeat for all the new high-frequency words.

INTERACTIVE WRITING: A Class Description

Model interactive writing.

- Point out that at the end of *Animals in the Cold,* the fox pups were warm.

- Model how to write this sentence: *The fox pups are not cold!* Encourage children to tell you what letters to write.

Introduce the topic for a class description.

- Tell children that today they will write a description of the neighborhood.

- If possible, take children on a neighborhood walk. Otherwise, have them take an imaginary walk by observing the neighborhood through the window.

Prompt children to contribute to the description.

- Ask, *What does the sky look like? What clothes are people wearing? What are they doing? What does the earth look like? What plants do you see? Are they changing in any way?*

- Have children contribute sentences as you write them on chart paper. Write the child's name after his/her sentence.

- Encourage children to participate by writing familiar letters, words, and punctuation.

- Remind children that a sentence is a group of words that tells about something. Ask, *Who can point to a sentence?*

Read the chart with the class.

- Call on each child to read aloud the sentence that he/she suggested.

- Save the chart. When the season changes, create a new neighborhood description and compare the two charts.

The sky is blue.	Roland
The sun is shining.	Patricia
There is green grass everywhere.	Joey
People are wearing shorts.	Linda

English Language Learners

Dictate Sentences

Work with English language learners as a group. First, make sure children understand the meaning of the sentence *Let's look around!* Encourage children to respond orally before they try to dictate sentences. You may want to provide a sentence frame, such as *I see a _____.* Help children dictate sentences about things they see around them.

DAY 3
week 1

Day at a Glance
pages T54–T71

Learning to Read

Reading the Main Story
Seasons

Responding

Comprehension Instruction
Topic, Main Idea,
Details/Summarizing

• • • • • • • • • • • • • • • • •

Leveled Readers, *T88–T91*
- ● *A Summer Day*
- ▲ *Fun in the Snow*
- ■ *Fall Leaves*
- ◆ *Summer*

Word Work

Spelling: The Short *a* Sound
Vocabulary: Seasons of the Year

Writing & Oral Language

Grammar: What Is a Sentence?
Writing: Responding

Daily Routines

Daily Message

Review skills. Use the Daily Message for a quick review of phonics, high-frequency words, and language skills. Read the message aloud, pointing to each word as it is read. Call on children to answer the question.

- Have children look for plurals ending with -*s*. Then choose children to circle the words.

- Ask children to look for the words *and, I, animals, do, you, cats, birds, The, full,* and *of.* Call on individuals to underline the words.

Hello, Boys and Girls!

I like animals! I like cats and birds and bugs. The world is full of animals. What animals do you like?

Model concepts of print. Point out that there are different kinds of sentences in the main part of the message. Have children find a sentence that ends with a question mark, a sentence that ends with an exclamation point, and a sentence that ends with a period.

Word Wall

KINDERGARTEN REVIEW **High-Frequency Words** Invite children to point to, read, and spell the high-frequency words *play* and *to.* Review the Word Wall words from days 1 and 2. Tell children they will work with these words this week.

play   to

Blackline Masters for these word cards appear in Theme 1 on pp. R39–R40.

Daily Phonemic Awareness

Blending and Segmenting Phonemes: The Name Game

Tell children that they are going to blend sounds together to make words.

- Ask children to say the sound that begins their first name. Have them practice making that sound whenever you point to them.

- Think of some single-syllable words that can be formed using the first sound of students' first names. For example, the word *man* might be formed by taking the first sound of the names M̲att, A̲nn, and N̲ick.

- Point to children in turn and have them say the first sound in their name. Example: Point to Matt, and he says /m̲/. Point to Ann, and she says /ă/. Point to Nick and he says /n̲/.

- Have the class repeat the individual sounds, blend them together, and say the word. If you are missing a sound, just fill it in yourself.

- Continue with other words, such as *bag, crash, dot, chat,* or *sled.*

Daily Language Practice

Grammar Skill: Punctuation

Spelling Skill: The Short *a* Sound

Have children correct the following sentence:

Cann you see the hen.

(**Can** you see the hen?)

Daily Writing Prompt

Have children draw and write about an animal they like, or have them write about self-selected topics.

I like elephants.
They have big ears.

Daily Independent Reading

Remind children to practice reading the Word Wall. Ask them to read from the following.

- Leveled Bibliography, pages T6–T7

Choose books from this list for children to read, outside class, for at least twenty minutes a day.

- Reread Phonics Library story *Fall Naps.*

- Leveled Readers

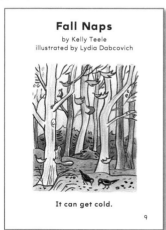

Fall Naps
by Kelly Teele
illustrated by Lydia Dabcovich

It can get cold.

9

Main Story

Vocabulary

Review the Words to Know with children.

Words to Know

New This Week

animals	full	is
birds	look	lots
cold	of	pick
fall	see	pups
flower	buds	will

Kindergarten Review

play

Use **Chart/Transparency 3–2** to introduce the Story Vocabulary. For practice, assign **Practice Book** page 130.

Vocabulary Preview

The Vocabulary Reader can be used to preteach or reinforce the story vocabulary.

Story Vocabulary

bear	rain	summer
insects	south	trees
leaves	spring	winter

Purpose Setting

• Have children share what they know about the seasons. Then ask children to read to decide whether the author does a good job telling about the seasons.

Journal ▶ Children can use their journals to write or draw what they like and don't like about the selection as they read.

Read Together

Meet the Author and Illustrator

Ashley Wolff grew up in the country. She has always loved to watch and draw animals.

20

Chart/Transparency 3–2

Seasons

fall

Leaves fall.
Birds go south.

winter

There are no leaves on the trees.
The bear can nap.

spring

Rain falls.
We can see the flowers.

summer

It is hot.
Insects buzz.
We have fun in the sun!

LET'S LOOK AROUND! Week 1, Day 3
Story Vocabulary Seasons
ANNOTATED VERSION

TRANSPARENCY 3-2
TEACHER'S EDITION PAGE T56

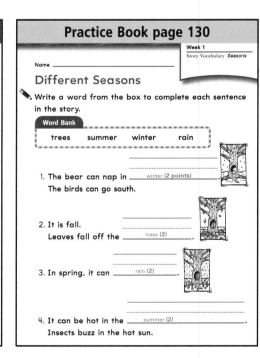

Practice Book page 130

Week 1
Story Vocabulary *Seasons*

Name _____

Different Seasons

✎ Write a word from the box to complete each sentence in the story.

Word Bank

trees	summer	winter	rain

1. The bear can nap in _____ winter (2 points)
   The birds can go south.

2. It is fall.
   Leaves fall off the _____ trees (2).

3. In spring, it can _____ rain (2)

4. It can be hot in the _____ summer (2).
   Insects buzz in the hot sun.

Main Story

Seasons

written and illustrated by
Ashley Wolff

21

Extra Support/Intervention

Preview the Selection

pages 22–25 What do animals do in the spring? What happens to plants in the spring?

pages 26–29 What do animals do in the summer? What happens to plants in the summer?

pages 30–33 What do animals do in the fall? What happens to plants in the fall?

pages 34–39 Point to the big animal on page 37 and explain that it is a woodchuck. What do animals do in the winter? What happens to plants in the winter?

COMPREHENSION STRATEGY

Evaluate

Teacher Modeling Read aloud the title and the author's name. Have children talk about the picture on Anthology page 21. Model how to evaluate a selection.

Think Aloud *As I read* Seasons, *I will try to decide why the author has written this selection. I will think about how she has written it—and whether or not it is easy to understand. If I can learn about the seasons from this selection, then I will know that the author did a good job writing.*

✓ **Test Prep** Children should always ask themselves how they think or feel about what they are reading, even on a test. If they form opinions and remember details that support their opinions, they will answer the questions more accurately.

COMPREHENSION SKILL

Topic, Main Idea, Details/ Summarizing

Explain that the topic of a selection is what the selection is about. Tell children to figure out the topic, or big idea, of this selection and pay attention to the details that tell about it as they read. This will help them summarize the selection after they read it.

Reading the Selection
(Anthology p. 21)

T57

Spring

It is spring.
Animals hop and run in the grass.

22

Trees are full of buds.
Nests are full of eggs.

23

CRITICAL THINKING

Guiding Comprehension

① **TOPIC, MAIN IDEA, DETAILS/SUMMARIZING** Look at
the title on page 21. What is the topic of this selection?
(the seasons)

READING STRATEGY

Phonics/Decoding

Plurals with -s

Teacher/Student Modeling Write *buds* on the board.
Underline *s* and remind children that this letter can stand for
the /z/ sound. Have children look carefully at the word, think
about the sounds for the letters *b, u, d, s*, and blend the word
sound by sound. Point out that an *s* at the end of a word can
mean more than one. Explain that a *bud* is a part of a plant from
which leaves or a flower will grow. Have children read the first
sentence on page 23 to see if *buds* makes sense.

English Language Learners

Supporting Comprehension

Introduce the names of the four seasons: *spring, summer,
fall,* and *winter.* Describe each season, providing some
information about weather, temperature, and events in
nature. Ask children if they have ever seen snow or colorful
fall leaves. Talk about the seasons where you live. If you
live in an area that does not have four distinct seasons,
briefly explain the kinds of weather you do experience.

Word Key

Decodable words with double final consonants; plurals with -s; short a _____

High-Frequency Words _____

Kindergarten High-Frequency Words ========

Story Vocabulary ▭

Note: Kindergarten High-Frequency Words
are reviewed in the Daily Routines on
pages T30 and T54.

THEME 3: Let's Look Around!
(Anthology pp. 22–23)

It <u>will</u> <u>rain</u> in the spring.
<u>Look</u> who <u>can</u> jump and <u>kick</u>
in the mud!

24

The <u>flower</u> buds are wet.
They will get big in the sun.

25

CRITICAL THINKING

Guiding Comprehension

② **FANTASY AND REALISM** How do you know whether this selection is about make-believe things or things that happen in real life? (The selection is about real life because it tells about things that could really happen.)

READING STRATEGY

Phonics/Decoding

Blending More Short *a* Words

Teacher/Student Modeling Write *can* on the board. Underline *a*. Remind children of the short *a* sound, /ă/. Have children look carefully at the word, think about the sounds for the letters *c*, *a*, *n*, and blend the word sound by sound. Repeat with other short *a* words from the selection: *quack, fat, nap*.

Story Vocabulary

spring the season after winter and before summer

trees tall, woody plants with one main stem

rain to fall in drops of water from clouds

DAY
3

MAIN STORY

WEEK 1

Reading the Selection
(Anthology pp. 24–25)

T59

It is <u>summer</u>.
Look who is here!
Three <u>birds</u> are in the nest.

26

<u>Insects</u> <u>see</u> <u>lots</u> of flowers.
They <u>buzz</u> and buzz in the
hot sun.

27

CRITICAL THINKING

Guiding Comprehension

3 **TOPIC, MAIN IDEA, DETAILS/SUMMARIZING** What do you learn about on pages 26 and 27? (some things that happen in summer)

 READING STRATEGY

Phonics/Decoding

Words with Double Final Consonants

Teacher/Student Modeling Write *buzz* on the board. Underline *zz*. Point out that some words have two of the same consonants at the end. Remind children of the sound for the letter *z*, /z/. Have children look carefully at the word, think about the sounds for the letters *b*, *u*, *z*, *z*, and blend the word sound by sound. Repeat with other selection words containing double final consonants: *grass*, *will*, *eggs*, *pass*.

Story Vocabulary

summer the hottest season of the year, between spring and fall

insects small animals with six legs and bodies divided into three main parts

 English Language Learners

Adjectives

Help children use adjectives from the selection, such as *wet*, *hot*, and *three*, to describe the illustrations up to this point. Then, as you continue, introduce new adjectives, such as *red* and *cold*.

THEME 3: Let's Look Around!
(Anthology pp. 26–27)

It is not too hot here.
Ducks quack and quack in
a pond.

28

Two fox pups get a sip.
Lots of animals are here at
the end of summer.

29

CRITICAL THINKING

Guiding Comprehension

4 **NOTING DETAILS** Which animals stay cool at the pond?
(ducks, turtles, foxes, a heron, frogs, a raccoon)

English Language Learners

Language Development

Find out what children know about pond animals. List
their ideas. Point to and name each animal in the picture
on pages 28–29. Have children repeat the word. Point to
the animals again and this time have children name the
animals on their own.

Reading the Selection
(Anthology pp. 28–29)

Fall

It is <u>fall</u>.

30

Lots and lots of red leaves fall.
Animals run and <u>play</u>.

31

CRITICAL THINKING

Guiding Comprehension

5 **COMPARE AND CONTRAST** How is the tree different in the fall and in the summer? (The tree has green leaves in the summer; in the fall, the leaves are red and they are falling off the tree.)

 **COMPREHENSION STRATEGY**

Evaluate

Teacher/Student Modeling Ask children to think about what they have read so far. Ask, *What order did the author put the seasons in? Do you think this is a good way to tell about the seasons?* If necessary, use the model in the Extra Support/Intervention box on this page.

Story Vocabulary

leaves thin, flat parts of plants that come in different shapes

 Extra Support/Intervention

Strategy Modeling: Evaluate

Use this example to model the strategy.

The author began by writing about spring. I learned about animals and plants. Then the author wrote about animals and plants in the summer and in the fall. By telling about the seasons in order, the author helped me understand how things change.

Concepts of Print

Headings Point out that the heading at the top of page 30 tells what these pages are about.

A <u>buck</u> <u>has</u> to get <u>fat</u> for a <u>cold</u> winter.

32

Look who can <u>pick</u> up <u>nuts</u>!
They get set for the cold, too.

33

Guiding Comprehension

6 **MAKING PREDICTIONS** What season will the author write about next? (winter) Why do you think so? (because winter comes after fall)

> ## Story Vocabulary
>
> **winter** the coldest season of the year, after fall and before spring

READING STRATEGY

Phonics/Decoding

Words with Final Consonants *ck*

Teacher/Student Modeling Write *buck* on the board. Underline *ck*. Remind children that the letters *ck* together stand for the /k/ sound. Have children look carefully at the word, think about the sounds for the letters *b, u, c, k,* and blend the word sound by sound. Explain that a male deer is called a *buck*. Have children read the sentence on page 32 to see if *buck* makes sense. Then guide children in reading other selection words with *ck: kick, ducks, quack, pick.*

Winter

It is winter.
It can get cold and wet.
Where do animals go?

34

Birds can go south.

35

CRITICAL THINKING

Guiding Comprehension

 TOPIC, MAIN IDEA, DETAILS/SUMMARIZING What do you learn about on pages 34 and 35? (what happens in winter)

Story Vocabulary

south the direction moving straight down from the North Pole on a globe

REACHING ALL LEARNERS   **On Level**   **Challenge**

Writing About the Seasons

Write the following sentence on the board: *I like _____ best.* Ask children to copy the sentence on a piece of paper. Have them fill in the blank with their favorite season, and then write and draw things they think are special about that season. Children may want to share some of the things they like with the class.

Lots of animals will <u>nap</u> in winter.
A bear will nap in a den.

36

Look who has a winter nap, too!
It is not cold and wet in here.

37

CRITICAL THINKING
Guiding Comprehension

8 **STORY STRUCTURE** How is this selection different from a story with characters, setting, and a problem that needs to be solved? (Sample answer: It gives information; it has a main idea and details rather than a problem and a solution.)

COMPREHENSION STRATEGY
Evaluate

Student Modeling Have children tell whether they think the author did a good job writing about the seasons. If necessary, ask, *Did the author make it easy to understand what happens during the seasons? Why do you think so?* If children need more help, use the model in the Extra Support/Intervention box on this page.

Story Vocabulary

bear a large animal with fur and claws

Extra Support/Intervention

Strategy Modeling: Evaluate

Use this example to model the strategy.

I learned a lot about the seasons. The selection was easy to understand because the author wrote about one season at a time. For each season, the author gave details about animals and plants. I think the author did a good job.

Reading the Selection
(Anthology pp. 36–37)

T65

The cold winter will pass.
Animals will look for spring.

38

39

Wrapping Up

Critical Thinking Questions

1. **DRAWING CONCLUSIONS** Why do you think the animals take naps during the winter? (Sample answers: because it is cold; because there isn't much food in the winter)

2. **COMPARE AND CONTRAST** What makes the seasons different from each other? (Sample answers: different weather; animals behave differently; plants are at different stages of growth)

Comprehension Check

Assign **Practice Book** page 131 to assess children's understanding of the selection.

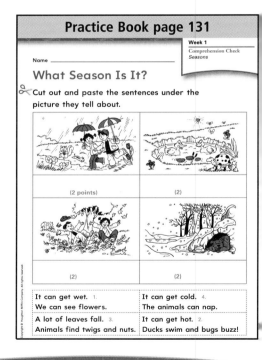

Practice Book page 131

Monitoring Student Progress

If . . .	Then . . .
children have difficulty identifying topic, main idea, or details in the selection,	have them fill in **Chart/Transparency 3–3** as they reread the selection with you.
children have difficulty reading decodable words,	coach them in using the Phonics/Decoding Strategy.

Think About the Story

Seasons

1 How did the animals get ready for the four seasons?

2 What did you learn about winter?

3 What happens during the seasons where you live?

40

Retell the Story

Work with three classmates. Each of you should choose a season. Tell what happens during your season.

 **Writing**

Write a Sentence

Write a sentence about your favorite season.

I can swim in the summer.

41

Responding

Think About the Story

Discuss the questions on Anthology page 40 and the starred question below. Accept reasonable responses.

1. **TOPIC, MAIN IDEA, DETAILS/SUMMARIZING** In spring, they hop, run, jump, and kick, and birds make nests; in summer, they keep cool by a pond; in fall, they run, play, eat to get fat, and collect food; in winter, some birds go south, and some animals nap.

2. **DRAWING CONCLUSIONS** Answers will vary but should include facts from the story.

3. **NOTING DETAILS** Answers will vary.

4. **Connecting/Comparing** How do some of the animals in *Animals in the Cold* and *Seasons* keep warm in the cold weather? (Possible answer: They stay in dens.)

Retell the Story

Tell children to reread the pages that describe the season they chose before they retell that part of the selection.

 Extra Support/Intervention

Responding: Writing Support

List the four seasons. Point to *fall,* and ask, *Who likes* fall *best?* Ask children who choose *fall* to tell why it is their favorite time of year. Continue with the other seasons. Then have children copy the name of the season they like best and draw pictures to show why.

English Language Learners

Supporting Comprehension

Beginning/Preproduction Display pictures representing the four seasons. Guide children in identifying and naming each season.

Early Production and Speech Emergence Have children draw pictures of activities they would like to do during each of the seasons. Help them label each season.

Intermediate and Advanced Fluency Have partners quiz each other about the seasons by asking questions such as, "What happens in the spring?" If necessary, children can refer to the selection.

OBJECTIVES

- Identify topic, main idea, and supporting details.
- Summarize expository text.

Target Skill Trace

Preview	p. T33, T50
Teach	pp. T68–T69
Reteach	p. R36
Review	p. T82
See	*Extra Support Handbook,* pp. 80–81, 86–87

INSTRUCTION

TARGET SKILL COMPREHENSION: Topic, Main Idea, Details/Summarizing

❶ Teach

Discuss topic, main idea, and details in *Counting on the Woods*. Explain that some stories give readers information. Ask children to look for the following information as you reread the Big Book:

- the topic, or what the story is about
- the main idea, or the big, important idea of the story
- the important details that tell more about the main idea

Explain that the topic, main idea, and details can help a reader summarize a story. A summary is a way to tell about a story in just a few sentences.

Modeling Demonstrate how to use topic, main idea, and details to summarize the story.

Think Aloud *I can summarize this selection by telling about the topic, main idea, and details. The topic of this selection is the woods. The main idea is that many different plants and animals live in the woods. The details that tell about those plants and animals are the birds, worms, trees, flowers, and bugs.*

❷ Guided Practice

Complete Chart/Transparency 3–3 with information from *Seasons*. Read the headings aloud and ask,

- *What is this selection about?* (the four seasons)
- *Can you think of a sentence that tells what you learned about the seasons?* If necessary, provide this sentence frame:
  Each season, the <u>weather</u> changes, and the <u>animals</u> do different things.
- *Name some details that tell how the four seasons are different.* (rain, buds, and eggs in spring; flowers, bees, and hot sun in summer; falling leaves and animals storing food in fall; birds going south and animals napping in winter)

Guide children in using topic, main idea, and details to summarize.

Chart/Transparency 3–3

Topic, Main Idea, Details/Summarizing

Title: _____ Seasons

Topic
the four seasons

Big Idea
Each season the weather changes, and animals do different things.

Details
rain, buds, and laying eggs in spring
flowers, insects, and hot sun in summer
falling leaves and animals storing food in fall
birds going south and animals napping in winter

TRANSPARENCY 3–3
TEACHER'S EDITION PAGE T68

LET'S LOOK AROUND! Week 1, Day 3
Comprehension
Topic, Main Idea, Details/Summarizing
ANNOTATED VERSION

❸ Apply

Choose one or more activities.

- Have pairs choose a nonfiction story and summarize with topic, main idea, and details. Distribute copies of **Chart/Transparency 3–3.** Children can complete the chart and summarize for classmates.
- Assign **Practice Book** page 133.
- Have children apply this skill as they read the Leveled Readers.

✓ **Test Prep** Tell children that test questions on nonfiction passages always focus on these elements:
- topic (what the passage is about)
- main idea (the big, important idea in the passage)
- details (information that tells more about the main idea)

Explain that children should begin looking for these elements as soon as they begin reading a nonfiction passage.

Leveled Readers and Leveled Practice

Children at all levels apply the comprehension skill as they read their Leveled Readers. See lessons on pages T88–T91.

| ● BELOW LEVEL | ▲ ON LEVEL | ■ ABOVE LEVEL | ◆ LANGUAGE SUPPORT |

Reading Traits

As children develop the ability to identify topic, main idea, and details, they are learning to "read the lines" of a selection. This comprehension skill supports the Reading Trait **Establishing Comprehension.**

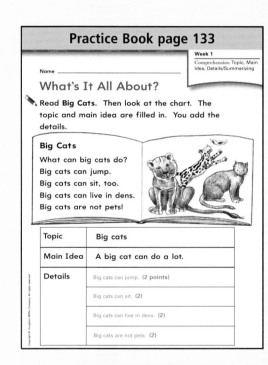

Practice Book page 133

Week 1
Comprehension Topic, Main
Idea, Details/Summarizing

Name _____

What's It All About?

Read **Big Cats.** Then look at the chart. The topic and main idea are filled in. You add the details.

Big Cats

What can big cats do?
Big cats can jump.
Big cats can sit, too.
Big cats can live in dens.
Big cats are not pets!

Topic	Big cats
Main Idea	A big cat can do a lot.
Details	Big cats can jump. (2 points)
	Big cats can sit. (2)
	Big cats can live in dens. (2)
	Big cats are not pets. (2)

Monitoring Student Progress

If . . .	Then . . .
children score 5 or below on **Practice Book** page 133,	use the Reteaching lesson on Teacher's Edition page R36.
children have met the lesson objectives,	have them do the Challenge/Extension activities on Teacher's Edition page R37.

OBJECTIVES

- Write the Basic Words.
- Categorize pictures according to the seasons.

Materials

- old magazines, safety scissors, yarn

Practice Book page 134

Name _____

The Short *a* Sound

Write a word from the box to complete each sentence in the story.

Spelling Words
an
at
can
cat
had
man

1. My pet is ___an (1 point)___ animal.

2. It is a ___cat (1)___ .

3. A ___man (1)___ let me have the cat.

4. He ___had (1)___ a lot of cats.

5. My cat ___can (1)___ do a lot.

6. Look ___at (1)___ my cat jump!

Week 1
Spelling The Short a Sound

SPELLING:
The Short *a* Sound

Story Sentences Write the sentences below.

- Have children read the sentences and brainstorm endings.

- Ask children to write and complete one or two sentences.

- Children can illustrate and share their sentences.

> A man had a cat.
> The cat had a ___.
> The cat can ___.
> The man can ___.

Practice/Homework Assign **Practice Book** page 134.

Penmanship Ball-and-stick *and* continuous-stroke penmanship models are available in the **Practice Book** (pp. 216–223) and the **Teacher's Resource Blackline Masters** (pp. 143–194).

VOCABULARY:
Seasons of the Year

TARGET SKILL

Teach Review *Seasons* on Anthology pages 21–39. Start a word web with *seasons* in the center cell. Ask children to name the four seasons. Write *spring*, *summer*, *fall*, *winter* in the outer cells.

Practice/Apply Pin the web in the center of a bulletin board. Have children cut out magazine pictures that show each of the seasons. Add these to the bulletin board. Use a piece of yarn to connect each picture to the web word it illustrates.

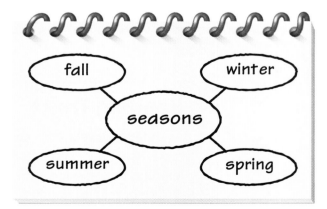

GRAMMAR:
What Is a Sentence?

OBJECTIVES
- Explain what sentences tell about.
- Tell sentences with a partner.

❶ Teach

Define a sentence.

- Write two sentences on the board.

> Dan got a flower pot.
>
> The fox ran to the den.

- Read the sentences. Tell children that a group of words that tells about something is a sentence.

- Call on a child to reread the first sentence. Ask, *Who is this sentence about?* (Dan) *What did Dan do?* (got a flower pot) Repeat for the second sentence.

Go over these points.

- A sentence expresses a complete thought. It tells what someone or something did.

- If a sentence tells what someone or something did, it is called a telling sentence.

❷ Guided Practice

Check children's understanding. Have partners take turns saying sentences that tell. Ask one child to name a person or object. Have another child tell what the person or object is doing or did.

❸ Apply

Assign Practice Book page 135. Have children match sentence parts and write the sentences they made.

Practice Book page 135

Week 1
Grammar What Is a Sentence?

Name _____

Make a Sentence

Draw a line from the part of the sentence that names a person or object to the part of the sentence that tells what the person or object can do.

1. We — can live in a den. (1 point)
2. A fox — can go to school. (1)

Write the sentences you made.

1. We can go to school. (1)

2. A fox can live in a den. (1)

Grammar **T71**

DAY 4
week 1

Day at a Glance
pages T72–T79

Learning to Read

Reading the Language Arts Link
Ha! Ha! Ha!
Phonics Review

• • • • • • • • • • • • • • • • • • • •

Leveled Readers, *T88–T91*
- ● *A Summer Day*
- ▲ *Fun in the Snow*
- ■ *Fall Leaves*
- ◆ *Summers*

Word Work

Spelling: The Short *a* Sound
Vocabulary: Months of the Year

Writing & Oral Language

Independent Writing

Daily Routines

Daily Message

Review high-frequency words and skills. Read the message aloud, pointing to each word as it is read. Call on children to answer the questions. Then ask individuals to underline the words *What, is, Do, you, fall, the, to, see, flowers,* and *in.*

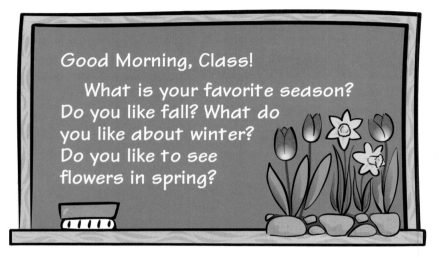

Good Morning, Class!

What is your favorite season?
Do you like fall? What do
you like about winter?
Do you like to see
flowers in spring?

Model concepts of print. Have all children look for the four question marks in the message. Then call on children to underline the question marks.

Word Wall

KINDERGARTEN REVIEW Write a chart similar to the one shown. Point to and read the word *see.* Ask a child to write the missing letter. Repeat with the other words. Next, read the words together. Finally, have children find each word on the Word Wall.

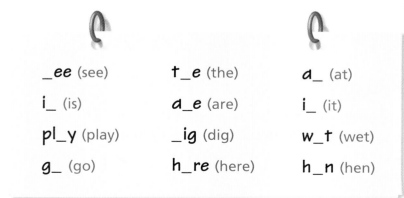

_**ee** (see)	t_**e** (the)	**a**_ (at)
i_ (is)	**a**_**e** (are)	**i**_ (it)
pl_**y** (play)	_**ig** (dig)	w_**t** (wet)
g_ (go)	h_**re** (here)	h_**n** (hen)

 Daily Phonemic Awareness

Blending and Segmenting Phonemes: Word Stretcher

Tell children that they will play a word game.

- Provide something stretchy, such as a short length of elastic, a balloon, or a rubber band. Tell children that it is a word stretcher that can help them stretch words out, and put them back together.

- Model how to stretch the elastic while you stretch a word. Say, *Listen. The sounds are /b/ /ă/ /g/.* Now release one end of the band as you put the word together. Say, *Together the sounds make bag.*

- Pass the elastic to a child. Whisper a single-syllable word to that player. The child stretches the band, says the separate sounds of the word, and asks classmates to signal when they know the word. The child confirms a classmate's response.

- Continue until everyone has had a chance to use the word stretcher.

Daily Language Practice

Grammar Skill: Capital Letters

Spelling Skill: The Short *a* Sound

Have children correct the following sentence:

the mman is my dad.

(The **man** is my dad.)

Daily Writing Prompt

Have children draw and write about a favorite seasonal activity, such as swimming in summer or sledding in winter. Children can also write on self-selected topics. Remind children to use a capital letter at the beginning of each sentence. An Activity Master for this writing activity appears on R49.

Daily Independent Reading

Daily independent exploration and reading of books will increase children's fluency. Ask children to read from the following.

- Leveled Bibliography, pages T6–T7

Choose books from this list for children to read, outside class, for at least twenty minutes a day.

- Leveled Theme Paperbacks

- Reread Anthology story *Seasons*.

Language Arts Link

Skill: How to Read Jokes and Lyrics

- **Introduce** Read aloud the title, "Ha! Ha! Ha!," and have children look at the pictures on all the pages. Ask children if they think these selections are going to be funny or serious. Then tell them that they will be reading some jokes and words to a song.

- **Explain** that jokes and songs are meant to be entertaining.

- **Model** how to read the first joke, stopping to give children a chance to guess the answer. As necessary, explain the humor of substituting the word *quacks* for *cracks*. Reread the first joke to the class, then ask children to read it with you. Model how to read the other jokes, stopping after each to have children take turns reading them aloud. Sing the "Seasons Song" with children to the tune of "Twinkle, Twinkle, Little Star."

Vocabulary

Write the Concept Vocabulary on the board, read the words, and discuss their meanings. Ask children how corn and carrots are alike, then ask them to name other vegetables.

Concept Vocabulary

planted	corn
growing	carrots

Review For children who need a review of phonics and high-frequency words, point out the Words to Know. Remind children that they can use what they've learned to read these words, and coach them to read the sentences in which the words occur.

Words to Know

birds	fall	is
cold	flowers	

Critical Thinking

Guiding Comprehension

1. **NOTING DETAILS** The joke about the duck's roof and the song about the seasons both mention something that happens a lot in spring. What is it? (They both say it rains in the spring.)

2. **FANTASY AND REALISM** Can people really plant corn, carrots, or any vegetables in their ears? (no)

3. **DRAWING CONCLUSIONS** Why do you think people like to tell jokes? (Sample answer: to make people laugh)

4. **CONNECTING/COMPARING**
Compare and Contrast What is something you read about in *Seasons* that you also read about in one of the jokes or the song? (Sample answers: It rains in the spring; the sun is hot in the summer; birds may go south for the winter.)

Language Arts Link
(Anthology pp. 44–45)

T75

OBJECTIVES

- Read and write words with short *u* and known consonants.

Review Skill Trace

Reteach	Theme 2, p. R24
▶ Review	pp. T76–T77

Materials

- **Large Letter Cards** for all consonants and *u*
- **Blending Routines Card 1**
- teacher-made word cards *bug, bus, but, cup, cut, dug, fun, fuss, fuzz, gum, hug, hum, hut, jug, jut, luck, mud, mug, nut, rub, rug, run, suds, sun, tuck*
- clothespins
- rope or string
- nine-square grid for each child
- counters

REVIEW

PHONICS:
Reading Short *u* Words

❶ Review

Review consonants and short *u*.

- Display **Large Letter Card** *u* and review the short *u* sound, /ŭ/.
- Display **Large Letter Cards** spelling *tug*. Using **Blending Routine 1,** review how to blend the sounds: /t//ŭ//g/, *tug*.
- Display *bud, tub,* and *yum*. Call on children to blend and read each word.

❷ Guided Practice/Apply

Have children play Tug-a-Word.

Tug-a-Word

- Using clothespins, hang all the word cards on a length of rope or string.
- Divide the class into two teams. Appoint a captain for each team and have the captains hold opposite ends of the string.
- The captain of one team asks a player on his/her team to tug on the nearest word card to remove it from the line. The player reads the word. If it is read correctly, the team keeps the card. If not, it is returned to the line.
- The captain of the other team then asks a player to remove and read the nearest card. Play continues until all cards have been removed from the line. The team with the most cards wins the game.

PHONICS:
Reading Short *u* Words

❶ Review

Have children listen for short *u* words.

- Write the word *up* on the board. Point to the letters as you blend the sounds. Remind children that the *u* in *up* has the short *u* sound, /ŭ/.

- Tell children to listen carefully as you say some words. Tell them to stand up each time they hear a word with the short *u* sound, as in *up*. Then say these words: *bug, cup, bat, gum, sad, nut, sun, lip, cat, hut, it, bus.*

❷ Guided Practice/Apply

Have children play Word-O.

Word-O

- Provide each child with a nine-square grid and nine counters.

- Display the short *u* word cards. Have children choose nine words to write in the squares on their grids.

- Hold up one word card and ask a child to read it aloud. Players who have that word on their grid cover it with a counter.

- Tell children to say "Word-O" when they cover three words in a row. The first child to say "Word-O" wins. Play for several rounds.

OBJECTIVES

- Spell the Basic Words.
- Make calendar pages with the months of the year.

Materials

- **Large Sound/Spelling Card** *apple*
- red, green, and brown construction paper; safety scissors; tape
- large calendar
- **Teacher's Resource Blackline Master** 202

Practice Book page 136

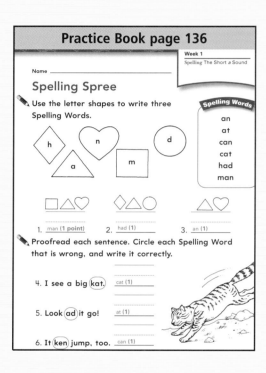

SPELLING:
The Short *a* Sound

Short *a* Apple Tree Review the short *a* sound, using **Large Sound/Spelling Card** *apple*.

- Have children cut one to three apple shapes from red or green construction paper. Give each child a Basic Word to write on each apple.
- Make a paper tree to display on a bulletin board.
- Tape the apples to the tree. Children take turns picking an apple, saying the word, and asking a classmate to spell it.

Practice/Homework Assign **Practice Book** page 136.

Penmanship Ball-and-stick *and* continuous-stroke penmanship models are available in the **Practice Book** (pp. 216–223) and the **Teacher's Resource Blackline Masters** (pp. 143–194).

VOCABULARY:
Months of the Year

Teach Page through a large calendar. Read aloud the name of each month, and point out any special days.

Practice/Apply Ask children to recite the names of the months with you. Write the names of the months on chart paper for reference.

- Ask each child to choose a favorite month and make a calendar page for that month. (See **Blackline Master** 202.)
- Children can add notes for special days.

INDEPENDENT WRITING: Writing About Favorite Seasons

Provide structured writing practice.

- Discuss seasons.
- Dictate this sentence: *It is hot in the sun.*

Ask children to choose a topic.

- Have each child choose a season to write about.

Have children use *Seasons* as a model and complete the following:

- Draw a picture to show something that happens during that season.
- Write the name of the season at the top of **Practice Book** page 137.
- Write one or more sentences telling about the season.

Remind children to look at their pictures if they need ideas for their writing.

Display children's work. Divide a bulletin board into four sections, one for each season. Post children's work and host a sharing time.

Winter

Animals take naps. Birds go south.

OBJECTIVES

- Write about seasonal events.

Practice Book page 137

Week 1
Writing Writing About
Favorite Seasons

Name _____

Which Season Is Your Favorite?

Write about your favorite season.

Season _____ Answers will vary. (2 points)

_____ Answers will vary. (6)

English Language Learners

Words About Seasons

Before English language learners begin to write about their favorite season, brainstorm words associated with each season. For spring, children may say *rain, bird, flower;* for winter, they may suggest *cold, snow, winter nap.* As needed, review words again by showing pictures from *Seasons.* Once children have finished drawing, help them label the objects and activities.

Writing T79

DAY 5 week 1

Day at a Glance
pages T80–T87

Learning to Read

Comprehension: Rereading for Understanding

Rereading for Fluency

Reading Decodable Text
Pam Can Pack

· ·

Leveled Readers, T88–T91

- ● *A Summer Day*
- ▲ *Fun in the Snow*
- ■ *Fall Leaves*
- ◆ *Summer*

Word Work

Spelling: The Short *a* Sound
Vocabulary: High-Frequency Words

Writing & Oral Language

Grammar Review: What Is a Sentence?

Independent Writing

Listening and Speaking

Daily Routines

Daily Message

NOTE: Before posting the Daily Message, place something new in the classroom, such as a new book or a picture of one of the four seasons.

Strategy Review Remind children of the Phonics/Decoding Strategy. Guide them in applying it to selected words in today's message. Then ask individuals to answer the questions.

> Good Morning, Boys and Girls!
>
> Look around the room. What do you see? Do you see anything new since yesterday? Tell me what you think it is.

Model concepts of print. Tell children to look for question marks and periods in the message. Then call on children to circle the punctuation marks.

Vocabulary

Speed Drill On index cards, write the words *animal, bird, cold, flower, fall, full, look, of, see, can, fat,* and *grass.* Have children take turns holding up the cards for a partner to read. After children have practiced, display the cards. Ask individuals to read them to you as quickly as they can.

animal	flower	look
bird	fall	of
cold	full	see
can	fat	grass

Daily Phonemic Awareness

Blending and Segmenting Phonemes: Riddles

- Say each clue below, and then say the separate sounds in the word. Have children blend the sounds and raise their hands when they know the answer. When most hands are up, say the sounds again. Have children whisper the word to a partner, and then have everyone say it together.

- Say these clues:

This is something that cools you off on a warm day: /b//r//ē//z/. (breeze)
This word describes a tire that has lost its air: /f//l//ă//t/. (flat)
This is another word for boat: /sh//ĭ//p/. (ship)
This is the opposite of front: /b//ă//k/. (back)
This is what you do with your hands after someone does a good job: /k//l//ă//p/. (clap)

- Now have children take turns segmenting the separate sounds in a word for others to blend. Some children might want to give a clue as well.

Daily Language Practice

Grammar Skill: Punctuation

Spelling Skill: The Short *a* Sound

Have children correct the following sentence:

We hadd to go

(We **had** to go.)

Daily Writing Prompt

Have children draw and write about something they like to do on weekends, or on self-selected topics. Remind children to use proper punctuation at the end of each sentence.

I go to art class.

Daily Independent Reading

Have children suggest favorite books to friends. They may wish to read from the following.

- Leveled Bibliography, pages T6–T7

Choose books from this list for children to read, outside class, for at least twenty minutes a day.

- Reread Phonics Library story *Fall Naps* or *Pam Can Pack*.

Fall Naps
by Kelly Teele
illustrated by Lydia Dabcovich

It can get cold.   9

Pam Can Pack
by Ruth Kwan
illustrated by Linda Wingerter

Look at Pam.   13

OBJECTIVES

- Review topic, main idea, details and summarizing in the week's selections.

Target Skill Trace	
Preview	p. T33
Teach	pp. T68–T69
Reteach	p. R36
▶ Review	p. T82
See	*Extra Support Handbook*, pp. 80–81; pp. 86–87

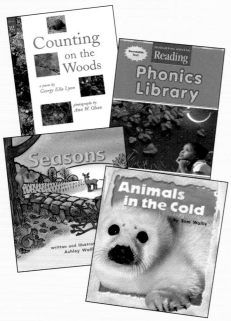

COMPREHENSION: Rereading for Understanding

Topic, Main Idea, Details/Summarizing

Display Chart/Transparency 3–4. Review the terms *topic, big idea,* and *details.* Have children recall *Seasons,* and model how to fill in the chart.

Think Aloud *From the title, I know that the topic of the selection is seasons. The big idea is that each season brings a change in the weather and in what animals do. The details are things that happen during each season. In fall, for example, lots of leaves fall, and animals run and play.*

- Have children identify a few more details from *Seasons* to complete the chart. Repeat for the selection *Animals in the Cold.*

- Then ask children what things were alike and different in the two selections.

Assign rereading and retelling.

- Have children think about topic, main idea, and details as they reread the other selections for the week: **On My Way Practice Reader, On Level/Challenge Theme Paperback, Phonics Library.**

- Have children demonstrate their understanding of topic, main idea, and details as they retell *Seasons.*

Chart/Transparency 3–4
Comparing Stories

Title: Seasons	**Title:** Animals in the Cold
Topic the seasons	**Topic** animals that live in cold places
Big Idea Each season brings a change in the weather and in what animals do.	**Big Idea** Animals do things in cold places.
Details In the spring, trees are full of buds, and nests are full of eggs. In the summer, insects buzz and ducks quack and swim. In the fall, animals look for food for winter. In the winter, some birds go south, and some animals nap in their dens.	**Details** Bears build dens, puffins flap in the water, and foxes live in their dens.

REREADING FOR FLUENCY

Rereading the Selection Have children reread *Animals in the Cold* or pages 30–33 of *Seasons* orally in small groups. Model fluent reading, and coach children to read with feeling and expression.

Singing a Song As an extension of the story, children may enjoy learning and singing the fall song "Five Little Pumpkins." Words and music are on page R54.

HOUGHTON MIFFLIN
Reading

Decodable Text

Phonics Library

Let's Look Around!

Pam Can Pack
by Ruth Kwan
illustrated by Linda Wingerter

Look at Pam.

13

PHONICS LIBRARY

End-of-Week Skills Check

Have children preview *Pam Can Pack*. Ask them to tell what the girl is doing on page 15.

Observe as children model the Phonics/Decoding Strategy.

- Have children read *Pam Can Pack*. As they read, ask individuals to tell how they use the strategy to figure out new words.

- Make note of children who have difficulty applying the strategy, and take oral reading records with these children.

Prompt children in rereading the story. For children who have difficulty, use prompts such as these.

- *Look at the letters from left to right.*

- *Say the sound for each letter and hold it until you say the next sound. What is the word?*

- *Is that a word you know? Does it make sense in the story?*

OBJECTIVES

- Apply the Phonics/Decoding Strategy to decode double final consonants; short *a* words; plurals with *-s*.
- Recognize high-frequency words in context.
- Reread to build fluency.

Word Key

Decodable words with double final consonants; short *a*; plurals with *-s* ———

High-Frequency Words ———

Monitoring Student Progress

Oral Reading Records Take oral reading records of a few children each week as they read the **Phonics Library** book individually or in small groups.

Alternative Assessment Use **Teacher's Resource Blackline Master** 39 to assess individual children's phonics and high-frequency word skills.

Reading Decodable Text **T83**

Pam <u>has</u> a big <u>tan</u> <u>sack</u>.

14

Pam <u>can</u> <u>pack</u> the big tan sack <u>full</u>.

15

Oral Language

Discuss these questions with children. Have them speak in complete sentences.

- Where does Pam pack the flowers? (She packs the flowers in a sack.)

- What does Pam do with the flowers at the end of the story? (She puts the flowers in ten big jugs.)

Pam can get ten big <u>jugs</u> of big, big <u>flowers</u>.

16

Build Fluency

Model fluent reading.

- Call attention to the period on page 14. Explain that this mark means to pause when reading.

- Read page 14 aloud. Have children read it aloud.

- Have children reread pages 14 and 15 several times until each child can read the pages effortlessly.

Home Connection

Hand out the take-home version of *Pam Can Pack*. Ask children to reread the story with their families. (See the **Phonics Library Blackline Masters**.)

OBJECTIVES

- Take a test on the Basic Words.
- Review the week's high-frequency words.

SPELLING: The Short *a* Sound

Test

Say each underlined word, read the sentence, and then repeat the word. Have children write only the underlined word.

Basic Words

1. Hal has **an** ax.
2. I am **at** the ranch.
3. My dad **can** clap.

4. The **cat** ran fast.
5. I **had** a plan.
6. That **man** has a hat.

Penmanship Ball-and-stick *and* continuous-stroke penmanship models are available in the **Practice Book** (pp. 216–223) and the **Teacher's Resource Blackline Masters** (pp. 143–194).

 VOCABULARY: High-Frequency Words

Review the Week's Words Review the words in the New Words section and the Kindergarten Review word *see* with "clap and spell." Remove each word as it is reviewed.

- Call on children to move the words to the permanent Word Wall. The class can chant the words as they are moved.

animal	bird	cold	fall	flower
full	look	of	see	

- Review some other words on the Word Wall.

Practice/Apply Have vocabulary speed drills. Assemble the Word Wall Cards for this week's new words, and make a few other cards for decodable words that feature the week's phonics elements.

- At small-group time, have children take turns holding up the cards for a partner to read.

- Then display the cards as a list. Have individuals read them to you as quickly as they can.

GRAMMAR:
What Is a Sentence?

Review Remind children that a sentence is a group of words that tells what someone or something did or is doing.

Write sentence parts on the board. Have children create sentences orally by using one part from each column. Ask children to write the complete sentences.

Birds	get a pet.
Leaves	go south.
Jan and Dot	fall.

Practice/Apply Coach children's writing. Dictate the following sentences for children to write: *The flower buds are wet. They will get big in the sun.* Have children add a third sentence. You may want to provide the sentence frame *Animals _____ in spring.*

Independent Writing Have children write a story about something they like to do in their favorite season or another story idea of their own. Remind them to write complete sentences.

LISTENING:
Fact or Opinion?

Define fact and opinion.

- Explain that a piece of information that is true is called a *fact*. Give this example: *Some birds fly south when the weather gets cool.*

- Explain that an opinion is what someone thinks about something. Give this example: *I think robins are funny-looking birds.* Point out that words like *I think* are clues that a sentence is an opinion.

Give opinions and facts.

- Have children say some opinions about summer, beginning with the words *I think.* Ask listeners to say, "That's your opinion" after each statement.

- State a few facts about summer, such as *Summer is a season of the year* or *Summer comes after spring.* Have listeners chant, "That's a fact!"

OBJECTIVES

- Identify and write complete sentences.
- Write a story independently.
- Note the difference between a fact and an opinion.

English Language Learners

Fact and Opinion

English language learners will need extra practice distinguishing between facts and opinions. Say, *Facts are things that everyone can see, or everyone can agree are true. Opinions are feelings.* Give some facts, such as *Birds have feathers* and *It often rains in the spring.* Then ask for other examples. Next, present words that signal opinions, including *like, hate, great, good, bad.* Tell children that these words are clues. Give examples, such as *I hate peas* and *That was a great movie!* Ask for other examples.

LEVELED READERS

WEEK 1

A Summer Day

Summary *In this nonfiction book, readers learn about summer and the wide range of things they can see and do during this warm season.*

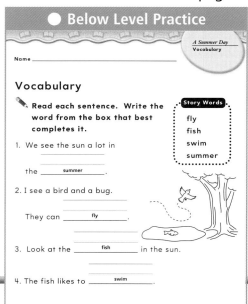

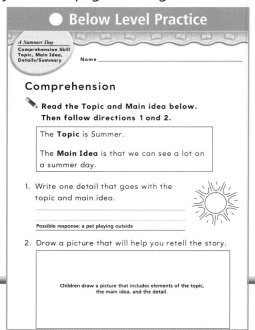

Story Words

Introduce the Story Words, one at a time, providing meaning with objects, pictures, gestures, and/or context sentences. Then ask children to complete the **Vocabulary Practice Master.**

fly *p. 2*

fish *p. 6*

swim *p. 6*

summer *(title), p. 8*

● BELOW LEVEL

Building Background and Vocabulary

Read the title and discuss the cover with children. Explain that this book is about the season of summer. Encourage children to talk about what they might see and do in the summer.

Comprehension Skill: Topic, Main Idea, Details/Summarizing

Read together the Strategy Focus on the book flap. Remind children to use the strategy and to identify the topic, main idea, and details as they read in order to retell the book later. (See the Leveled Readers Teacher's Guide for **Vocabulary and Comprehension Practice Masters.**)

Responding

Have partners discuss how to answer the questions on the inside back cover.

Think About What You Have Read Sample answers:

1. a bird, a bug, flowers, an animal, a fish, a pet, and people
2. Answers may include spring or summer, because flowers are blooming, the garden has lots of bugs in it, and people are doing things outdoors.
3. Answers will vary.

Making Connections Answers will vary.

Building Fluency

Model Reread pages 2 and 3 to children. Point out that the author uses the word *We* to include the reader in what is being told about the summer day. Invite children to locate the repeated words *We can* on other pages.

Practice Ask children to reread pages 4–8 aloud. Have one half of the group read all the sentences that begin with the words *We can*, and the other half read the second sentence on each page. They can read page 8 all together.

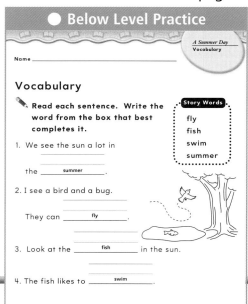

● Below Level Practice

Name _____

A Summer Day
Vocabulary

Vocabulary

✏ **Read each sentence. Write the word from the box that best completes it.**

Story Words
fly
fish
swim
summer

1. We see the sun a lot in

   the ____summer____.

2. I see a bird and a bug.

   They can ____fly____.

3. Look at the ____fish____ in the sun.

4. The fish likes to ____swim____.

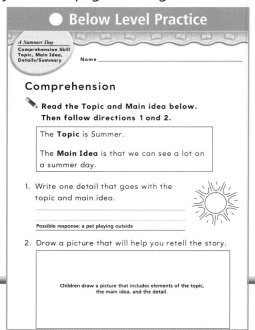

● Below Level Practice

A Summer Day
Comprehension Skill
Topic, Main Idea,
Details/Summary

Name _____

Comprehension

✏ **Read the Topic and Main idea below. Then follow directions 1 and 2.**

The **Topic** is Summer.

The **Main Idea** is that we can see a lot on a summer day.

1. Write one detail that goes with the topic and main idea.

   _____

   Possible response: a pet playing outside

2. Draw a picture that will help you retell the story.

   Children draw a picture that includes elements of the topic, the main idea, and the detail.

▲ ON LEVEL

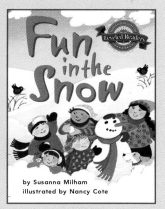

by Susanna Milham
illustrated by Nancy Cote

Fun in the Snow

Summary *This realistic account of winter fun focuses on what people do and see in the snow. The text and illustrations describe activities including making a snowman, feeding birds, looking at animal tracks, making tracks, and just having fun outside in the snow.*

Building Background and Vocabulary

Read the title aloud and have children tell about the cover picture. Ask them to share their own experiences playing in snow. Then take a picture walk through the book discussing the activities children see.

Comprehension Skill: Topic, Main Idea, Details/Summarizing

Read together the Strategy Focus on the book flap. Remind children to use the strategy and to identify the topic, main idea, and details as they read in order to retell the book later. (See the Leveled Readers Teacher's Guide for **Vocabulary and Comprehension Practice Masters.**)

Responding

Have partners discuss how to answer the questions on the inside back cover.

Think About What You Have Read Sample answers:

1. some things you can do and see in the snow
2. Possible answers: squirrels, a dog, birds, rabbits, and a person because they are shown making tracks and the words say so
3. Answers will vary.

Making Connections Answers will vary.

Building Fluency

Model Write the word *We* on the chalkboard and ask the group to read the word aloud. Then ask them to follow along in their books, watching for the word *We* as you reread page 2 to them.

Practice Invite children reread pages 3 through 8 aloud together and to stand each time they read the word *We*.

Story Words

Introduce the Story Words, one at a time, providing meaning with objects, pictures, gestures, and/or context sentences. Then ask children to complete the **Vocabulary Practice Master.**

snow *p. 2*

cold *p. 3*

make *p. 4*

snowman *p. 4*

tracks *p. 6*

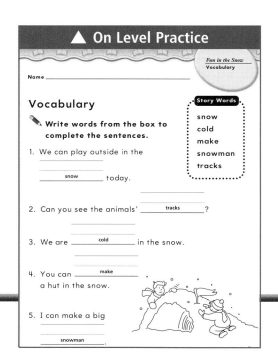

▲ On Level Practice

Fun in the Snow
Vocabulary

Name _____

Vocabulary

Story Words
snow
cold
make
snowman
tracks

✏ Write words from the box to complete the sentences.

1. We can play outside in the
   ____snow____ today.

2. Can you see the animals' ____tracks____ ?

3. We are ____cold____ in the snow.

4. You can ____make____ a hut in the snow.

5. I can make a big
   ____snowman____

▲ On Level Practice

Fun in the Snow
Comprehension Skill
Topic, Main Idea,
Details/Summarize

Name _____

Comprehension

✏ In the chart below, the topic and main idea of <u>Fun in the Snow</u> are filled in for you. Add some details that tell more about the topic and main idea.

Topic	Main Idea
Snow	There's a lot to see and do in the snow.

Details
Answers should include one or all of the following: Snow is cold and wet. We can jump in the snow; make a snowman and snowballs; see bird and animal tracks; make tracks; ski; sled.

Leveled Readers

Fall Leaves

Summary *This nonfiction book shows a family walking through the woods in the fall season. They are looking at the brightly colored leaves. Both text and photos feature different kinds of trees and the shape and color of their leaves in the fall.*

Story Words

Introduce the Story Words, one at a time, providing meaning with objects, pictures, gestures, and/or context sentences. Then ask children to complete the **Vocabulary Practice Master.**

leaves *p. 2*

change *p. 2*

maple *p. 6*

bright *p. 6*

points *p. 6*

syrup *p. 6*

Building Background and Vocabulary

Read the title aloud and discuss the cover with children. Explain that in this book they will read about and see photos of trees and leaves that change color in the fall season. Then invite children to share what they know about different kinds of trees and how they change throughout the year.

Comprehension Skill: Topic, Main Idea, Details/Summarizing

Read together the Strategy Focus on the book flap. Remind children to use the strategy and to identify the topic, main idea, and details as they read so they can retell the book later. (See the Leveled Readers Teacher's Guide for **Vocabulary and Comprehension Practice Masters.**)

Responding

Have partners discuss how to answer the questions on the inside back cover.

Think About What You Have Read Sample answers:

1. different kinds of trees and leaves and what they look like in the fall
2. Possible answer: to dry them out and to keep their colors bright
3. Answers will vary.

Making Connections Answers will vary.

Building Fluency

Model Invite children to reread page 2 aloud with you. Then have them tell the word that names a color. Write *green* on the chalkboard and have the group read it aloud together.

Practice Have children reread pages 3 through 8 aloud with partners, and watch as they read for other words that name colors. Add the color words they find to the chalkboard (*red, gold, dark red, white, gray*).

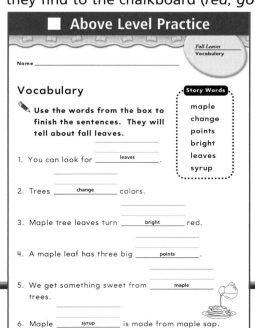

Summer

Summary *This selection presents visual scenes of summer. The photographs include a bird flying, a bug flying, a flower in the sun, a cow basking in the sunshine, a fish swimming in the water, a dog playing, and a group of children and adults enjoying the beautiful summer weather.*

Story Words

Introduce the Story Words. Then ask children to complete the **Story Words Master.**

fly to move in the air, *p. 2*

likes to enjoys, takes pleasure in, *p. 6*

swim to move in water by using fins, arms, or legs, *p. 6*

◆ **LANGUAGE SUPPORT**

Building Background and Vocabulary

Display a picture from the book or another source that shows a summer day. Ask: *How do you know that this is a picture of a summer day?* Guide children to notice the sun, the foliage, perhaps a particular summer activity. Then distribute the **Build Background Practice Master,** read aloud the directions, and have children complete the page. (See the Leveled Readers Teacher's Guide for **Build Background and Story Words Masters.**)

 ## Reading Strategy: Evaluate

Have children read the Strategy Focus on the book flap. Remind children to use the strategy as they read the book.

Responding

Have partners discuss how to answer the questions on the inside back cover.

Think About What You Have Read Sample answers:

1. summer
2. Possible answer: yes, because there is a lot to see and enjoy in the summer
3. Answers will vary.

Making Connections Answers will vary.

 ## Building Fluency

Model Have children point to each word as they listen to pages 2–3 on the audio CD.

Practice Have children read aloud with the recording until they are able to read the text with accuracy and expression.

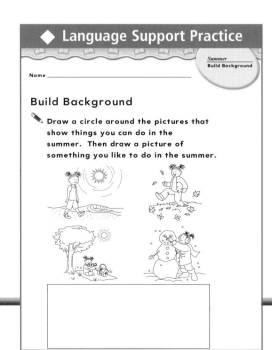

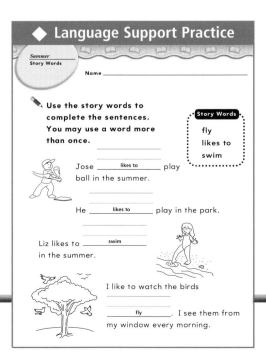

Lesson Overview

Literature

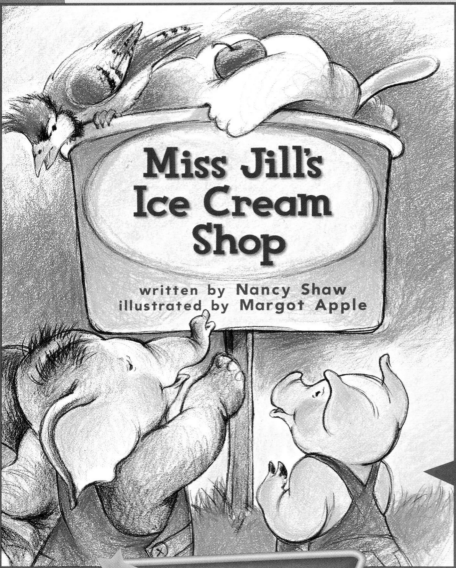

Miss Jill's Ice Cream Shop

written by Nancy Shaw
illustrated by Margot Apple

Selection Summary

One mishap leads to another in Miss Jill's ice cream shop.

1 Big Book

- *Pearl's First Prize Plant*

2 Decodable Text

Phonics Library
- *Lots of Picking*
- *Bill Bird*
- *Tim's Cat*

3 Get Set Story

4 Main Story

Miss Jill's Ice Cream Shop
Genre: Fantasy

Vocabulary Reader

Nonfiction

5 Social Studies Link

Instructional Support

Planning and Practice

Teacher's Edition

Practice Book

Teacher's Resources

Transparencies

Decodable Text

Differentiated Instruction

Intervention Strategies for Extra Support

Instructional Activities for Challenge

Instructional Strategies for English Language Learners

Ready-Made Centers

Building Vocabulary Flip Chart
- center activities
- word skills practice

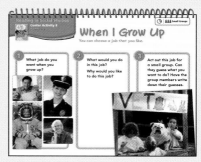

Reading in Science and Social Studies Flip Chart
- books and center activities
- support for state content standards

Hands-On Literacy Centers for Week 2
- activities
- manipulatives
- routines

Technology

Audio Selections
Ham and Eggs
Miss Jill's Ice Cream Shop

www.eduplace.com
- over 1,000 Online Leveled Books

Accelerated Reader®

Leveled Books for Reaching All Learners

Fluency

Increase children's reading fluency using these activities.

● BELOW LEVEL

Model fluent reading of a page. Have each child practice a page and then read it to you.

▲ ON LEVEL

In small groups, have children read a page silently. After each child practices reading the page, have them read it aloud chorally.

■ ABOVE LEVEL

Model fluent reading. Ask each child to read a page of the book to others in small groups. Then have the groups discuss the book.

◆ LANGUAGE SUPPORT

Have children follow along silently while listening to an audio CD. Then have them read aloud two pages while playing back the CD.

Skills Practice

- Topic, comprehension strategy, and vocabulary linked to main selection
- Lessons in Teacher's Edition, pages T160–T163

● BELOW LEVEL

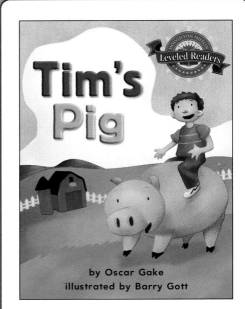

Tim's Pig
by Oscar Gake
illustrated by Barry Gott

▲ ON LEVEL

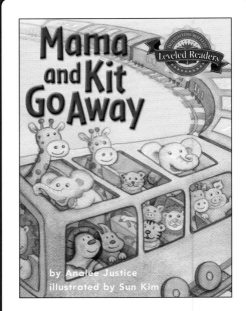

Mama and Kit Go Away
by Analee Justice
illustrated by Sun Kim

● Below Level Practice

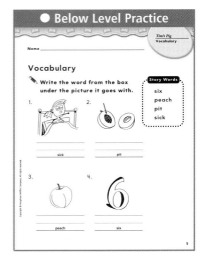

▲ On Level Practice

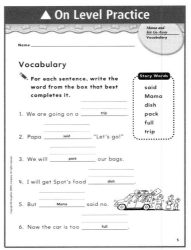

● Below Level Practice

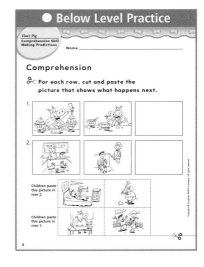

▲ On Level Practice

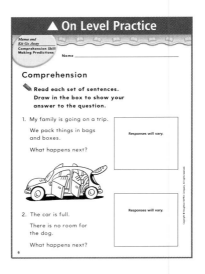

■ ABOVE LEVEL

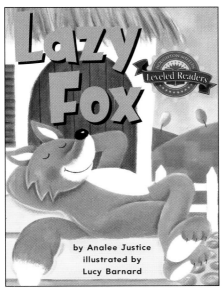

Lazy Fox

Leveled Readers

by Analee Justice
illustrated by
Lucy Barnard

■ Above Level Practice

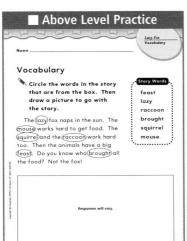

Lazy Fox
Vocabulary

Name _____

Vocabulary

✎ Circle the words in the story that are from the box. Then draw a picture to go with the story.

Story Words
feast
lazy
raccoon
brought
squirrel
mouse

The (lazy) fox naps in the sun. The (mouse) works hard to get food. The (squirrel) and the (raccoon) work hard too. Then the animals have a big (feast). Do you know who (brought) all the food? Not the fox!

Responses will vary.

■ Above Level Practice

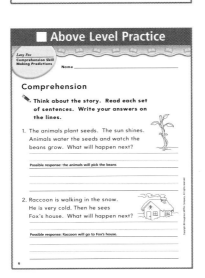

Lazy Fox
Comprehension Skill
Making Predictions

Name _____

Comprehension

✎ Think about the story. Read each set of sentences. Write your answers on the lines.

1. The animals plant seeds. The sun shines. Animals water the seeds and watch the beans grow. What will happen next?

Possible response: the animals will pick the beans

2. Raccoon is walking in the snow. He is very cold. Then he sees Fox's house. What will happen next?

Possible response: Raccoon will go to Fox's house.

◆ LANGUAGE SUPPORT

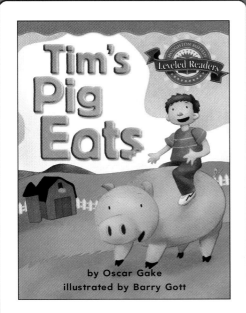

Tim's Pig Eats

Leveled Readers

by Oscar Gake
illustrated by Barry Gott

◆ Language Support Practice

Tim's Pig Eats
Build Background

Name _____

Build Background

✎ Some things really could NOT happen. They are make believe. But some things could happen. Look at the list below and write down the items from the list into the correct column.

A pig eats nuts.
Pigs wear pretty hats.
Pigs eat vegetables.
Pigs walk on two feet.
A pig eats hats.

MAKE BELIEVE Could NOT Happen	Could Really Happen
Pigs wear pretty hats. Pigs walk on two feet. A pig eats hats.	A pig eats nuts. Pigs eat vegetables.

◆ Language Support Practice

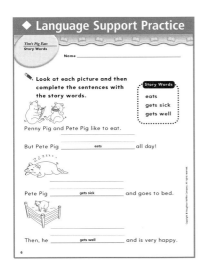

Tim's Pig Eats
Story Words

Name _____

✎ Look at each picture and then complete the sentences with the story words.

Story Words
eats
gets sick
gets well

Penny Pig and Pete Pig like to eat.

But Pete Pig _____ eats _____ all day!

Pete Pig _____ gets sick _____ and goes to bed.

Then, he _____ gets well _____ and is very happy.

Leveled Theme Paperbacks

- Extended independent reading in theme-related paperbacks
- Lessons in Teacher's Edition, pages R6–R9

Apple Picking
by Irma Singer
illustrated by Darcy Schwartz

Houghton Mifflin

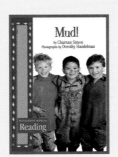

Mud!
by Charnan Simon
Photographs by Dorothy Handelman

Reading

● **BELOW LEVEL**   ▲ **ON LEVEL**

Reading

Pearl's First Prize Plant
Story and Illustrations by A. Delaney

■ **ABOVE LEVEL**

Technology

HOUGHTON MIFFLIN
Online Leveled Books
www.eduplace.com

- over 1,000 Online Leveled Books

Leveled Readers
Audio available

Daily Lesson Plans

Technology

Lesson Planner CD-ROM allows you to customize the chart below to develop your own lesson plans.

T Skill tested on Integrated Theme Test and/or Weekly or Theme Skills Test

80–90 minutes

Learning to Read

Phonemic Awareness
Phonics
Comprehension

Leveled Readers
- Fluency Practice
- Independent Reading

20–30 minutes

Word Work

Spelling
High-Frequency Words
Vocabulary

20–30 minutes

Writing and Oral Language

Writing
Grammar
Listening/Speaking/Viewing

DAY 1

Daily Routines, T102–T103
Phonics, High-Frequency Words,
Phonemic Awareness,
Independent Reading, Writing

Sharing the Big Book, T104–T107

Comprehension Strategy, T104
Predict/Infer

Comprehension Skill, T105
Making Predictions

Phonics, T108–T110
Verb Endings -s, -ed, -ing **T**
Blending More Short *i* Words **T**
Possessives with *'s* **T**

Reading Decodable Text,
T111–T113
Lots of Picking

Leveled Readers
Tim's Pig
Mama and Kit Go Away
Lazy Fox
Tim's Pig Eats

Lessons and Leveled Practice, T160–T163

Spelling, T114
The Short *i* Sound

Vocabulary, T114
Spelling Patterns -ip, -in

Daily Language Practice
1. i see a bird
   (I see a bird.)

Shared Writing, T115
A Persuasive Letter

Viewing, T115
Nonverbal Cues

DAY 2

Daily Routines, T116–T117
Phonics, High-Frequency Words,
Phonemic Awareness,
Independent Reading, Writing

High-Frequency Words, T118–T119
all, call, eat, every, first, never, paper, shall, why **T**

Reading the Get Set Story, T120–T123
Building Background, T120

Vocabulary: all, called, eating, every, first, never, paper, shall, why, fixed, Jack's, licked, yelled

Comprehension Skill, T121
Making Predictions **T**

Leveled Readers
Tim's Pig
Mama and Kit Go Away
Lazy Fox
Tim's Pig Eats

Lessons and Leveled Practice, T160–T163

Spelling, T124
The Short *i* Sound

Vocabulary, T124
High-Frequency Words

Daily Language Practice
2. can you find himm?
   (Can you find him?)

Interactive Writing, T125
A Persuasive Letter

Target Skills of the Week

Phonemic Awareness	Blending and Segmenting Phonemes
Phonics	Verb Endings *-s, -ed, -ing*; Blending Short *i* Words; Possessives with *'s*
Comprehension	Making Predictions
Vocabulary	Spelling Patterns; High-Frequency Words; Possessives; Size Words
Fluency	Decodable Text: Phonics Library; Leveled Readers

DAY 3

Daily Routines, T126–T127

Phonics, High-Frequency Words,

Phonemic Awareness,
Independent Reading, Writing

Vocabulary Reader

Reading the Main Story, T128–T137

Comprehension Strategy, T129
Predict/Infer

Comprehension Skill, T129, T140–T141
Making Predictions **T**
Responding, T138–T139

Leveled Readers
Tim's Pig
Mama and Kit Go Away
Lazy Fox
Tim's Pig Eats

Lessons and Leveled Practice, T160–T163

Spelling, T142
The Short *i* Sound

Vocabulary, T142
Possessives

Daily Language Practice
3. pam has a bg cat.
   (**Pam** has a **big** cat.)

Writing: Responding, T139
Write a Menu

Grammar, T143
Naming Part of a Sentence

Speaking, T139
Retelling

DAY 4

Daily Routines, T144–T145

Phonics, High-Frequency Words,

Phonemic Awareness,
Independent Reading, Writing

Reading the Social Studies Link, T146–T147

Comprehension:
How to Read a Social Studies Article
Visual Literary: Using Photographs, T147

Phonics Review, T148–T149
More Short *a* Words,
Double Final Consonants,
Final *ck*, Plurals with *-s*

Vocabulary Reader

Leveled Readers
Tim's Pig
Mama and Kit Go Away
Lazy Fox
Tim's Pig Eats

Lessons and Leveled Practice, T160–T163

Spelling, T150
The Short *i* Sound

Vocabulary, T150
Size Words

Daily Language Practice
4. sitt here with me.
   (**Sit** here with me.)

Independent Writing, T151
Writing About Favorite Foods

DAY 5

Daily Routines, T152–T153

Phonics,

High-Frequency Words,

Phonemic Awareness,
Independent Reading, Writing

Comprehension: Rereading for Understanding
(Making Predictions **T**) T154

Rereading for Fluency, T154

Reading Decodable Text,
T155–T157
Tim's Cat
End-of-the-Week Skills Check

Vocabulary Reader

Leveled Readers
Tim's Pig
Mama and Kit Go Away
Lazy Fox
Tim's Pig Eats

Lessons and Leveled Practice, T160–T163

Spelling, T158
The Short *i* Sound

Vocabulary, T158
Review: High-Frequency Words

Daily Language Practice
5. What didd jack do?
   (What **did** Jack do?)

Independent Writing, T159
Writing a Story

Grammar, T159
Review: Naming Part of a Sentence

Listening and Speaking, T159
Retelling a Story

Managing Flexible Groups

Leveled Instruction and Leveled Practice

	DAY 1	DAY 2
WHOLE CLASS	• Daily Routines (TE pp. T102–T103) • Read Aloud the Big Book *Pearl's First Prize Plant.* (TE pp. T104–T107) • Phonics lesson (TE pp. T108–T110)	• Daily Routines (TE pp. T116–T117) • High-Frequency Words lesson (TE pp. T118–T119) • Building Background, Vocabulary (TE p. T120)
SMALL GROUPS		
Extra Support	**TEACHER-LED** • Preview vocabulary; support reading with Vocabulary Reader. • Read Phonics Library: *Lots of Picking.* (TE pp. T111–T113) • Read Books 28–30, I Love Reading Books.	**TEACHER-LED** • Read Anthology: Get Set Story. (TE pp. T120–T123) • Read Phonics Library: *Bill Bird.* (TE p. T119) ————————————— **Partner or Individual Reading** • **Fluency Practice** Reread Phonics Library: *Lots of Picking.* (TE pp. T111–T113)
On Level	**TEACHER-LED** • Read Phonics Library: *Lots of Picking.* (TE pp. T111–T113) • Begin Leveled Theme Paperback: On Level. (TE p. R7)	**Partner or Individual Reading** • Read Anthology: Get Set Story. (TE pp. T120–T123) • Read Phonics Library: *Bill Bird* (TE p. T119) AND Leveled Theme Paperback: On Level. (TE p. R3) • **Fluency Practice** Reread Phonics Library: *Lots of Picking* (TE pp. T111–T113) AND read Books 28–30, I Love Reading Books.
Challenge	**Partner or Individual Reading** • Read Phonics Library: *Lots of Picking.* (TE pp. T111–T113) • Read Leveled Theme Paperback: On Level. (TE p. R7)	**TEACHER-LED** • Read silently, Anthology: Get Set Story. • Reread aloud to answer Guiding Comprehension. (TE p. T123) • Read Little Big Book *Pearl's First Prize Plant.* (TE pp. R8–R9) • **Fluency Practice** Read Phonics Library: *Bill Bird.* (TE p. T119) ✔
English Language Learners	**TEACHER-LED** • Preview vocabulary; support reading with Vocabulary Reader. • Together, read Phonics Library: *Lots of Picking.* (TE pp. T111–T113) • Together, read Books 28–30, I Love Reading Books.	**TEACHER-LED** • Reread Phonics Library: *Lots of Picking.* (TE pp. T111–T113) • Read Phonics Library: *Bill Bird.* (TE p. T119) ————————————— **Partner or Individual Reading** • Read with audio CD of Anthology: Get Set Story.

Independent Activities

• Complete, review **Practice Book** pages (138–152) and **Leveled Readers Practice Blackline Masters** (TE pp. T160–T163).
• Reread familiar selections.
• Read trade book from Leveled Bibliography (TE pp. T6–T7).

✔ Opportunity to informally assess oral reading rate.

- Daily Routines (TE pp. T126–T127)
- Vocabulary, Purpose Setting, Comprehension Strategy and Skill (TE pp. T128–T129)

After Reading at Small Group Time
- Responding (TE pp. T138–T139)
- Comprehension lesson (TE pp. T140–T141)

- Daily Routines (TE pp. T144–T145)
- Science Link (TE pp. T146–T147)
- Phonics Review (TE pp. T148–T149)

- Daily Routines (TE pp. T152–T153)
- Rereading (TE p. T154)

TEACHER-LED
- Read Anthology: Main Story. (TE pp. T128–T137)
- **Fluency Practice** Reread Get Set Story (TE pp. T120–T123) AND Phonics Library: *Bill Bird*. (TE p. T119) ✔

TEACHER-LED
- Read the On My Way Practice Reader. (TE p. R 6)
- **Fluency Practice** Reread Books 28–30, I Love Reading Books. ✔

TEACHER-LED
- Read Phonics Library: *Tim's Cat*. (TE pp. T 155–T157)
- Read Leveled Reader: Below Level. (TE p. T160)
- **Fluency Practice** Reread the On My Way Practice Reader (TE p. R6) OR Books 28–30, I Love Reading Books. ✔

TEACHER-LED
- Read silently, Anthology: Main Story.
- Reread aloud to answer Guiding Comprehension. (TE pp. T123, T128–T137)
- **Fluency Practice** Reread Phonics Library: *Bill Bird* (TE p. T119) ✔ OR begin Leveled Reader: On Level. (TE p. T161)

Partner Reading
- **Fluency Practice** Reread Anthology: Main Story (TE pp. T128–T137) OR complete Leveled Reader: On Level. (TE p. T161)

TEACHER-LED
- Reread Anthology: Link. (TE pp. T146–T147)
- Read Phonics Library: *Tim's Cat*. (TE pp. T 155–T157)
- Respond to Leveled Theme Paperback: On Level. (TE p. R7)
- **Fluency Practice** Reread week's Phonics Library books OR Leveled Reader: On Level. (TE p. T161) ✔

Partner or Individual Reading
- Read Anthology: Main Story. (TE pp. T128–T137)
- **Fluency Practice** Reread Anthology: Main Story OR read Leveled Reader: Above Level. (TE p. T162)

TEACHER-LED
- Reread silently, Anthology: Link.
- Reread aloud to answer Guiding Comprehension. (TE pp. 128–T137, T146–T147)
- **Fluency Practice** Reread Little Big Book *Pearl's First Prize Plant*. (TE pp. R8–R9) ✔

Individual Reading
- **Fluency Practice** Reread Anthology: Main Story and Link (TE pp. T128–T137, T146–T147) OR Leveled Reader: Above Level. (TE p. T162)
- Read Phonics Library: *Tim's Cat*. (TE pp. T 155–T157)

TEACHER-LED
- Reread Phonics Library: *Bill Bird*. (TE p. T119)
- Together, reread Anthology: Get Set Story. (TE pp. T120–T123)

Partner or Individual Reading
- Read with audio CD of Anthology: Main Story.

TEACHER-LED
- Together, reread Anthology: Main Story. (TE pp. T128–T137)
- Begin Leveled Reader: Language Support (TE p. T163) OR On My Way Practice Reader. (TE p. R6)

Individual Reading
- **Fluency Practice** Read with audio CD of Anthology: Get Set Story, Main Story.

TEACHER-LED
- Read Phonics Library: *Tim's Cat*. (TE pp. T155–T157)
- Complete Leveled Reader: Language Support (TE p. T163) OR On My Way Practice Reader. (TE p. R6)
- **Fluency Practice** Reread Books 28–30, I Love Reading Books. ✔

Turn the page for more independent activities.

Ready-Made Small Group Activities

Word Work

Cross Curricular

Building Vocabulary Center Activity 8
● ▲ ■ *How Much Is That?*

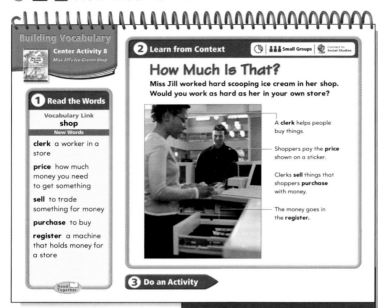

Leveled Activities on side 2

Game Board 2
● ▲ ■ *Toy Store*

Key Vocabulary Cards 38–46

green

Spelling Word Cards 7–12

sit

Reading in Social Studies Independent Boo
● *A Job for You*

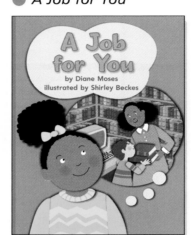

Reading in Social Studies Center Activity 8
● ▲ ■ *When I Grow Up*

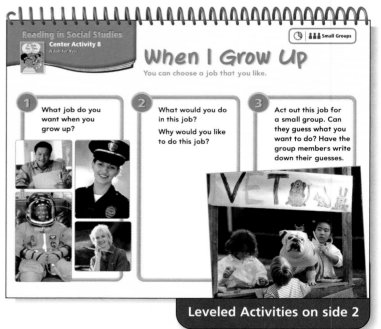

Leveled Activities on side 2

Leveled for ● Below Level, ▲ On Level, ■ Above Level

SMALL GROUP ACTIVITIES

Reading

Routine Card 3
● ▲ ■ *Independent Reading*

RC•3

Independent Reading

1. Choose a book.
2. Read quietly.

Materials
• a book

Show What You Know
Draw and write about the book.
Write the title on your Reading Log.

Grade 1 • Routine Card RC-3 • Side 1   Copyright © Houghton Mifflin Co. All rights reserved.

Challenge Card 3–8
▲ ■ *What Do You Predict?*

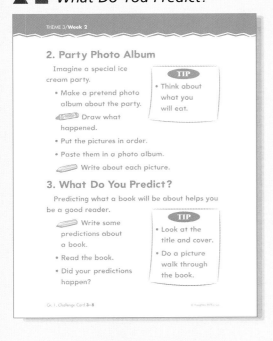

THEME 3/**Week 2**

2. Party Photo Album

Imagine a special ice cream party.

• Make a pretend photo album about the party.

✎ Draw what happened.

• Put the pictures in order.

• Paste them in a photo album.

✎ Write about each picture.

TIP
• Think about what you will eat.

3. What Do You Predict?

Predicting what a book will be about helps you be a good reader.

✎ Write some predictions about a book.

• Read the book.

• Did your predictions happen?

TIP
• Look at the title and cover.
• Do a picture walk through the book.

Gr. 1, Challenge Card **3–8**   © Houghton Mifflin Co.

Writing

Routine Card 6
● ▲ ■ *Write in Your Journal*

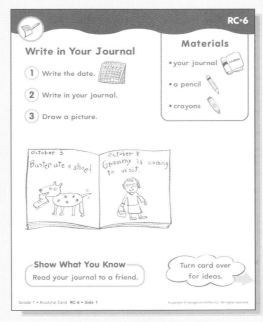

RC•6

Write in Your Journal

1. Write the date.
2. Write in your journal.
3. Draw a picture.

Materials
• your journal
• a pencil
• crayons

october 3
Buster ate a shoe!

october 4
Grammy is coming to visit.

Show What You Know
Read your journal to a friend.

Turn card over for ideas.

Grade 1 • Routine Card RC-6 • Side 1   Copyright © Houghton Mifflin Co. All rights reserved.

Challenge Card 3–5
▲ ■ *Mud!*

THEME 3/**Week 2**

1. *Mud!*

DAY 1

Responding

✎ Write your ideas about the story.

• The boys in the book had fun by

_____

_____

• One time I had fun . . .

_____

Gr. 1, Challenge Card **3–5**   © Houghton Mifflin Co.

Multiple Tiers of Intervention

Core Program Intervention

• research-based
• systematic
• assessment-driven
• extra support
• English learner support
• reteaching

Small Group Intervention

Daily lessons and activities for differentiated instruction

Intervention Strategies for Extra Support, pages 88–97

Instructional Activities for Challenge, pages 34–37

Instructional Strategies for English Learners, pages 92–101

Intensive Intervention

Proven efficacy for struggling readers

Reading Intervention for Early Success

For these materials and more, see **Small Group Independent Activities Kit.**

DAY 1
week 2

Day at a Glance
pages T102–T115

Learning to Read

Sharing the Big Book
Phonics Instruction
Verb Endings *-s, -ed, -ing*
Blending More Short *i* Words
Possessives with *'s*

Reading Decodable Text
Lots of Picking

• • • • • • • • • • • • • • • • • • • •

Leveled Readers, T160–T163

● *Tim's Pig*
▲ *Mama and Kit Go Away*
■ *Lazy Fox*
◆ *Tim's Pig Eats*

Word Work

Spelling: The Short *i* Sound
Vocabulary: Spelling Patterns *ip, in*

Writing & Oral Language

Shared Writing
Viewing

Daily Routines

Daily Message

Review phonics and language skills. Read the message aloud, pointing to each word as it is read. Call on children to answer the question. As they respond, list their answers on chart paper. Then ask children to underline the high-frequency words *and, we, are, to, a, the, in, flowers, of,* and *you.* Children can find and underline two words that end with *-s* to name more than one. Review that the *-s* ending means more than one.

Hi, Boys and Girls!
   Today we are going to read a story about spring and a girl named Pearl. Flowers bloom in the spring. A lot of things begin to grow then. What do you like about spring?

Model concepts of print. Write *Today, going, bloom, grow,* and *story* on index cards. Have children match each card with a word in the message. Then choose a child to point to the word.

Word Wall

(KINDERGARTEN REVIEW) **High-Frequency Words** Have children point to, read, and spell the high-frequency words *go, here, is, a, and, have, I, said,* and *to.* Remind children that they learned these words in kindergarten. Tell children they will read these words this week in new stories.

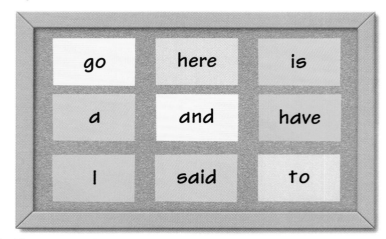

Blackline Masters for these word cards appear in Theme 1 on pp. R39–R40.

Daily Phonemic Awareness

Blending and Segmenting Phonemes: Echo

Tell children that you will say some sounds and that they should listen and repeat the sounds like an echo.

- Have them blend the sounds together, and say the word they make. Say,

/s//ē//d/ (seed)　　　/g//r//ō///z/ (grows)
/g//r//ō/ (grow)　　　/p//r//ī//z/ (prize)
/g//o͞o//d/ (good)　　　/b//ĕ//s//t/ (best)
/t//o͞o//k/ (took)　　　/m//ĭ//l//k/ (milk)

- Continue by reading aloud each of the unsegmented words above. Ask children to segment each word by saying the individual sounds in the proper sequence.

Daily Language Practice

Grammar Skills: Punctuation, Capitalize First Word in a Sentence

Have children correct the following sentence:

i see a bird

(I see a bird.)

Daily Writing Prompt

Ask children to write about something that grows, or have them write on self-selected topics. Encourage children to tell how the thing they have chosen changes as it grows.

Daily Independent Reading

Daily independent exploration and reading of books will increase children's reading fluency. Ask them to read the following.

- Leveled Bibliography, pages T6–T7

Choose books from this list for children to read, outside class, for at least twenty minutes a day.

- Little Big Book *Pearl's First Prize Plant*

Sharing the Big Book

Building Background

Read the title and the name of the author/illustrator. Ask children to tell what they know about how seeds grow.

 ## Fluency Modeling

Tell children you will read a selection about a girl and her plant. Explain that you will model how to read with expression.

COMPREHENSION STRATEGY

Predict/Infer

Teacher Modeling Read aloud the Strategy Focus question on Big Book page 33. Model how to make predictions about the story.

Think Aloud *To predict what will happen, I will read the title and look for clues in the picture on the cover. These things give me hints about what might happen.*

Meet the Author and Illustrator

A. Delaney's first name is Antoinette, but she likes A better. She started drawing before she could read or write. Many of her ideas for books come from things she sees outdoors.

Pearl's First Prize Plant
Story and illustrations by A. Delaney

Strategy Focus
What do you think will happen to Pearl's plant?

32

33

32   **33**

One day in spring,
Pearl planted a seed.

34

35

34   **35**

Day by day, Pearl watched the seed grow into a little green plant.

36

37

36   **37**

Pearl took very good care of her plant.

It grew and grew.

38

39

38   **39**

One day, the little green plant grew a little white flower.

40

41

"Wow!" said Pearl.

"You are the best plant I ever saw!"

42

43

Pearl took the little green plant to the county fair.

44

45

She knew it would win First Prize at the Flower Show.

"Oh, no!" said Pearl.

46

47

COMPREHENSION SKILL

Making Predictions

Tell children to make predictions about what might happen to Pearl's plant. Record their predictions on chart paper, and return to them as you read.

Oral Language and Fluency

Read Aloud: Big Book

Ask children to listen as you read to see if their predictions match the story. Pause occasionally and ask children if they still think their predictions will come true.

Concepts of Print

(Big Book, page 33) Explain that the 's in *Pearl's First Prize Plant* shows that the plant belongs to Pearl.
(Big Book, pages 50–51) Demonstrate how to track print when a sentence begins on one page and ends on the following page.

English Language Learners

Develop Comprehension

Find out what children know about gardens and gardening. If children have experiences with gardening, ask what kinds of plants they grow. If children don't have gardening experience, show a picture of a garden. Point out flowering plants and food plants that grow.

Read Aloud **T105**

Oral Language: Discussion Options

Retelling Remind children that as they read a story, they may need to revise, or change, their predictions. Ask these questions:

- *Did your predictions match what happened in the story?*
- *Did you change your mind about what would happen to the plant during the story? When?*

Literature Discussion Circle Quickly review the speaking and listening etiquette in these Discussion Tips:

- Think about what you want to say.
- Raise your hand before talking, and wait your turn.
- Listen politely when other people are talking.

Then discuss the following questions as a class:

- Why didn't Pearl enter her plant in the flower show?
- Why did Pearl give her plant a blue ribbon?

Pearl looked at the red flowers.

48

She looked at the orange flowers.

49

48   **49**

She looked at the yellow flowers

50

and at the blue flowers.

51

50   **51**

She looked at the purple flowers.

52

Then Pearl looked at her own little green plant, with its little white flower.

53

52   **53**

"Hmph!" she said. And that was that!

54

55

54   **55**

Pearl took her plant home and planted it by an old tree.

56

57

56

57

"You're *my* First Prize Plant!" she said.

58

The rain rained. The sun shone.

59

58

59

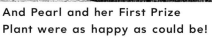

And Pearl and her First Prize Plant were as happy as could be!

60

60

61

REACHING ALL LEARNERS

Challenge

Write a New Ending

Have children suggest an alternative ending to the story. Tell them to imagine that Pearl does enter her plant in the flower show. Ask, *What will Pearl tell the judges? What will the judges say when they see Pearl's plant? What will happen in the end?*

Extra Support/Intervention

Discussing Feelings

Discuss with children why Pearl said "Hmph!" (page 55) and walked away from the flower show. Ask how a person may feel about something he or she tries hard to make or do—even if that thing doesn't win any prizes.

OBJECTIVES

● Read verbs with *-s, -ed, -ing.*

Target Skill Trace

Preteach, Teach	p. T108
Reteach	p. R20
Review	p. T221
See	*Handbook for English Language Learners,* p. 99; *Extra Support Handbook,* pp. 88, 94.

Practice Book page 138

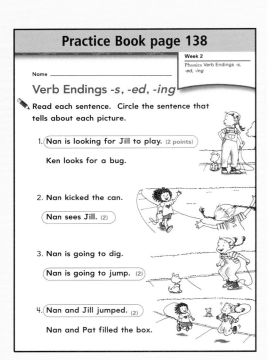

PHONICS: Verb Endings *-s, -ed, -ing*

❶ Teach Phonics

Connect sounds to letters. Write the words as shown.

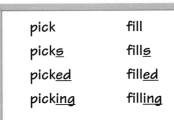

pick	fill
pick<u>s</u>	fill<u>s</u>
pick<u>ed</u>	fill<u>ed</u>
pick<u>ing</u>	fill<u>ing</u>

● Blend and read *pick*: /p/ /ĭ/ /k/, *pick*. Then say, *I pick flowers.* Point out that *pick* is an action word—it tells what someone or something does.

● Explain that the endings *-s, -ed,* and *-ing* can be added to action words. Point to *picks.* Remind children that the letter *s* can stand for /s/ or /z/. Tell them that in this word the *-s* stands for /s/. Together, blend and read the word.

● Point to *picked.* Explain that *-ed* can stand for /d/ or /t/, and in this word *-ed* stands for /t/. Together, blend and read the word.

● Point to *picking.* Explain that the ending *-ing* stands for /ĭng/. Together, blend and read the word.

● Call on children to use each word in a sentence.

● Repeat with the words in the second column, pointing out that *-s* stands for /z/, *-ed* stands for /d/, and *-ing* stands for /ĭng/.

Extend. Have children blend *asked.*

❷ Guided Practice

Check understanding. Write *zips, going, wins, fixed, falling, passed, digs, packing, puffed, passing.* Call on a child to read each word, point to the ending, and use the word in a sentence.

Connect sounds to spelling and writing. Write *kick.*

● Read *kick* aloud. Ask, *What ending should I write to change this word to* kicks? (*s*) Model writing *-s.* Repeat for *kicked* and *kicking.*

● Write *sip, mix, pack, sit, fix, wax, rip.* Call on children to add the endings to make *sips, mixed, packing, sits, fixing, waxed,* and *rips.*

Extend. Have children write *asked.*

❸ Apply

Have children complete **Practice Book** page 138.

Monitoring Student Progress

If . . .	Then . . .
children score 2 or below on **Practice Book** page 138,	use the Reteaching lesson on **Teacher's Edition** page R20.
children have met the lesson objectives,	use the Challenge/ Extension activities on **Teacher's Edition** page R21.

TARGET SKILL PHONICS: Blending More Short *i* Words

❶ Phonemic Awareness

Model how to blend and segment phonemes.

- Have children repeat after you: /l/ /ĭ/ /k/, *lick*. Have them repeat these sounds and blend to say each word: /p/ /ĭ/ /n/ (*pin*), /s/ /ĭ/ /k/ (*sick*), /J/ /ĭ/ /l/ (*Jill*), /m/ /ĭ/ /t/ (*mitt*).

- Have children repeat after you: *pit,* /p/ /ĭ/ /t/. Have them repeat these words and say the sounds: *miss* (/m/ /ĭ/ /s/), *tick* (/t/ /ĭ/ /k/), *hiss* (/h/ /ĭ/ /s/), *pill* (/p/ /ĭ/ /l/).

❷ Teach Phonics

Connect sounds to letters: *i* /ĭ/. Display **Large Sound/Spelling Card** *igloo*. Remind children that *i* is a vowel that stands for the /ĭ/ sound at the beginning of *igloo* and in the middle of *pig*.

Model how to blend short *i* words. Using **Large Letter Cards** and **Blending Routine 1,** model how to blend *kiss*. See instructional Routines, p. T11. Repeat with *Rick* and *sill*.

Extend. Have children blend *mint* and *went*.

| k | i | s | s |

❸ Guided Practice–Word Building

Check understanding. Write *will*. Have children blend *will* as you point to the letters. Repeat for *zips, missed, sick, ticking, ill, licks* and the sentence *Mick and Bill pick up pins.*

Connect sounds to spelling and writing. Say *kick*. Have children repeat it, say its sounds, and build it with punchout letters. Write the word and have children check their work. Repeat with *mill, hissed, digs, ticking, wigs, Bill, sick.*

Extend. Have children build *mint* and *went*.

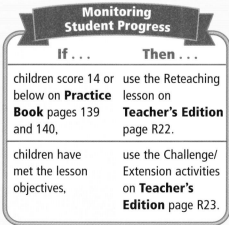

Practice Book page 139

❹ Apply

Have children complete **Practice Book** pages 139–140.

OBJECTIVES

- Blend and segment phonemes.
- Blend and read words with short *i*.

Target Skill Trace	
Preteach, Teach	p. T109
Reteach	p. R22
Review	p. T220

Materials

- **Large Sound/Spelling Card** *igloo*
- **Large Letter Cards** *c, e, i, k, l, l, m, n, R, s, s, t, w*
- **Blending Routines Card 1**
- **Practice Book** punchout trays and letter cards: *B, c, d, e, g, h, i, i, k, k, l, l, m, n, s, s, t, w*

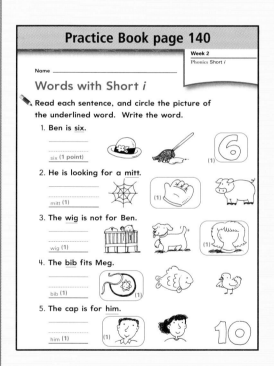

Practice Book page 140

Monitoring Student Progress

If . . .	Then . . .
children score 14 or below on **Practice Book** pages 139 and 140,	use the Reteaching lesson on **Teacher's Edition** page R22.
children have met the lesson objectives,	use the Challenge/Extension activities on **Teacher's Edition** page R23.

OBJECTIVES

● Read nouns with the possessive ending 's.

Target Skill Trace

Preteach, Teach	p. T110
Reteach	p. R24
Review	p. T221
See	*Handbook for English Language Learners,* p. 97; *Extra Support Handbook,* pp. 89, 95.

 PHONICS:
Possessives with '*s*

❶ Teach Phonics

Connect sounds to letters.

Write and read the sentences shown.

> Kim's pet is a pig.
> The vet's kit is big.

● Circle the '*s* in each sentence.

● Explain that in these sentences the apostrophe followed by *s* means that something belongs to someone.

● Remind children that '*s* stands for the sound /z/ or /s/. Model how to blend and read each possessive: /k/ /ĭ/ /m/ /z/, *Kim's;* /v/ /ĕ/ /t/ /s/, *vet's.*

● Underline and reread the phrase *Kim's pet.* Ask, *Whose pet is it?* (Kim's) Repeat for the phrase *vet's kit.*

❷ Guided Practice

Check understanding. Write these phrases on the board: *Jill's pig, two big cats, six dads, the man's hat, Tim's pen, Jim's mitt, a big bass, two pets, my pet's bed, four birds.* Call on a child to read each one. Tell children to raise their hands if the phrase tells that someone owns something. Ask a child to name the owner and what is owned.

Connect sounds to spelling and writing. Write the following sentence frame on the board: _____ mitt fits.

● Ask children to help you write the word *Nick's* to complete the sentence.

● Then have children complete the sentence with as many names as they can. Remind them to include the apostrophe to show that the mitt belongs to someone.

❸ Practice/Apply

Have children complete **Practice Book** page 141.

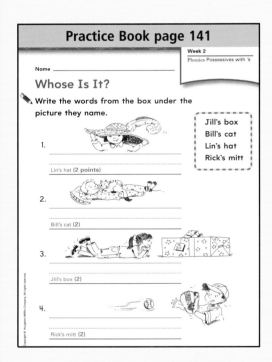

Practice Book page 141

Week 2
Phonics Possessives with '*s*

Name _____

Whose Is It?

✎ Write the words from the box under the picture they name.

| Jill's box |
| Bill's cat |
| Lin's hat |
| Rick's mitt |

1.

Lin's hat **(2 points)**

2.

Bill's cat **(2)**

3.

Jill's box **(2)**

4.

Rick's mitt **(2)**

Monitoring Student Progress

If . . .	Then . . .
children score 6 or below on **Practice Book** page 141,	use the Reteaching lesson on **Teacher's Edition** page R24.
children have met the lesson objectives,	use the Challenge/ Extension activities on **Teacher's Edition** page R25.

Lots of Picking

by Kelly Teele
illustrated by Lars Leetaru

Kim is picking.

17

PHONICS LIBRARY

Reading Decodable Text

Have children preview *Lots of Picking*. Ask them to tell what the girl is doing on page 17.

Model the Phonics/Decoding Strategy. Read the steps of the strategy on **Poster B** and use the strategy to read the story title.

Think Aloud *I see a word I know,* Lot. *I add the /s/ and get* Lots. *I know the next word,* of. *The last word has an ending:* -ing. *I blend the sounds* /p//ĭ//k//ĭng/, picking. *The title is* Lots of Picking.

Apply the Phonics/Decoding Strategy. Have children read *Lots of Picking.* If they have difficulty, remind them to look at each letter and sound out the word. If necessary, use prompts such as these:

- *Look at the letters from left to right.*
- *Think about the sounds for the letters and look for word parts you know.*
- *Say each sound and hold it until you say the next sound. What is the word?*
- *Is that a word you know? Does it make sense in the story?*

OBJECTIVES

- Apply the Phonics/Decoding Strategy to decode verb endings *-s, -ed, -ing;* short *i* words; possessives with *'s.*
- Reread to build fluency.

Word Key

Decodable words with verb endings *-s, -ed, -ing;* short *i;* possessives with *'s* ————

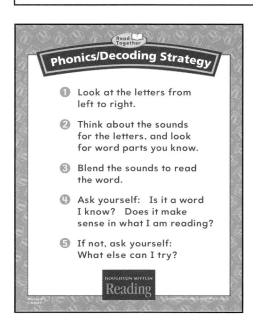

Phonics/Decoding Strategy

1. Look at the letters from left to right.
2. Think about the sounds for the letters, and look for word parts you know.
3. Blend the sounds to read the word.
4. Ask yourself: Is it a word I know? Does it make sense in what I am reading?
5. If not, ask yourself: What else can I try?

Reading Decodable Text **T111**

Kim's Dad <u>picks</u>, too.

18

Kim can get lots.
Kim's Dad <u>gets</u> lots, too.

19

Oral Language

Discuss these questions with children. Have them speak in complete sentences.

- What are Kim and her Dad picking? (They are picking apples.)

- Where do they put the apples? (They put them in baskets and bins.)

- What is a bin? Describe the bins in the story. (Sample answer: A bin is like a box. The bins in the story look like big wooden boxes.)

They filled big bins.

20

Build Fluency

Model fluent reading.

- Read aloud pages 19 and 20. Then have children read the pages aloud.

- Have children reread the same pages several times until each child can read them aloud effortlessly.

Home Connection

Hand out the take-home version of *Lots of Picking*. Ask children to reread the story with their families. (See the **Phonics Library Blackline Masters**.)

OBJECTIVES

- Identify the sound and letter for short *i* in VC and CVC words.
- Spell words with spelling patterns *-ip, -in*.

Materials

- teacher-made word cards *sip, in*

SPELLING WORDS

Basic

big*	it*
in*	him
did	sit

Challenge

dish*	milk*

Forms of these words appear in the literature.

Practice Book page 227

Take-Home Word List	Take-Home Word List
Miss Jill's Ice Cream Shop	Seasons
The Short *i* sound in it him	The Short *a* sound an at can
Spelling Words 1. in 2. it 3. him 4. big 5. sit 6. did	**Spelling Words** 1. an 2. at 3. can 4. cat 5. had 6. man
Challenge Words 1. dish 2. milk	**Challenge Words** 1. catch 2. add
My Study List Add your own spelling words on the back. →	My Study List Add your own spelling words on the back. →

Take-Home Word List

SPELLING: The Short *i* Sound

❶ Teach the Principle

Pretest Say each underlined word, read the sentence, and repeat the word. Have children write only the underlined word.

Basic Words

1. The ant is **in** the grass.
2. What is **it**?
3. I can see **him**.
4. That is a **big** fish.
5. Can I **sit** with you?
6. He **did** not run.

Teach Write the Basic Words, and read them with children.

- Point out that in each word, the vowel *i* is followed by a consonant. Have children identify each final consonant.
- Say that in this vowel-consonant pattern, the short *i* sound, /ĭ/, is usually spelled *i*.

❷ Practice/Apply

Listen for Short *i* Write *bat, it, nap, big, pat, did, dad, him, has, sit*. Have children read each word and raise a hand if they hear /ĭ/.

Practice/Homework Assign **Practice Book** page 227, the Take-Home Word List.

Penmanship Ball-and-stick *and* continuous-stroke penmanship models are available in the **Practice Book** (pp. 216–223) and the **Teacher's Resource Blackline Masters** (pp. 143–194).

VOCABULARY: Spelling Patterns *-ip, -in*

Teach Post *sip* and *in* on the Word Wall. Read the words and explain that these words will help children read and spell other *-ip* and *-in* words.

Practice/Apply Give small groups a paper labeled *sip* or *in*. Have groups write rhyming words. Work together to list all the words on chart paper. (*sip, dip, drip, hip, lip; in, pin, tin, thin, chin*)

SHARED WRITING: A Persuasive Letter

Introduce the topic for a persuasive letter.

- Remind children that in *Pearl's First-Prize Plant,* Pearl went to the county fair.
- Tell children that they will write a letter to their school principal suggesting that the school have a school fair.

Prompt children to contribute to the persuasive letter.

- On chart paper, write the date and greeting. Add a topic sentence such as, *We would like our school to have a school fair.*
- Ask, *Why should our school have a fair?* Write the sentences children contribute to form the body of the letter.
- Add a closing and have children sign the letter.

Display the persuasive letter and read it aloud.

- You may wish to invite the principal to your classroom and have children read the letter aloud.

VIEWING: Nonverbal Cues

Introduce using pictures to interpret nonverbal cues.
Display *Pearl's First Prize Plant.* Tell children that sometimes you can tell a lot about what story characters feel and think by looking at pictures. Use the pictures in the Big Book to help children understand how Pearl is feeling.

- **pages 40–41** (Pearl looks both surprised and pleased at seeing the little white flower on her little green plant.)
- **pages 44–45** (Pearl looks excited to go to the fair.)
- **pages 54–55** (Pearl and the pig look proud and a little mad.)

Ask children to pretend to be Pearl. They can use facial expressions and body motions to show how Pearl feels when she does the following:

- takes her plant home and plants it by an old tree
- awards her plant a blue ribbon

OBJECTIVES

- Contribute ideas for a persuasive letter.
- Interpret nonverbal cues.

Materials

- chart paper
- Big Book *Pearl's First Prize Plant*

English Language Learners

Riddles

English language learners will benefit from repeated opportunities to view the illustrations in the Big Book. Name objects pictured, and have children point to them. Have children repeat the names of the objects; check for correct pronunciation. Make up easy riddles that describe objects. Call on individuals to identify the objects in the riddles. Have more proficient children make up riddles for others to solve.

DAY 2
week 2

Day at a Glance
pages T116–T125

Learning to Read

High-Frequency Words
Reading the Get Set Story
Ham and Eggs
Reading Decodable Text
Bill Bird
. . . .
Leveled Readers, *T160–T163*

- ● *Tim's Pig*
- ▲ *Mama and Kit Go Away*
- ■ *Lazy Fox*
- ◆ *Tim's Pig Eats*

Word Work

Spelling: The Short *i* Sound
Vocabulary: High-Frequency Words

Writing & Oral Language

Interactive Writing

Daily Routines

Daily Message

Review skills. Point to each word as you read the message aloud. Invite children to answer the question. Then call on children to find and circle examples of words with short *i*.

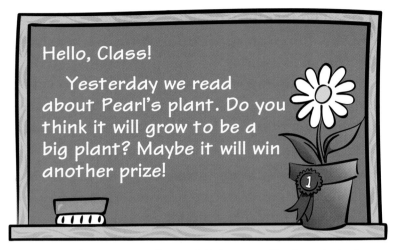

Hello, Class!
 Yesterday we read about Pearl's plant. Do you think it will grow to be a big plant? Maybe it will win another prize!

Model concepts of print. Call on children to find and circle a period that shows the end of a sentence, an exclamation point that shows excitement, and an apostrophe that shows that something belongs to someone.

Word Wall

KINDERGARTEN REVIEW **Pattern Words** Have children find the word *it* on the Word Wall. Ask children to identify each letter and the sound it stands for. (/ĭ//t/) Model blending the sounds. Next, model blending the words *an, pot, wet, at, hen,* and *dig.* Tell children they will work with words that rhyme with these words this week.

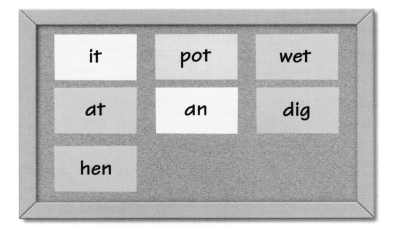

it	pot	wet
at	an	dig
hen		

Blackline Masters for these word cards appear in Theme 1 on pp. R39–R41.

Daily Phonemic Awareness

Blending and Segmenting Phonemes: Silly Story

Read the following silly story aloud, segmenting selected words as shown and pausing for children to blend and say the words.

Once, I sent a little /ă//n//t/ a /g//ĭ//f//t/. I bent to hear it talk. It said "Thank you for the /r//ă//f//t/. Now I do not have to walk! I /l//ĭ//f//t/ myself onto it and ride /ĭ//t/ home!"

Now read naturally, stopping after *ant, gift, raft, it,* and *lift.* This time have children repeat the word and say the sounds in it.

Daily Language Practice

Grammar Skill: Capitalize a Sentence
Spelling Skill: The Short *i* Sound
Have children correct the following sentence:

can you find himm?

(**C**an you find **him**?)

Daily Writing Prompt

Have children draw a picture of a first-prize plant. Then ask them to write a sentence telling about the plant. Children can also write on self-selected topics.

An Activity Master for this writing activity appears on R50.

The plant is yellow, green, and purple.

Daily Independent Reading

Have children read with partners from the following.

● Leveled Bibliography, pages T6–T7

Choose books from this list for children to read, outside class, for at least twenty minutes a day.

● Reread Phonics Library story *Lots of Picking.*

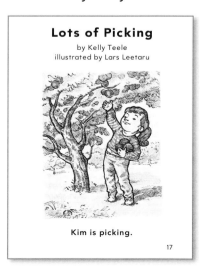

Lots of Picking
by Kelly Teele
illustrated by Lars Leetaru

Kim is picking.

17

OBJECTIVES

- Read and write *all, call, eat, every, first, never, paper, shall, why.*

Target Skill Trace

Teach	pp. T118–T119
Reteach	pp. R32
Review	p. T158
See	*Handbook for English Language Learners,* pp. 95, 97; *Extra Support Handbook,* pp. 92–93.

Materials

- Word Wall Cards and **Practice Book** punchout word cards: *all, call, eat, every, first, never, paper, shall, why*

Chart/Transparency 3–5

Lots to Eat

I get up <u>first</u>.

I <u>call</u> Bill and Tim. They <u>never</u> get up first.

My mom looks at the <u>paper</u>.

My dad and I get the eggs.

We have a lot!

<u>Shall</u> we <u>eat</u> <u>all</u> of the eggs?

<u>Why</u> not?

We will eat <u>every</u> one!

 # HIGH-FREQUENCY WORDS

❶ Teach

Introduce the high-frequency words. Hold up the Word Wall Card *all.*

- Read the word aloud and have children repeat it after you. Point out that the *a* in this word stands for /â/, and the letters *ll* together stand for /l/. Blend /â/ /l/, *all.*

- Call on a child to use *all* in a sentence.

- Post *all* in the New Words section of the Word Wall.

- Lead the class in a cheer in which you clap on each letter as you spell and say the word, *a-l-l, all!*

- Repeat the procedure for *call, eat, every, first, never, paper, shall,* and *why.*

- Remind children to look on the Word Wall when they are writing these words.

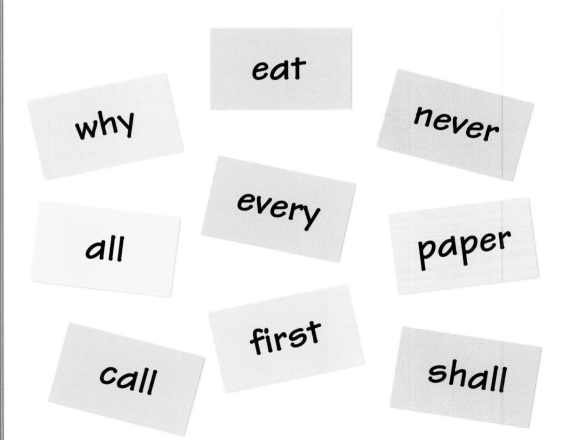

❷ Guided Practice

Have children read the words in context.

Display **Chart/Transparency 3–5.**

- Tell children to follow along as you read the title and the sentences.

- Display the Word Wall Cards one at a time. Choose a child to read each word and read the sentence in which the word appears.

- Tell children to read the sentences to themselves.

- Call on children to read the sentences aloud.

❸ Apply

- Have children complete **Practice Book** pages 142 and 143 independently, in pairs, or in small groups.

- Have partners read their punchout word cards *all, call, eat, every, first, never, paper, shall, why* to one another. Then have them take turns using the words in sentences.

- Have children read the **Phonics Library** story *Bill Bird* independently, with partners, or in small groups.

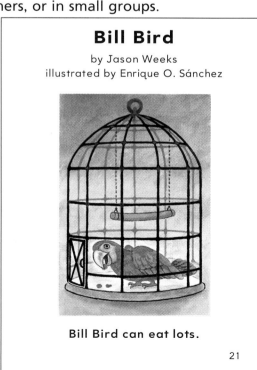

Bill Bird

by Jason Weeks
illustrated by Enrique O. Sánchez

Bill Bird can eat lots.

21

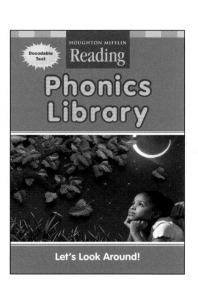

Practice Book page 142

Week 2
High-Frequency Words

Name _____

Words to Know

✎ Draw a line from each sentence to the picture it tells about.

1. Bill got the paper first.

2. "Look at the paper, Dad!" said Bill.
The paper said, "Come eat at Kit's! All kids can have a dip and a bit to eat."

3. "Shall I call Kit's?" said Bill. "I have never had a dip at Kit's."

4. "Why not?" said Dad. "Every kid will go. Get set."

(2 points)
(2)
(2)
(2)

Practice Book page 143

Week 2
High-Frequency Words

Name _____

Words to Know

✎ Circle the sentence that tells about each picture.

1. "Why do we jump?" said Dot Hen.

"Look at the paper first," said Dot Hen.
(2 points)

2. Call all the hens to eat.

"Call all the hens to eat," it said.
(2)

"I never see all the animals," said Fox.

3. "Every flower looks tan," said Fox.

"Shall I call Pig to eat, too?" said Dot Hen.
(2)

Monitoring Student Progress

If . . .	Then . . .
children score 8 or below on **Practice Book** pages 142 and 143,	use the Reteaching lesson on **Teacher's Edition** page R32.
children are ready for more challenging material,	have them do the Challenge/ Extension activities on **Teacher's Edition** page R33.

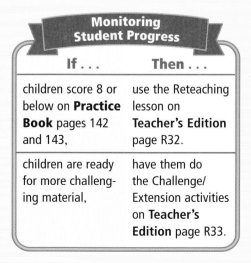

High-Frequency Words **T119**

For This Week

Stories to Read

❶ Get Set Story   ❷ **Main Story**   ❸ Social Studies Link

Realistic Fiction   Fantasy   Nonfiction

Words to Know

all	first	fixed
called	never	Jack's
eat	paper	licked
eating	shall	yelled
every	why	

46

Get Set Story

Ham and Eggs

by Kathryn Mitter

47

Get Set Story

Building Background: Foods We Like

Tell children that this week they will read stories about different kinds of foods. Ask them to name some of their favorite foods.

• Have children tell the story setting on Anthology page 47. (outside a diner or restaurant) Ask, *What do people do at a restaurant?* (order something to eat)

Vocabulary

Have children look at Words to Know on Anthology page 46.

• Read the words with children. Point out that some of these words are on the Word Wall.

• Reread the words *fixed* and *licked*. Point out that these words have the short *i* sound, /ĭ/. Then point out the *-ed* endings.

• Have children find and read other words in the list with *-ed* or *-ing* endings. (*called, eating, yelled*)

• Have children read to a partner the title of the story on Anthology page 47. Ask how they figured out how to say the words.

Words to Know

High-Frequency Words

all	every	paper
called	first	shall
eat	never	why
eating		

Words with verb endings *-s*, *-ed*, *-ing*; possessives with *'s*; short *i*

fixed	licked
Jack's	yelled

English Language Learners

Quotation Marks

Remind children that quotation marks show the exact words of a speaker. On Anthology pages 48–49, point out the words said by the characters in the story. Have children look through the story and find other examples of quotation marks.

"Dad, can we eat at Jack's?" I said.
"Why not?" said Dad.

48

"I never go to Jack's," said Ted.
"It is fun here."

49

TARGET SKILL

COMPREHENSION SKILL

Making Predictions

Remind children that they can make predictions by thinking about what they know in real life and what they know from the story. Explain that as they read and get more information, readers sometimes need to change their predictions. Have children look at Anthology page 49 and describe what is happening in the story. (Sample answers: They are sitting at the table. They are looking at menus.) Ask, *What do you think the children will do?* (Sample answers: order food, order ice cream)

REACHING ALL LEARNERS

Extra Support/Intervention

Making Predictions

If children have trouble making predictions, ask them to describe the illustrations on Anthology pages 48–49. Then help them make a prediction by asking, *What are the children holding? What are menus for? What do you think the children will do next?*

"Here is Jack," said Dad.
Jack had a pen and paper.
"What will you have?" Jack said.
"Let Ted go first," Dad said.

50

"I shall have ham and eggs,"
Ted said.
"Ham and eggs! Ham and eggs!"
we yelled.

51

 **READING STRATEGY**

Phonics/Decoding

Verb Ending -ed

Teacher/Student Modeling Write *fixed*. Cover the
-*ed* and have children use sound-by-sound blending to read
/f/, /ĭ/, /x/, *fix*. Uncover the ending and remind children that
the -*ed* ending can stand for /d/ or /t/. Then have children
finish blending *fixed*.

 Extra Support/Intervention

Phonics/Decoding Strategy

If children have trouble decoding, review the short *i*
sound and the verb ending -*ed*. Then help them use what
they know to decode *fixed, lips,* and *bit,* using sound-by-
sound blending.

Jack fixed us ham and eggs.
"Eat up!" called Jack.
"Yum, yum!" said Ted.

52

Ted licked his lips.
We had every bit of ham and eggs.
We ALL had fun eating at Jack's.

53

CRITICAL THINKING

Guiding Comprehension

1 **DRAWING CONCLUSIONS** Why do you think the children were hungry? (They just finished practicing/playing soccer.)

2 **MAKING INFERENCES** Do you think Ted likes the diner? Why? (Yes; he says it is fun, and he likes to eat ham and eggs.)

3 **MAKING PREDICTIONS** What do you think the children will do after their *next* soccer practice or game? (Sample answers: They will come back to Jack's. They will go get pizza.)

OBJECTIVES

- Spell the Basic Words.
- Write sentences with high-frequency words.

Materials

- **Practice Book** punchout trays and letters *b, d, d, g, h, i, m, n, s, t*

Challenge

Completing Sentences

Have children write a Challenge Word to complete each sentence.

1. Please put the ____ on the table. (*dish*)
2. I will drink a glass of ____. (*milk*)

SPELLING:
The Short *i* Sound

Review the Principle Remind children that *i* spells /ĭ/ at the beginning of *it* and in the middle of *sit*. Also remind them that /ĭ/ is a vowel sound called *short i*.

Practice/Apply Provide punchout letters and trays. Have children work in pairs to build words by following the directions below. Write each word for children to check their work.

- Build the word *in*. Change the last letter to build *it*.
- Add *s* to build *sit*.
- Build the word *did*.
- Now build *big*. Which letter remained the same? (*i*)
- Change the first and last letters to build *him*.

Penmanship Ball-and-stick *and* continuous-stroke penmanship models are available in the **Practice Book** (pp. 216–223) and the **Teacher's Resource Blackline Masters** (pp. 143–194).

VOCABULARY:
High-Frequency Words

Review the Week's Words Point to each word in the New Words section of the Word Wall, and have a child read it.

Practice/Apply Dictate some of the following sentences: *Shall we eat first? You never call me. Why is the paper here? I see every bird.*

- Have children write the sentences.
- After children finish each sentence, write the sentence on the board or use the cards from the Word Wall to build the sentence. Have children check their work.

INTERACTIVE WRITING: A Persuasive Letter

OBJECTIVES
- Contribute sentences for a persuasive letter.
- Participate by writing letters, words, and punctuation in a persuasive letter.

Model interactive writing.

- Point out that Pearl likes her plant.
- Model how to write the sentence *I like my flower!* Encourage children to tell you what letters to write.

Introduce the topic for a persuasive letter.

- Discuss why Pearl thought her plant was a first-prize plant. Talk about Pearl's hard work and her proud feelings about her plant.
- Tell children that today they will write a letter to the judges, telling why Pearl's plant should win a prize.

Prompt children to contribute to the persuasive letter.

- Write the date, greeting, and a topic sentence on chart paper.
- Ask, *Why should Pearl and her plant get a prize?*
- Write the sentences children contribute to complete the body of the letter. Add the closing.
- Encourage children to participate by writing familiar letters, words, and punctuation.

Read the letter with the class.

- Call on children to help read the letter.
- Post the letter in the classroom for children to read.

Dear Judges,

    We think Pearl worked hard to care for her plant. She watered it and gave it vitamins. Pearl played music for her plant. You should give Pearl's plant the prize for Best-Loved Plant.

        Sincerely,

        The students in Room 203

DAY 3
week 2

Day at a Glance
pages T126–T143

Learning to Read

Reading the Main Story
Miss Jill's Ice Cream Shop

Responding

Comprehension Instruction
Making Predictions

• • • • • • • • • • • • • • • • • • •

Leveled Readers, *T160–T163*

● *Tim's Pig*

▲ *Mama and Kit Go Away*

■ *Lazy Fox*

◆ *Tim's Pig Eats*

Word Work

Spelling: The Short *i* Sound

Vocabulary: Possessives

Writing & Oral Language

Grammar: Naming Part of a Sentence

Writing: Responding

Daily Message

Review skills. Use the Daily Message for a quick review of phonics, high-frequency words, and language skills. Read the message aloud, pointing to each word as it is read. Invite children to answer the question.

• Ask children to find an action word that ends with *-s*. (*eats*)

• Ask children to underline the high-frequency words *to, a, and, eats, too,* and *is*. Then ask them to circle any other words they can read.

Good Morning to All of You!

We are going to read a story about Jack and Bill. In the story, Jack eats ice cream. Bill eats ice cream, too. What is your favorite ice cream flavor?

Model concepts of print. Point out the commas in the message. Then reread the message to show how commas tell readers to pause.

Word Wall

KINDERGARTEN REVIEW **High-Frequency Words** Invite children to point to, read, and spell the high-frequency words *she, for, he,* and *the*. Review the Word Wall words from days 1 and 2. Tell children they will work with these words this week.

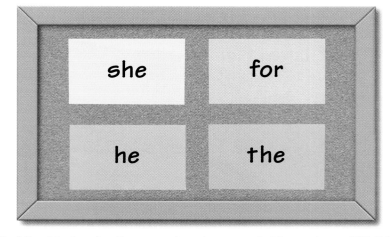

she   for

he   the

Blackline Masters for these word cards appear in Theme 1, pp. R39–R41.

Daily Phonemic Awareness

Blending and Segmenting Phonemes: Simon Says Blend

Play "Simon Says" by giving instructions and calling out the sounds for one of the key words. Children blend to form the word and follow the instruction.

- Say these commands:

Simon says to /k/ /ĭ/ /k/ your leg. (kick)
Simon says to /h/ /ŏ/ /p/ one time. (hop)
Simon says to /s/ /k/ /ĭ/ /p/ to the side. (skip)
Simon says to /b/ /ĕ/ /n/ /d/ down and touch your toes. (bend)
Simon says to /t/ /ĭ/ /p/ your head to one side. (tip)

- Now have children form small groups. Members take turns playing Simon, segmenting commands for others to blend.

Daily Language Practice

Grammar Skill: Capitalizing Names
Spelling Skill: The Short *i* Sound
Have children correct the following sentence:

pam has a bg cat.

(**P**am has a **big** cat.)

Daily Writing Prompt

Have children draw and write about a special day, such as a birthday or a day they did something fun with their family or friends. Children can also write on self-selected topics.

We ate chocolate cake.

Daily Independent Reading

Remind children to practice reading the Word Wall. Ask them to read from the following.

- Leveled Bibliography, pages T6–T7

Choose books from this list for children to read, outside class, for at least twenty minutes a day.

- Reread Phonics Library story *Bill Bird*.

- Leveled Readers

Bill Bird
by Jason Weeks
illustrated by Enrique O. Sánchez

Bill Bird can eat lots.

21

Main Story

Vocabulary

Review the Words to Know with children.

Words to Know

New This Week

all	first	fixed
call	never	Jack's
eat	paper	licked
eating	shall	yelled
every	why	

Kindergarten Review

she

Use **Chart/Transparency 3–6** to introduce the Story Vocabulary. For practice, assign **Practice Book** page 144.

Vocabulary Preview

Vocabulary Reader

The Vocabulary Reader can be used to preteach or reinforce the story vocabulary.

Story Vocabulary

cone	ice cream	shop
dish	kind	try
green	napkins	wish

Purpose Setting

• Ask children to talk about experiences they have had at an ice cream shop. Have them predict what might happen at an ice cream shop for animals when a pig and an elephant want ice cream.

Journal ▶ Children can use their journals to draw or write their predictions about what happens at the ice cream shop.

THEME 3: Let's Look Around!
(Anthology p. 54)

Read Together

Meet the Author
Nancy Shaw likes to write stories that make children laugh. Many of her stories are about animals doing silly things.

Meet the Illustrator
Margot Apple has four cats and three horses. She loves spending time with her horses and drawing pictures.

54

Chart/Transparency 3–6

The Ice Cream Shop

We can go to the ice cream <u>shop</u>.
We can all eat ice cream.
What <u>kind</u> will you <u>try</u>?

I will try <u>green</u> ice cream.
It is mint.

I can have a <u>dish</u>.
I can have a <u>cone</u>.
I can lick the cone.

I <u>wish</u> I had a <u>napkin</u>!

TRANSPARENCY 3–6
TEACHER'S EDITION PAGE T128

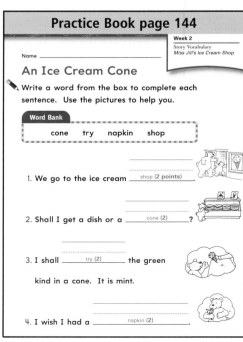

Practice Book page 144

Week 2
Story Vocabulary
Miss Jill's Ice Cream Shop

Name _____

An Ice Cream Cone

Write a word from the box to complete each sentence. Use the pictures to help you.

Word Bank

cone	try	napkin	shop

1. We go to the ice cream _____ shop (2 points)

2. Shall I get a dish or a _____ cone (2) ?

3. I shall _____ try (2) the green kind in a cone. It is mint.

4. I wish I had a _____ napkin (2) .

Main Story

Miss Jill's Ice Cream Shop

written by Nancy Shaw
illustrated by Margot Apple

55

Extra Support/Intervention

Preview the Selection

pages 56–57 Where are Jack and Bill?

pages 58–61 What do Jack and Bill get from Miss Jill?

pages 62–63 What does Jack have now?

pages 64–67 What happens to the ice cream?

pages 68–71 What happens in the shop at the end of the story?

Concepts of Print

Apostrophe Review that the apostrophe in the title shows ownership.

COMPREHENSION STRATEGY
Predict/Infer

Teacher Modeling Read aloud the story title and author's name. Have children look at the pictures on Anthology pages 56–57. Model how to predict what might happen in the story by previewing some of the illustrations.

Think Aloud *As I look at the pictures on these pages, I see a panda behind the counter. That is probably Miss Jill. I also see that there are many ice cream flavors. Maybe the pig and the elephant will have trouble deciding which flavor to choose. As I read, I will check to see if my predictions are right.*

✔ **Test Prep** Tell children to use the Predict/Infer strategy before reading each test passage. First, they should use the title and any pictures to predict whether the passage is fiction or nonfiction. Then they should predict what will happen or what they will learn.

COMPREHENSION SKILL
Making Predictions

Explain that children can make good predictions by thinking about what they know in real life and what they know from the story. Remind children that if they change their minds about their predictions, they can make new ones as they read. Suggest that if children do make new predictions, they should write them in their journals so they can refer to them later on.

Reading the Selection
(Anthology p. 55)

T129

DAY
3

MAIN STORY

WEEK 2

Bill and Jack went to Miss Jill's shop.

56

"Look at all the ice cream!" said Jack. "What shall I eat first?"

57

Guiding Comprehension

1 **FANTASY AND REALISM** How do you know that this story is a fantasy? (Animals are in an ice cream shop; they talk.)

READING STRATEGY

Phonics/Decoding

Possessives with 's

Teacher/Student Modeling Write *Jill's* on the board. Circle the *'s* and remind children that the apostrophe followed by *s* means that something belongs to Jill. Remind children that the letter *s* can stand for the /z/ sound. Have children look carefully at the word, think about the sounds for the letters *J, i, l, l, s,* and blend the word sound by sound. Ask them to read the sentence on page 56 to see if it makes sense.

English Language Learners

Language Development

Before reading the story, preview the meanings of important nouns. Say the word *shop*, and have children repeat it as they point to the shop in the picture. Preview these other nouns: *ice cream, cone, dish, nuts, animals, napkins.*

Word Key

Decodable words with verb endings *-s, -ed, -ing;* possessives with *'s;* short *i* _____

High-Frequency Words _____

Kindergarten High-Frequency Words ═══

Story Vocabulary ▭

Note: Kindergarten High-Frequency Words are reviewed in the Daily Routines on pages T102 and T126.

"Try eating the green ice cream,"
said Bill.
"Why not?" said Jack.
"Miss Jill, what do you call it?"

58

"It is mint," said Miss Jill.
She fixed Jack a mint cone.

59

CRITICAL THINKING

Guiding Comprehension

2 STORY STRUCTURE Who are the characters in this story?
(Miss Jill, Jack, Bill) **What is the setting?** (an ice cream shop)

TARGET SKILL

READING STRATEGY

Phonics/Decoding

Blending More Short *i* Words

Teacher/Student Modeling Write *mint* on the board.
Underline *i*. Remind children of the short *i* sound, /ĭ/. Have
children look carefully at the word, think about the sounds
for the letters *m, i, n, t,* and blend the word sound by sound.
Explain that *mint* is a flavoring made from the leaves of certain
plants. Have children read page 59 to see if *mint* makes sense.

Story Vocabulary

shop a small store

ice cream a sweet frozen food made
from milk or cream and sugar

try taste or sample

green a color made from mixing yellow
and blue

cone an ice cream holder that looks like
an upside-down triangle

"I will have plum in a dish," said Bill.
"He likes lots of nuts on top,"
said Jack.

60

Miss Jill filled Bill's dish and
dumped nuts on top.

61

READING STRATEGY

Phonics/Decoding

Verb Ending -*s*

Teacher/Student Modeling Write *likes* on the board.
Underline *s*. Remind children that the ending -*s* can be added
to a word to make a new word. Remind them that the letter *s*
can stand for the /s/ sound. Have children look carefully at the
word, think about the sounds for the letters *l, i, k, e, s,* and blend
the word sound by sound. Ask them to read the second sentence
on page 60 to see if *likes* makes sense.

Story Vocabulary

dish a flat or shallow container for
holding food

"Yum!" said Jack.
"I will have plum, too."
"Here you go!" said Miss Jill.

62

Jack licked his lips.
"I will have every kind," he said.
Miss Jill added ice cream to
Jack's cone.

63

CRITICAL THINKING
Guiding Comprehension

3 DRAWING CONCLUSIONS Why do you think Jack orders plum ice cream, too? (Sample answer: When he sees that Bill has plum ice cream, he wants the same thing.)

Story Vocabulary

kind flavor

English Language Learners

Language Development

Children may have trouble with some of the past-tense verbs in this story. Model reading some of the *-ed* words, and have children repeat them after you: *fixed, filled, dumped, licked, bumped, yelled, asked.* Listen carefully for the correct pronunciation of the ending. Help children make a list of past-tense verbs they encounter in selections in this theme for future reference.

"You will <u>never</u> eat it all," said Bill.
"Yes, I will!" said Jack.

64

Jack had his first <u>big</u> lick.
"Look!" <u>yelled</u> Bill. "It is <u>falling</u>!"

65

CRITICAL THINKING

Guiding Comprehension

4 **COMPARE AND CONTRAST** How is this story different from a selection that you read to get information? (It has characters, a setting, and a problem for characters to solve. It is a fantasy.)

 COMPREHENSION STRATEGY

Predict/Infer

Teacher/Student Modeling Ask children to think about what has happened in the story so far. Have them predict what Jack will do next. Ask, *Has Jack done everything he said he would do? Do you think he will eat all of his ice cream?* If necessary, use the model in the Extra Support/Intervention box on this page.

Strategy Modeling: Predict/Infer

Use this example to model the strategy.

Jack wanted mint ice cream, and he got it. He wanted every kind of ice cream, and he got that, too. So when Jack says he will eat all of his ice cream, I predict that he will do it.

THEME 3: Let's Look Around!
(Anthology pp. 64–65)

Jack bumped Bill.
Bill fell, and up went his ice cream.
Ice cream fell on all of the animals.

66

Miss Jill ran to get paper napkins.
She fell, too.

67

CRITICAL THINKING

Guiding Comprehension

5 **MAKING PREDICTIONS** What do you think the other animals in the shop will do after the ice cream falls?
(Sample answer: They will run out the door.)

Story Vocabulary

napkins pieces of soft paper used to wipe the mouth and fingers while eating

READING STRATEGY

Phonics/Decoding

Verb Ending *-ed*

Teacher/Student Modeling Write *bumped* on the board. Underline *ed*. Remind children that the ending *-ed* can be added to an action word to make a new word. Remind them that the letters *ed* can stand for the /t/ sound. Have children look carefully at the word, think about the sounds for the letters *b, u, m, p, e, d,* and blend the word sound by sound. Ask them to read the first sentence on page 66 to see if it makes sense.

"What a mess!" yelled Bill.
"I can help!"

68

"Run! Run!" yelled the animals.

69

CRITICAL THINKING

Guiding Comprehension

6 NOTING DETAILS How does Bill try to help? (He sprays water from his trunk to try to clean up the mess.)

 COMPREHENSION STRATEGY

Predict/Infer

Student Modeling Have children predict how they think the story will end. If necessary, ask, *Did Jack and Bill make a mess on purpose? Will Miss Jill be upset with them?* If children need more help, use the model in the Extra Support/Intervention box on this page.

Story Vocabulary

wish to want something

REACHING ALL LEARNERS **Extra Support/Intervention**

Strategy Modeling: Predict/Infer

Use this example to model the strategy.

Jack and Bill have made a big mess, but it was an accident. Bill did try to help clean up. I don't think Miss Jill will be too upset. I predict Jack and Bill will feel bad at the end of the story.

"I wish I had asked for a dish," said Jack.

70

71

Wrapping Up

Critical Thinking Questions

1. **DRAWING CONCLUSIONS** How do you think Jack and Bill feel at the end of the story? (Sample answer: sorry for the mess they have made)

2. **MAKING PREDICTIONS** What will the characters do next? (Sample answer: Jack and Bill will help Miss Jill clean up the mess.)

Comprehension Check

Assign **Practice Book** page 145 to assess children's understanding of the selection.

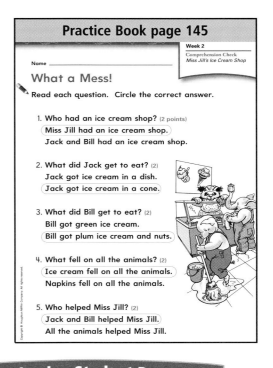

Practice Book page 145

Week 2
Comprehension Check
Miss Jill's Ice Cream Shop

Name _____

What a Mess!

Read each question. Circle the correct answer.

1. Who had an ice cream shop? (2 points)
   (Miss Jill had an ice cream shop.)
   Jack and Bill had an ice cream shop.

2. What did Jack get to eat? (2)
   Jack got ice cream in a dish.
   (Jack got ice cream in a cone.)

3. What did Bill get to eat? (2)
   Bill got green ice cream.
   (Bill got plum ice cream and nuts.)

4. What fell on all the animals? (2)
   (Ice cream fell on all the animals.)
   Napkins fell on all the animals.

5. Who helped Miss Jill? (2)
   (Jack and Bill helped Miss Jill.)
   All the animals helped Miss Jill.

Monitoring Student Progress

If . . .	Then . . .
children have difficulty making predictions about the story,	reread the story with them, pausing to ask what they think will happen next and why.
children have difficulty reading decodable words,	coach them in using the Phonics/Decoding Strategy.

Reading the Selection
(Anthology pp. 70–71)

T137

Responding

Think About the Story

Miss Jill's Ice Cream Shop

1 What kind of ice cream did Jack get first?

2 How did ice cream get on all of the animals?

3 What do you think Jack will get at Miss Jill's next time? Why?

72

Retell the Story

Act out the story with two classmates. Use masks.

 Writing ▶

Write a Menu

Write a menu for Miss Jill's shop. Draw pictures for the menu.

dish

cone

brownie sundae

73

Responding

Think About the Story

Discuss the questions on Anthology page 72 and the starred question below. Accept reasonable responses.

1. **NOTING DETAILS** mint

2. **CAUSE AND EFFECT** Bill fell, his ice cream went up into the air and hit the fan, and the ice cream landed on the animals.

3. **MAKING PREDICTIONS** Possible answer: He will get a dish because it might not tip over.

4. **Connecting/Comparing** Is *Miss Jill's Ice Cream Shop* a good story for the theme *Let's Look Around!*? Why? (Answers will vary.)

Retell the Story

See **Teacher's Resource Blackline Masters 40–42** for masks.

OBJECTIVES

- Make predictions based on personal knowledge and story details.

Target Skill Trace

Preview	p. T105, p. T121
Teach	pp. T140–T141
Reteach	p. R38
Review	p. T154
See	*Extra Support Handbook,* pp. 90–91, 96–97

COMPREHENSION: Making Predictions

❶ Teach

Discuss making predictions. Explain that people can use clues and what they know to predict what might happen in life or in stories.

- Blow up a balloon. Move a pin toward the balloon. Ask children to predict what will happen. Then push the pin into the balloon.
- Ask children what clues they used to make their predictions. (The balloon has a thin skin. The pin is sharp.)

Explain that readers make predictions about stories in a similar way.

Modeling Demonstrate how to make predictions about *Miss Jill's Ice Cream Shop.*

Think Aloud *When I read that Jack got every kind of ice cream in a cone, I predicted he would eat all the ice cream. Then I saw that the ice cream cone was very tall. I changed my prediction. I predicted that the ice cream would fall.*

Explain that readers make good predictions by thinking about what they know in real life and what they know from the story. Point out that readers review and change their predictions if they get new information.

❷ Guided Practice

Make predictions about other fiction books.

- Display the covers of a few books and ask children to predict what each story will be about.
- Record the predictions and discuss the reasons for them.
- Read or page through the stories with children. Review the predictions and discuss whether any need to be changed.

Title	We predict...
We Hide, You Seek	The animals will not be able to find each other.
I Went to the Bay	The boy will ~~go sailing on a ship~~ look for frogs.

❸ Apply

Choose one or more activities.

- Have partners choose a fiction story, make predictions about it, and then read and revise their predictions.
- Assign **Practice Book** page 147.
- Have children apply this skill as they read the Leveled Readers.

Test Prep Tell children that they can read the test questions for a given passage before they read the passage itself. They can use the questions to predict what the passage will be about and what important information they should look for in order to answer the questions.

Leveled Readers and Leveled Practice

Children at all levels apply the comprehension skill as they read their Leveled Readers. See lessons on pages T160–T163.

● BELOW LEVEL ▲ ON LEVEL ■ ABOVE LEVEL ◆ LANGUAGE SUPPORT

Reading Traits

As children develop the ability to predict outcomes, they are learning to "read between the lines" of a selection. This comprehension skill supports the Reading Trait **Realizing Context**.

Practice Book page 147

Week 2
Comprehension Making Predictions

Name _____

What Happens Next?

Cut out and paste a picture to show what happens next.

Monitoring Student Progress

If . . .	Then . . .
children score 3 or below on **Practice Book** page 147,	use the Reteaching lesson on Teacher's Edition page R38.
children have met the lesson objectives,	have them do the Challenge/Extension activities on Teacher's Edition page R39.

Practice Book page 149

Name _____

Week 2
Spelling The Short *i* Sound

The Short *i* Sound

Write a word from the box to complete each sentence in the story.

Spelling Words

in
it
him
big
sit
did

1. Dad ___did (1 point)___ not see me.

2. I filled a box for ___him (1)___ .

3. The ___big (1)___ box looked full.

4. I said to Dad, "You can ___sit (1)___ here."

5. Dad said, "What is ___in (1)___ the box?"

6. I said, "Look in ___it (1)___ and see!"

SPELLING:
The Short *i* Sound

Big Word Books Give each child three pieces of paper. Tell children they are going to write the spelling words in big letters.

• Have children hold their papers horizontally. Dictate the words as children write a word on each side of the paper.

• Write each word so children can check their spelling.

• Help children staple the pages together to make a book. Children can use their books to review the spelling words.

Practice/Homework Assign **Practice Book** page 149.

Penmanship Ball-and-stick *and* continuous-stroke penmanship models are available in the **Practice Book** (pp. 216–223) and the **Teacher's Resource Blackline Masters** (pp. 143–194).

TARGET SKILL

VOCABULARY:
Possessives

Teach Ask children to draw a favorite thing and label it following this model: *Jan's cat*. Point out that *'s* shows to whom something belongs.

• Write and read aloud *my, mine, yours, her, hers, his, their,* and *theirs*. Explain that these words tell to whom things belong.

• Choose a child's picture and ask questions using possessives: *Is this* my *hat*? *Is it* his *hat*? *Is it* her *hat*?

• Repeat for a few more pictures.

Practice/Apply Have small groups write sentences about other children's pictures. Ask children to use some of the words on the board.

Dinosaurs

My dinosaur book is cool.

GRAMMAR:
Naming Part of a Sentence

OBJECTIVES

- Distinguish naming parts from action parts in sentences.
- Match naming and action parts to make complete sentences.

Materials

- blank sentence strips
- safety scissors

❶ Teach

Define the naming part of a sentence.

- Write the following sentences on the board.

> Ken jumps.
> The animals ran.
> Van picks flowers.
> The pot is hot!
> Ben calls and calls.
> The paper is in the box.

- Read the first sentence with children.

- Explain that a sentence has two parts: a naming part and an action part. Tell children that the naming part names someone or something.

- Ask children to find the naming part in the first sentence. (*Ken*) Draw a vertical line between *Ken* and *jumps*.

- Repeat for the remaining sentences. (Naming parts are *The animals, Van, The pot, Ben, The paper.*)

Go over these points.

- Each sentence has a naming part and an action part.

- The naming part names someone or something.

❷ Guided Practice

Check children's understanding.

- Make copies of one or two of the sentences from the board and distribute them to children. Have them cut apart each sentence to separate the naming part from the action part.

- Tell children to put the sentences back together. They can refer to the the board for help. Make corrections as needed.

- Ask individuals to read their sentences.

❸ Apply

Assign Practice Book page 150. Have children write the naming part of each sentence.

Practice Book page 150

Name _____

Week 2
Grammar Naming Part of a Sentence

Naming Parts

✎ Read each sentence, and write the naming part.

1. Tim runs.   Tim (2 points)

2. The cat sits.   cat (2)

3. The pot falls.   pot (2)

4. Dad gets the flowers.   Dad (2)

DAY 4
week 2

Day at a Glance
pages T144–T151

Learning to Read

Reading the Science Link
Making Ice Cream

Phonics Review
• •

Leveled Readers, *T160–T163*
- ● *Tim's Pig*
- ▲ *Mama and Kit Go Away*
- ■ *Lazy Fox*
- ◆ *Tim's Pig Eats*

Word Work

Spelling: The Short *i* Sound
Vocabulary: Size Words

Writing & Oral Language

Independent Writing

Daily Routines

Daily Message

Review phonics and language skills. Read the message aloud, pointing to each word as it is read. Call on children to complete the sentence. Then have children look for a word that ends with *-ing,* and call on a child to underline it. Have children look for each of the high-frequency words *all, call, every,* and *shall* before calling on individuals to underline them.

Hello to All of You!

   Today is going to be a big day.
We have a lot of work to do. We
are going to _____.
I shall call on each and
every one of you to help.

Model concepts of print. Ask children to show how to track the print in the message from top to bottom and from left to right. Ask them to show how to make the return sweep.

Word Wall

KINDERGARTEN REVIEW Write a chart similar to the one shown. Point to and read the word *for.* Ask a child to write the missing letter. Repeat with the other words. Next, read the words together. Finally, have individuals find each word on the Word Wall.

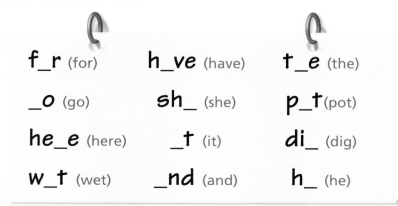

f_r (for)	h_ve (have)	t_e (the)
_o (go)	sh_ (she)	p_t (pot)
he_e (here)	_t (it)	di_ (dig)
w_t (wet)	_nd (and)	h_ (he)

Daily Phonemic Awareness

Blending and Segmenting Phonemes: Name the Picture

In a pocket chart, turn over the **Picture Cards** *braid, crow, dress, gray, prize, train.*

- Tell children that you will say the sounds in a word slowly, and that they should blend the sounds together to name your hidden picture.

- Say each of the sets of sounds shown here. Then choose a child to blend the sounds and name the **Picture Card** that matches the word.

- Have children work in pairs. One child can segment the sounds, and a partner can blend them to name the picture.

/g//r//ā/ (gray)   /b//r//ā//d/ (braid)
/d//r//ĕ//s/ (dress)   /p//r//ī//z/ (prize)
/t//r//ā//n/ (train)   /k//r//ō/ (crow)

Daily Language Practice

Grammar Skill: Beginning Sentences with Capital
               Letters

Spelling Skill: The Short *i* Sound

Have children correct the following sentence:

sitt here with me.

(**Sit** here with me.)

Daily Writing Prompt

Have children draw and write about a favorite book they recently read, or have them write on self-selected topics.

An Activity Master for this writing activity appears on R51.

Mr. Bear met some bees.

Daily Independent Reading

Remind children to practice reading the Word Wall. They can select books to read from the following.

- Leveled Bibliography, pages T6–T7

Choose books from this list for children to read, outside class, for at least twenty minutes a day.

- Leveled Theme Paperbacks

- Reread Anthology story *Miss Jill's Ice Cream Shop.*

Mud!
By Charnan Simon
Photographs by Dorothy Handelman

HOUGHTON MIFFLIN
Reading

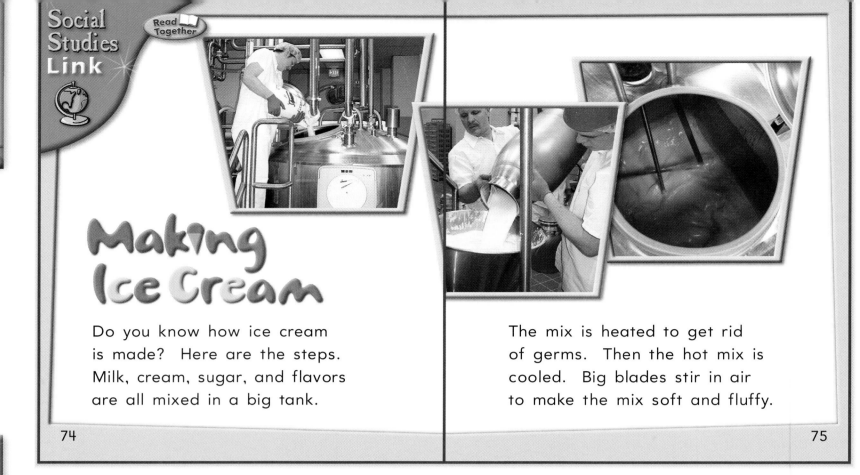

Making
Ice Cream

Do you know how ice cream
is made? Here are the steps.
Milk, cream, sugar, and flavors
are all mixed in a big tank.

The mix is heated to get rid
of germs. Then the hot mix is
cooled. Big blades stir in air
to make the mix soft and fluffy.

74

75

Social Studies Link

Skill: How to Read a Social Studies Article

- **Introduce** the article by reading the title and asking children to look at the photographs.

- **Explain** to children that "Making Ice Cream" is an article. Remind them that an article does not tell a story; instead, it gives information about a topic.

- **Point out** that the title of this article tells what the article is about. As children read the article, they will learn the steps involved in the process of making ice cream.

- **Model** how to read this article. Reread the title. With children, create a sequence chart. Write the heading. Read page 74 with children; write the first step on the chart. Tell children this is the first step in the process. Continue reading, asking children to identify consecutive steps. List them on the chart.

Steps for Making Ice Cream

1. Mix milk, cream, sugar, and flavors in a big tank.
2. Heat the mixture to get rid of germs.
3. Stir the mixture until it's soft and fluffy.
4. Add cookie bits and chips.
5. Put into tubs, then in the freezer.

Vocabulary

Write the Concept Vocabulary on the board and read each word. Ask children to find each item in the photographs on pages 74–76 and to tell how it is used in making ice cream.

Concept Vocabulary

tank	tubs
blades	freezer

Review For children who need a review of phonics and high-frequency words, point out the Words to Know. Remind children that they can use what they've learned to read these words, and coach them to read the sentences in which the words occur.

Words to Know

all	eat

THEME 3: Let's Look Around!
(Anthology pp. 74–75)

Things like cookie bits and chips get added last. The ice cream is put into tubs. The tubs go into a freezer.

76

Trucks bring the ice cream to stores. What flavor will you eat?

Critical Thinking

Guiding Comprehension

1. **MAIN IDEA/DETAILS** What is this article mostly about? (how to make ice cream)

2. **CAUSE AND EFFECT** Why is the ice cream heated? (to get rid of germs)

3. **NOTING DETAILS** What words describe the mixture after blades stir air in? (soft, fluffy)

4. **CONNECTING/COMPARING**
   Making Predictions What flavors do you predict Jack and Bill, from *Miss Jill's Ice Cream Shop,* would mix into the ice cream? (Sample answer: They might mix in mint and plums.)

Visual Literacy

Using Photographs

Teach

Have children revisit the photographs on pages 74–76. Together, read aloud the sentences on each page. Then ask children to point out each of the ingredients in the photographs.

Practice/Apply

Ask children to look at the photographs on pages 75–77. For each page, have children describe how the photos show what the text explains.

Social Studies Link

DAY 4

OBJECTIVES

- Write and sort words with short *a*.
- Read words with double final consonants, final *ck*.
- Read plurals with –*s* as /s/, /z/.

Review Skill Trace

| Reteach | pp. R4, R6, R8 |
| Review | pp. T148–T149 |

Materials

- **Picture Cards** *bat, cab, can, cat, fan, hat, man, map, mat, pad, pan, sad, tag, van, yam*
- paper word slips
- pencils
- colored 8 1/2″ x 11″ construction paper
- tape or glue
- teacher-made word cards *bass, hill, kiss, lass, legs, lick, mass, Matt, miss, mugs, nuts, pots, pads, quack, quick, sack, shall, sick, tack, tags*

PHONICS: More Short *a* Words

TARGET SKILL

❶ Review

Review consonants and short *a*.

- Display the **Picture Cards** along the chalkboard ledge.
- Name each picture with children and ask what all the names have in common. (All have the short *a* sound, /ă/.)
- Have children take turns coming to the board, choosing a **Picture Card,** and writing the word that names the picture above the card.
- Once all picture names have been written, have children sort for words that begin the same and words that rhyme.

❷ Guided Practice/Apply

Have children play Fill the Cone.

Fill the Cone

- Have children form small groups. Give each group a supply of word slips and a piece of colored construction paper.
- Tell each group to roll its piece of construction paper into a cone shape, and tape or glue it closed.
- Ask the groups to spend five minutes or so brainstorming short *a* words, writing them on their paper slips, and filling their cones with word slips.
- After time has expired, have groups read their words aloud and then count them to see which group wrote the most words.

PHONICS: Double Final Consonants, Final *ck*, Plurals with *-s*

❶ Review

Review double final consonants, final *ck*, and plurals with *-s*.

- Write *pass, mitt, pill, back, muff, egg,* and *jazz* on the board.
- Have children read the words with you. Underline and review the sounds for the final consonants.
- Write *cats, pots, bags,* and *wigs* on the board. Circle the *s* at the end of each word. Remind children that we can add an *s* to form words that name more than one, and that *s* at the end of a word can stand for /s/ or /z/.

❷ Guided Practice/Apply

Have children play Step Right Up.

Step Right Up

- Display the word cards.
- Divide the class into two teams. Have each team designate a "stepper," who stands at the back wall of the room. Players take turns rolling a number cube and reading a word card. If the word is read correctly, the "stepper" advances that number of steps (toe to heel) from the back of the room toward the front.
- The winning team is the one whose "stepper" gets to the front of the room first.

hill   bass   miss   Matt

sack   mugs   pots   pads

OBJECTIVES

- Write the Basic Words in sentences.
- Make a class chart of size words.

Materials

- Large Sound/Spelling Card *igloo*

Practice Book page 151

Name _____

Week 2
Spelling The Short *i* Sound

Spelling Spree

Write the missing letter to complete each Spelling Word. Then write the word.

Spelling Words

in
it
him
big
sit
did

1. d _i_ d   did (1 point)

2. h _i_ m   him (1)

3. _i_ t   it (1)

Proofread each sentence. Circle each Spelling Word that is wrong, and write it correctly.

4. The pig is (bige).   big (1)

5. The pig is (en) a pen!   in (1)

6. The pig can (zit).   sit (1)

SPELLING:
The Short *i* Sound

Short *i* Sentences Use **Large Sound/Spelling Card** *igloo* to review the sound for short *i*.

- Display the Basic Words and have children use them in sentences about an igloo: *I can sit in it. It is big.*

- Award a point for each Basic Word that children are able to use. Challenge children to try to earn six points.

Practice/Homework Assign **Practice Book** page 151.

Penmanship Ball-and-stick *and* continuous-stroke penmanship models are available in the **Practice Book** (pp. 216–223) and the **Teacher's Resource Blackline Masters** (pp. 143–194).

VOCABULARY:
Size Words

Teach Explain that *big* and *little* tell about the size of something. Ask children to point out big and little things.

Practice/Apply Work with children to generate size words.

- Ask children what other words they might use to describe something big. (*huge, gigantic, enormous, great*) List suggestions on chart paper in a column under *big*.

- Follow a similar procedure for *little*. (*tiny, wee, itsy-bitsy, small*)

- Post the chart. Remind children to write with these words.

INDEPENDENT WRITING: Writing About Favorite Foods

OBJECTIVES
- Write about favorite foods.
- Match descriptions of foods to pictures.

Provide structured writing practice.

- Discuss favorite foods.
- Dictate this sentence: *I like big figs.*

Ask children to choose favorite foods.

- Ask children what they like to eat for breakfast, lunch, and dinner.
- Have children choose a food and think about why they like it.

Have children make favorite food pictures. They can cut out magazine pictures of favorite foods, and then paste the pictures on drawing paper.

Assign Practice Book page 152.

- Have children write one or more sentences about their favorite food.
- Suggest that they name the food and write about how it looks and tastes.

Display children's pictures and sentences. Challenge the class to match up each sentence with its picture.

Practice Book page 152

English Language Learners

Food Words

Help English language learners brainstorm a list of foods they like. Write *Breakfast, Lunch, Dinner* on the board. Direct children to name appropriate foods by asking questions such as *What do you like to eat for breakfast?* Accept all possible answers, and write the responses on the board under the appropriate heading. Encourage more proficient children from the same language background to help with vocabulary. Model any structures that are causing trouble.

Day at a Glance
pages T152–T159

Learning to Read

Comprehension: Rereading for Understanding

Rereading for Fluency

Reading Decodable Text
Tim's Cat

• •

Leveled Readers, *T160–T163*
- ● *Tim's Pig*
- ▲ *Mama and Kit Go Away*
- ■ *Lazy Fox*
- ◆ *Tim's Pig Eats*

Word Work

Spelling: The Short *i* Sound
Vocabulary: High-Frequency Words

Writing & Oral Language

Grammar Review: Naming Part of a Sentence
Independent Writing
Listening and Speaking

Daily Routines

Daily Message

Strategy Review Remind children of the Phonics/Decoding Strategy. Guide them in applying it to selected words in today's message. Then ask children to answer the questions.

> Good Morning Boys and Girls!
>
> The book we will read today is about Tim and his cat. Tim's cat is called Miss Hiss. Do you have a cat? What is your cat's name?

Model concepts of print. Point out that two sentences in the message are questions. Have a child find and circle the question mark at the end of each question.

Vocabulary

Speed Drill On index cards, write the words *all, call, eat, every, first, never, paper, shall, why, Bill, him,* and *his.* Have children take turns holding up the cards for a partner to read. After children have practiced, display the cards. Ask individuals to read them to you as quickly as they can.

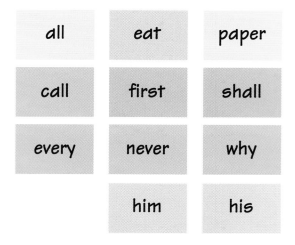

all	eat	paper
call	first	shall
every	never	why
	him	his

Daily Phonemic Awareness

Blending and Segmenting Phonemes: Cheer Short *i* Words

- Lead a cheer to help children blend and segment the words *dig, tip, chin, ship, thin, think, giggle, little, fiddle*. First say the word to be segmented.

- Lead the class in the cheer, as follows:

Teacher: *Let's cheer the sounds in* dig. *Give me the first one.*
Class: /d/!
Teacher: *Give me the next one.*
Class: /i/!
Teacher: *Give me the last one.*
Class: /g/!
Teacher: *What's the word?*
Class: Dig!

- Continue with the other words listed above. If children have difficulty segmenting the sounds, try a blending cheer first. Segment the word, and ask for each sound in turn: "Give me a /d/!" End with "What's the word?"

Daily Language Practice

Grammar Skill: Capitalize a Name
Spelling Skill: The Short *i* Sound
Have children correct the following sentence:

What didd jack do?

(What **did** **J**ack do?)

Daily Writing Prompt

Have children draw and name a pet they know, or have them write on self-selected topics. Remind them to use a capital letter at the beginning of the pet's name.

Hopper

Daily Independent Reading

Have children read with partners from the following.

- Leveled Bibliography, pages T6–T7

Choose books from this list for children to read, outside class, for at least twenty minutes a day.

- Reread Phonics Library story *Bill Bird* or *Tim's Cat.*

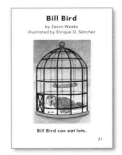

Bill Bird
by Jason Weeks
illustrated by Enrique O. Sánchez

Bill Bird can eat lots.
21

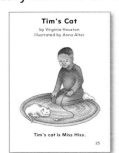

Tim's Cat
by Virginia Houston
illustrated by Anna Alter

Tim's cat is Miss Hiss.
25

OBJECTIVES

- Review making predictions in the week's selections.

Target Skill Trace	
Preview	p. T105
Teach	pp. T140–T141
Reteach	p. R38
▶ Review	p. T154
See	*Extra Support Handbook,* pp. 90–91; pp. 96–97

 # COMPREHENSION: Rereading for Understanding

Making Predictions

Discuss making predictions. Remind children that the first time they make predictions about a story, they read the title and look at the cover illustration. They may also read the first few sentences of the story.

Point out that we often need to revise, or change, our predictions as we read a story.

Think Aloud *Sometimes a story has a surprise ending. We think one thing is going to happen, but then something else happens instead. That makes a story fun to read.*

Ask children to tell what, if anything, surprised them in *Pearl's First Prize Plant.* Then ask if anything surprised them in *Miss Jill's Ice Cream Shop* and in *Ham and Eggs.* Ask at what point in each story a reader might need to revise predictions made earlier.

Assign rereading and retelling.

- Have children reread the other selections for the week: **On My Way Practice Reader, On Level/Challenge Theme Paperback, Phonics Library.** Ask them to think about the early predictions they made, and tell whether they had to revise their predictions later.

- Have children demonstrate making predictions through retelling *Miss Jill's Ice Cream Shop,* using the masks from **Teacher's Resource Blackline Masters 40–42.**

 # REREADING FOR FLUENCY

Rereading the Selection Have children reread *Ham and Eggs* or pages 66–69 of *Miss Jill's Ice Cream Shop* orally in small groups. Model fluent reading, and coach children to read with feeling and expression.

Tim's Cat

by Virginia Houston
illustrated by Anna Alter

Tim's cat is Miss Hiss.

25

PHONICS LIBRARY

End-of-Week Skills Check

Have children preview *Tim's Cat*. Ask them to describe the cat on page 26.

Observe as children model the Phonics/Decoding Strategy.

- Have children read *Tim's Cat*. As they read, ask individuals to tell how they use the strategy to figure out new words.
- Make note of children who have difficulty applying the strategy, and take oral reading records with these children.

Prompt children in rereading the story. For children who have difficulty, use prompts such as these.

- *Look at the letters from left to right.*
- *Think about the sounds for the letters and look for word parts you know.*
- *Say each sound and hold it until you say the next sound. What is the word?*
- *Is that a word you know? Does it make sense in the story?*

OBJECTIVES

- Apply the Phonics/Decoding Strategy to decode verb endings *-s, -ed, -ing;* short *i* words; possessives with *'s*.
- Recognize high-frequency words in context.
- Reread to build fluency.

Word Key

Decodable words with verb endings *-s, -ed, -ing;* short *i;* possessives with *'s* —————

High-Frequency Words —————

Monitoring Student Progress

Oral Reading Records Take oral reading records of a few children each week as they read the **Phonics Library** book individually or in small groups.

Alternative Assessment Use **Teacher's Resource Blackline Master** 43 to assess individual children's phonics and high-frequency word skills.

<u>Why</u> is <u>his</u> cat
<u>called</u> Miss Hiss?

26

Look at Miss Hiss
<u>hissing</u> at the <u>paper</u>!

27

Oral Language

Discuss these questions with children. Have them speak in complete sentences.

• Why is the cat named *Miss Hiss?* (She hisses at things.)

• What does Tim give Miss Hiss at the end of the story? (He gives her a hug.)

**But Miss Hiss has
never hissed at Tim!**

28

Build Fluency

Model fluent reading.

- Call attention to the question mark on page 26. Explain that this mark means a question is being asked.

- Read page 26 aloud. Have children read it aloud.

- Have children reread pages 26 and 27 several times until each child can read the pages effortlessly.

Home Connection

Hand out the take-home version of *Tim's Cat.* Ask children to reread the story with their families. (See the **Phonics Library Blackline Masters.**)

OBJECTIVES

- Take a test on the Basic Words.
- Review the week's high-frequency words.

SPELLING: The Short *i* Sound

Test

Say each underlined word, read the sentence, and then repeat the word. Have children write only the underlined word.

Basic Words

1. The ant is **in** the grass.
2. What is **it**?
3. I can see **him**.
4. That is a **big** fish.
5. Can I **sit** with you?
6. He **did** not run.

Penmanship Ball-and-stick *and* continuous-stroke penmanship models are available in the **Practice Book** (pp. 216–223) and the **Teacher's Resource Blackline Masters** (pp. 143–194).

VOCABULARY: High-Frequency Words

Review the Week's Words Review the New Words section with "clap and spell." Remove each word as it is reviewed.

- Call on children to move the words to the permanent Word Wall. The class can chant the words as they are moved.

all	call	eat	every	first

never	paper	shall	why

- Point to several other words on the Word Wall and have children read them and use them in sentences.

Practice/Apply Have vocabulary speed drills. Assemble the Word Wall Cards for this week's new words, and for decodable words that feature this week's phonics elements.

- At small-group time, have children take turns holding up the cards for a partner to read.
- Then display the cards as a list. Have individuals read them to you as quickly as they can.

GRAMMAR:
Naming Part of a Sentence

- Provide naming parts to complete sentences.
- Write a story independently.
- Retell familiar stories.

Review Remind children that a sentence has a naming part, which names someone or something.

- Write incomplete sentences on the board.
- Write each naming part that children suggest.

> _____ finds a flower.
> _____ sees a box.
> _____ gets wet!

Practice/Apply Have children write *Nan hops. Ken jumps.* Ask children to underline the naming part in each sentence.

Independent Writing Have children write a story about how the animals clean up the ice cream store or another story idea of their own. Remind them to include a naming part in each sentence.

LISTENING AND SPEAKING:
Retelling a Story

Review the parts of a story. Remind children that a story has characters, a setting, and a problem that needs to be solved.

Write the following questions on a chart. Read the questions aloud.

Who is in the story?

Where and when does it take place?

What is the problem?

How is it solved?

- Have children choose a story. Ask them to copy the underlined words from the chart and complete the charts based on their stories.

Have children retell their stories. Remind children to use the notes from their charts. Ask listeners to check that the storyteller answered the questions *who, where, when, what,* and *how.*

English Language Learners

Completing the Story Map

Help children complete the story map chart. Simplify the second question by writing it as *Where does the story take place? When does the story take place?* Rephrase the last question as *How do the characters solve the problem?* Model using the wording of the questions as part of an oral response. Example: "The story takes place in a forest." Check for correct use of prepositions.

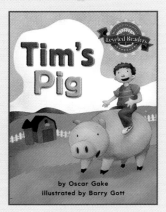

Tim's Pig

Summary *Tim's pig eats six of everything, including peach pits and hats, even though Tim keeps trying to pull him away. Tim's pig eventually gets sick from his unusual diet but Tim helps him get well.*

Building Background and Vocabulary

Read the title and discuss the cover picture. Explain that this is a make-believe story about a boy and his pet pig. Preview the illustrations, having the children look for the boy and his pig on each page.

Comprehension Skill: Making Predictions

Read together the Strategy Focus on the book flap. Remind children to use the strategy and to make predictions about what will happen next as they read the story. (See the Leveled Readers Teacher's Guide for **Vocabulary and Comprehension Practice Masters.**)

Responding

Have partners discuss how to answer the questions on the inside back cover.

Think About What You Have Read Sample answers:

1. He keeps eating everything he sees.
2. Answers may include: Tim is upset and angry at his pig.
3. Answers will vary.

Making Connections Answers will vary.

Building Fluency

Model Have children reread page 2 aloud with you. Tell them that the pattern of words in the sentence is repeated on pages 3 through 7. Explain that only the things that the pig eats change.

Practice Have children take turns with partners to reread the story. Tell them to reread the last sentence on page 7 and all of page 8 together.

Story Words

Introduce the Story Words, one at a time, providing meaning with objects, pictures, gestures, and/or context sentences. Then ask children to complete the **Vocabulary Practice Master.**

six *p. 2*

peach *p. 4*

pits *p. 4*

sick *p. 7*

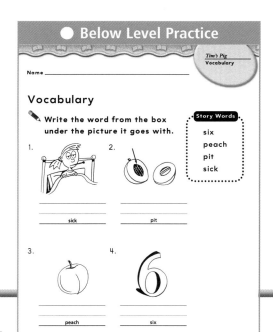

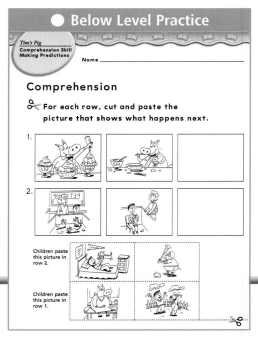

Leveled Readers

Mama and Kit Go Away

Summary *In this fantasy story, Mama Kangaroo and her baby, Kit, are getting ready to take a trip. Once they have packed Mama's hat, every map, every pot, and every dish into Mama's pouch, there's no room for Kit. Mama solves the problem by having Kit travel in a bag on Mama's back.*

Story Words

Introduce the Story Words, one at a time, providing meaning with objects, pictures, gestures, and/or context sentences. Then ask children to complete the **Vocabulary Practice Master.**

trip *p. 2*

said *p. 2*

Mama (title), *p. 2*

pack *p. 3*

dish *p. 5*

full *p. 6*

Building Background and Vocabulary

Read the title aloud and discuss the illustration. Explain that this make-believe story tells about a mother kangaroo and her baby as they pack to go on a trip. Have children tell about preparations they have made for a trip and what they know about real kangaroos.

Comprehension Skill: Making Predictions

Read together the Strategy Focus on the book flap. Remind children to use the strategy and to make predictions about what will happen next as they read the story. (See the Leveled Readers Teacher's Guide for **Vocabulary and Comprehension Practice Masters.**)

Responding

Have partners discuss how to answer the questions on the inside back cover.

Think About What You Have Read Sample answers:

1. Answers should include mama's hat, maps, pots, and dishes.
2. She's afraid there isn't room for her in Mama's pocket.
3. Answers will vary.

Making Connections Answers will vary.

Building Fluency

Model Copy the words from page 2 on the chalkboard and read the lines aloud. Point out the set of quotation marks and remind children that these show the words the characters say. Ask children to find other words in the story that are set in quotation marks and to identify who said the words.

Practice Have children reread the remaining pages aloud together. Ask one group to read the words *Mama said,* another group to read the words *Kit said,* and a third group to reread the words that neither Mama nor Kit said.

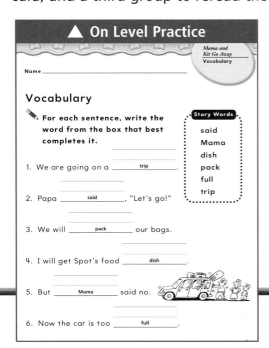

▲ On Level Practice

Mama and Kit Go Away
Vocabulary

Name _____

Vocabulary

✏ **For each sentence, write the word from the box that best completes it.**

Story Words
said
Mama
dish
pack
full
trip

1. We are going on a ___trip___.

2. Papa ___said___, "Let's go!"

3. We will ___pack___ our bags.

4. I will get Spot's food ___dish___.

5. But ___Mama___ said no.

6. Now the car is too ___full___.

▲ On Level Practice

Mama and Kit Go Away
Comprehension Skill
Making Predictions

Name _____

Comprehension

✏ **Read each set of sentences. Draw in the box to show your answer to the question.**

1. My family is going on a trip.
   We pack things in bags and boxes.
   What happens next?

   Responses will vary.

2. The car is full.
   There is no room for the dog.
   What happens next?

   Responses will vary.

Leveled Readers

Lazy Fox

Summary *In this adaptation of an Aesop's fable, a lazy fox naps in the sun rather than work gathering food for the winter, as the other animals do. When he gets hungry, the fox asks the other animals to bring him food. They all bring food to the lazy fox but it is not the kind of food the fox expects or likes.*

Story Words

Introduce the Story Words, one at a time, providing meaning with objects, pictures, gestures, and/or context sentences. Then ask children to complete the **Vocabulary Practice Master.**

lazy *p. 2*

Raccoon *p. 3*

brought *p. 4*

Squirrel *p. 4*

Mouse *p. 5*

feast *p. 6*

■ ABOVE LEVEL

Building Background and Vocabulary

Read the title and discuss the cover. Explain that this fantasy story is about a fox who is too lazy to collect food for the winter, so he asks his friends to bring him food. Preview the illustrations and invite children to tell about other stories in which animals talk and act like people.

⟳ Comprehension Skill: Making Predictions

Read together the Strategy Focus on the book flap. Remind children to use the strategy and to make predictions about what will happen next as they read the story. (See the Leveled Readers Teacher's Guide for **Vocabulary and Comprehension Practice Masters.**)

Responding

Have partners discuss how to answer the questions on the inside back cover.

Think About What You Have Read Sample answers:

1. He was lazy and didn't want to work to gather it.
2. Answers should include: He was upset. The food in the bags was what the other animals liked to eat, not what he liked.
3. Answers will vary.

Making Connections Answers will vary.

⟳ Building Fluency

Model Write the word *thought* on the chalkboard. Invite children to reread page 2 aloud with you to find out what the fox thought. Point out the thought balloon over the fox's head on page 3 and explain that this also shows what the fox thought about.

Practice Ask children to reread pages 3 through 8 aloud together, pausing after reading each page to tell what the words say the fox thought and what the thought balloons show the fox thought about.

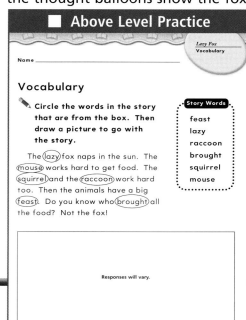

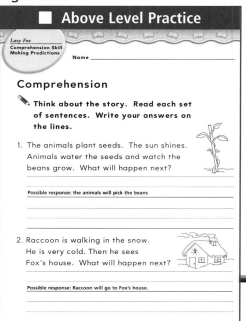

Leveled Readers

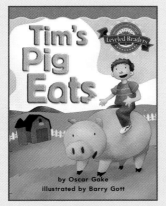

Tim's Pig Eats

by Oscar Gake
illustrated by Barry Gott

Tim's Pig Eats

Summary *This story is about a boy's pet pig. Tim's pig eats nuts, figs, pits, hats, cans, and bugs. The pig of course becomes ill from overeating, but recovers with the boy's solicitous care.*

Story Words

Introduce the Story Words. Then ask children to complete the Story Words Master.

eats takes food into the mouth, chews, and swallows, *p. 2*

gets sick becomes ill, is not well, *p. 7*

gets well regains health, is no longer sick, *p. 8*

◆ LANGUAGE SUPPORT

Building Background and Vocabulary

Discuss with children what they know about pigs. Elicit that pigs are usually found on farms. Ask, *Do you think it is a good idea to have a pig as a pet? Why should you keep a pig out of the house?* Then distribute the **Build Background Practice Master,** read aloud the directions, and have children complete the page. (See the Leveled Readers Teacher's Guide for **Build Background and Story Words Masters.**)

Reading Strategy: Predict/Infer

Have children read the Strategy Focus on the book flap. Remind children to use the strategy as they read the book.

Responding

Have partners discuss how to answer the questions on the inside back cover.

Think About What You Have Read Sample answers:

1. nuts, figs, pits, hats, cans, and bugs

2. No, because Tim tries to pull the pig away and because he looks upset.

3. Answers will vary.

Making Connections Answers will vary.

Building Fluency

Model Read aloud the text, pointing to the objects Tim's pig eats.

Practice Have small groups of children listen to the audio CD and point to the pictures in the book.

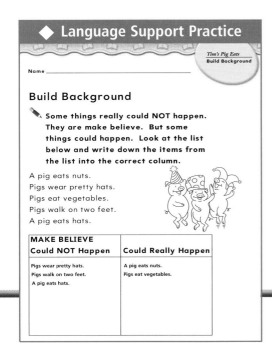

◆ Language Support Practice

Tim's Pig Eats
Build Background

Name _____

Build Background

✎ Some things really could NOT happen. They are make believe. But some things could happen. Look at the list below and write down the items from the list into the correct column.

A pig eats nuts.
Pigs wear pretty hats.
Pigs eat vegetables.
Pigs walk on two feet.
A pig eats hats.

MAKE BELIEVE Could NOT Happen	Could Really Happen
Pigs wear pretty hats. Pigs walk on two feet. A pig eats hats.	A pig eats nuts. Pigs eat vegetables.

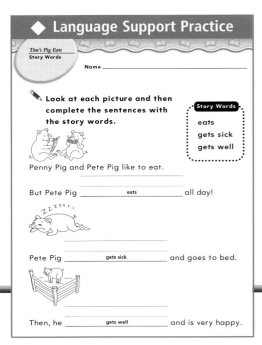

◆ Language Support Practice

Tim's Pig Eats
Story Words

Name _____

✎ Look at each picture and then complete the sentences with the story words.

Story Words
eats
gets sick
gets well

Penny Pig and Pete Pig like to eat.

But Pete Pig _____eats_____ all day!

Pete Pig _____gets sick_____ and goes to bed.

Then, he _____gets well_____ and is very happy.

Lesson Overview

Literature

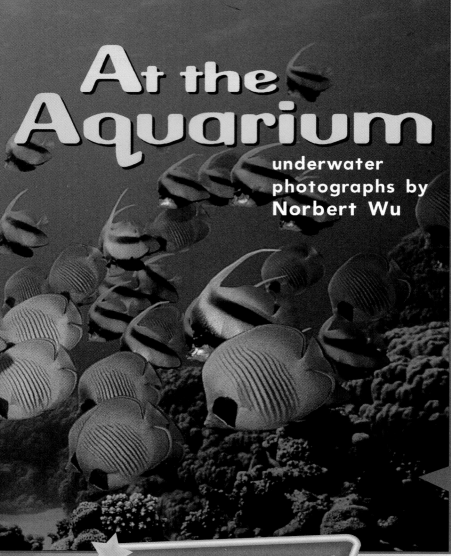

At the Aquarium
underwater photographs by Norbert Wu

Selection Summary

On a trip to the aquarium, children learn about fish, small sea animals, otters, and dolphins.

1 Big Book

- *Hilda Hen's Scary Night*

2 Decodable Text

Phonics Library

- *Let's Trim the Track!*
- *Brad's Quick Rag Tricks*
- *Fran Pig's Brick Hut*

3 Get Set Story

 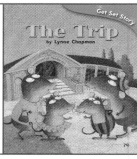

4 Main Story

At the Aquarium
Genre: Nonfiction

Vocabulary Reader

Sea Animals

Nonfiction

5 Drama Link

Instructional Support

Planning and Practice

Teacher's Edition

Practice Book

Teacher's Resources

Transparencies

Decodable Text

Differentiated Instruction

Intervention Strategies for Extra Support

Instructional Activities for Challenge

Instructional Strategies for English Language Learners

Ready-Made Centers

Building Vocabulary Flip chart
- center activities
- word skills practice

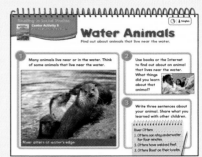

Reading in Science and Social Studies Flip Chart
- books and center activities
- support for state content standards

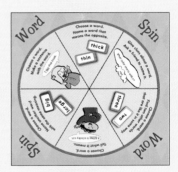

Hands-On Literacy Centers for Week 3
- activities
- manipulatives
- routines

Technology

Audio Selections
The Trip
At the Aquarium

www.eduplace.com
- over 1,000 Online Leveled Books

Accelerated Reader®

Leveled Books for Reaching All Learners

Fluency

Increase children's reading fluency using these activities.

● BELOW LEVEL
Model reading aloud with expression. Have children read the same passage aloud two or more times.

▲ ON LEVEL
Have each child practice a passage until fluent. Then have the child record the passage for teacher feedback.

■ ABOVE LEVEL
Have children read a passage to a partner. Then have both children read the passage several times in unison and discuss its meaning.

◆ LANGUAGE SUPPORT
Model fluent reading while children follow in the book, pointing to words. Have children echo read the same passage two or more times.

Skills Practice

- Topic, comprehension strategy, and vocabulary linked to main selection
- Lessons in Teacher's Edition, pages T232–T235

● BELOW LEVEL

Let's Grab It!
by Sally Schultz
illustrated by Betina Ogden

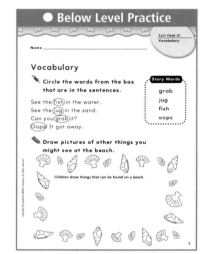

● Below Level Practice

Let's Grab It!
Vocabulary

Name _____

Vocabulary

✎ Circle the words from the box that are in the sentences.

Story Words
grab
jug
fish
oops

See the fish in the water.
See the jug in the sand.
Can you grab it?
Oops! It got away.

✎ Draw pictures of other things you might see at the beach.

Children draw things that can be found on a beach.

● Below Level Practice

Let's Grab It!
Comprehension Skill
Categorize and Classify

Name _____

Comprehension

✎ Write each word from the box where it belongs under Animals or Holds Something.

pot cat box bug bird cup

Animals	Holds Something
Order of responses in each column may vary.	
bug	pot
cat	box
bird	cup

✎ On the other side of this page, draw one more thing that is an animal and one more thing that holds something.

Responses should show an animal and a container such as a glass, a can, or a basket.

6

▲ ON LEVEL

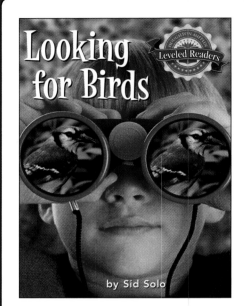

Looking for Birds
by Sid Solo

▲ On Level Practice

Looking for Birds
Vocabulary

Name _____

Vocabulary

✎ Circle the words in the story that are from the box.

Story Words
looking
green
flower
blue
brown
found

I am looking for a flower. First, I found a big bush. It had big green leaves and lots of brown buds. I did not see a flower on it. Then I saw a big blue one on a plant in a pot.

✎ Draw a picture to go with the story.

Possible response: Children draw a green bush with brown buds on it and a tall blue flower growing in a pot.

5

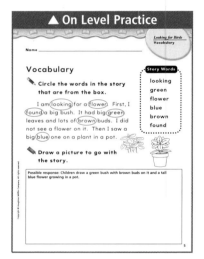

▲ On Level Practice

Looking for Birds
Comprehension Skill
Categorize and Classify

Name _____

Comprehension

✎ Write each word from the box where it belongs under Can Fly or under Can Not Fly.

| cat | jet | crab | bug |
| bird | bag | pig | |

Can Fly	Can Not Fly
jet	cat
bug	crab
bird	pig
	bag

6

■ ABOVE LEVEL

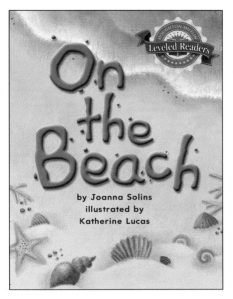

On the Beach

by Joanna Solins
illustrated by
Katherine Lucas

■ Above Level Practice

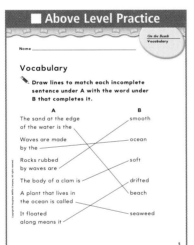

Vocabulary

Draw lines to match each incomplete sentence under A with the word under B that completes it.

■ Above Level Practice

Comprehension

◆ LANGUAGE SUPPORT

Grab It!

by Sally Schultz
illustrated by Betina Ogden

◆ Language Support Practice

Build Background

Circle the pictures that show activities that you can do at the beach.

Use the back of this paper to draw a picture of something you like to do at the beach.

◆ Language Support Practice

Leveled Theme Paperbacks

- Extended independent reading in theme-related paperbacks
- Lessons in Teacher's Edition, pages R10–R13

The Crab
by Alice E. Lisson
illustrated by Dennis Hackerman

Houghton Mifflin

WHEN TINY WAS TINY
by Cari Meister
illustrated by Rich Davis

● BELOW LEVEL ▲ ON LEVEL

Reading

HILDA HEN'S SCARY NIGHT

MARY WORMELL

■ ABOVE LEVEL

Technology

HOUGHTON MIFFLIN
Online Leveled Books
www.eduplace.com

- over 1,000 Online Leveled Books

Leveled Readers
Audio available

Daily Lesson Plans

 **Technology**
Lesson Planner CD-ROM allows you to customize the chart below to develop your own lesson plans.

T Skill tested on Integrated Theme Test and/or Weekly or Theme Skills Test

 80–90 minutes

Learning to Read

Phonemic Awareness
Phonics
Comprehension

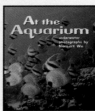

Leveled Readers
• Fluency Practice
• Independent Reading

DAY 1

Daily Routines, T174–T175
Phonics, High-Frequency Words,
Phonemic Awareness,
Independent Reading, Writing

Sharing the Big Book, T176–T179

Comprehension Strategy, T176
Question

Comprehension Skill, T177
Categorize and Classify

Phonics, T180–T182
Clusters with *r* **T**
Contractions with *'s* **T**

Reading Decodable Text,
T183–T185
Let's Trim the Track!

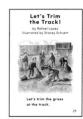

Leveled Readers
Let's Grab It!
Looking for Birds
On the Beach
Grab It!

Lessons and Leveled Practice, T232–T235

DAY 2

Daily Routines, T188–T189
Phonics, High-Frequency Words,
Phonemic Awareness,
Independent Reading, Writing

High-Frequency Words, T190–T191
also, blue, brown, color, funny, green, like, many, some **T**

Reading the Get Set Story, T192–T195
Building Background, T192

Vocabulary: *also, blue, brown, colors, funny, green, like, many, some, grab, grass, it's, let's, trip*

Comprehension Skill, T194
Categorize and Classify **T**

Leveled Readers
Let's Grab It!
Looking for Birds
On the Beach
Grab It!

Lessons and Leveled Practice, T232–T235

 20–30 minutes

Word Work

Spelling
High-Frequency Words
Vocabulary

DAY 1

Spelling, T186
Clusters with *r*

Vocabulary, T186
Spelling Patterns *-ick, -ill*

DAY 2

Spelling, T196
Clusters with *r*

Vocabulary, T196
High-Frequency Words

 20–30 minutes

Writing and Oral Language

Writing
Grammar
Listening/Speaking/Viewing

DAY 1

Daily Language Practice
1. where do you live
   (Where do you live?)

Shared Writing, T187
A Class Story

Viewing, T187
Main Ideas and Details

DAY 2

Daily Language Practice
2. let's go on a tripe
   (Let's go on a **trip**.)

Interactive Writing, T197
A Class Story

Target Skills of the Week

Phonemic Awareness	Blending and Segmenting Phonemes
Phonics	Clusters with *r*; Contractions with *s*
Comprehension	Categorize and Classify
Vocabulary	Spelling Patterns; High-Frequency Words; Color Words; Word That Show Position
Fluency	Decodable Text: Phonics Library; Leveled Readers

DAY 3

Daily Routines, T198–T199

Phonics, High-Frequency Words,

Phonemic Awareness,

Independent Reading, Writing

Vocabulary Reader

Reading the Main Story, T200–T210

Comprehension Strategy, T201
Question

Comprehension Skill, T201, T212–T213
Categorize and Classify **T**

Responding, T211

Leveled Readers
Let's Grab It!
Looking for Birds
On the Beach
Grab It!

Lessons and Leveled Practice, T232–T235

Spelling, T214
Clusters with *r*

Vocabulary, T214
Color Words

Daily Language Practice
3. do you see the crab.
   (Do you see the crab?)

Writing: Responding, T211
Write a Description

Grammar, T215
Action Part of a Sentence

Speaking, T211
Retelling

DAY 4

Daily Routines, T216–T217

Phonics, High-Frequency Words,

Phonemic Awareness,

Independent Reading, Writing

Reading the Drama Link, T218–T219

Comprehension:
How to Read a Play
Genre: Reading a Play

Phonics Review, T220–T221
More Short *i* Words
Verbs ending with *-s, -ed, -ing*, Possessives with *'s*

Vocabulary Reader

Leveled Readers
Let's Grab It!
Looking for Birds
On the Beach
Grab It!

Lessons and Leveled Practice, T232–T235

Spelling, T222
Clusters with *r*

Vocabulary, T222
Words That Show Position

Daily Language Practice
4. liz will grabb it.
   (Liz will **grab** it.)

Independent Writing, T223
Writing About Trips

DAY 5

Daily Routines, T224–T225

Phonics,

High-Frequency Words,

Phonemic Awareness,

Independent Reading, Writing

Comprehension: Rereading for Understanding
(Categorize and Classify **T**) T226

Rereading for Fluency, T226

Reading Decodable Text,
T227–T229
Fran Pig's Brick Hut
End-of-the Week Skills Check

Fran Pig's Brick Hut
by Mark Dempsey
illustrated by Amy Walrod

Fran Pig got some big, fat bricks.
37

Vocabulary Reader

Leveled Readers
Let's Grab It!
Looking for Birds
On the Beach
Grab It!

Lessons and Leveled Practice, T232–T235

Spelling, T230
Clusters with *r*

Vocabulary, T230
Review: High-Frequency Words

Daily Language Practice
5. do not trapp animals.
   (Do not **trap** animals.)

Independent Writing, T231
Writing a Story

Grammar, T231
Review: Action Part of a Sentence

Listening, T231
To Gather Information

Managing Flexible Groups

Leveled Instruction and Leveled Practice

	DAY 1	DAY 2
WHOLE CLASS	• Daily Routines (TE pp. T174–T175) • Read Aloud the Big Book *Hilda Hen's Scary Night.* (TE pp. T176–T179) • Phonics lesson (TE pp. T180–T182)	• Daily Routines (TE pp. T188–T189) • High-Frequency Words lesson (TE pp. T190–T191) • Building Background, Vocabulary (TE p. T192)

SMALL GROUPS

	DAY 1	DAY 2
Extra Support	**TEACHER-LED** • Preview vocabulary; support reading with Vocabulary Reader. • Read Phonics Library: *Let's Trim the Track!* (TE pp. T183–T185) • Read Book 31, I Love Reading Books.	**TEACHER-LED** • Read Anthology: Get Set Story. (TE pp. T192–T195) • Read Phonics Library: *Brad's Quick Rag Tricks.* (TE p. T191) **Partner or Individual Reading** • **Fluency Practice** Reread Phonics Library: *Let's Trim the Track.* (TE pp. T183–T185)
On Level	**TEACHER-LED** • Read Phonics Library: *Let's Trim the Track!* (TE pp. T183–T185) • Begin Leveled Theme Paperback: On Level. (TE p. R11)	**Partner or Individual Reading** • Read Anthology: Get Set Story. (TE pp. T192–T195) • Read Phonics Library: *Brad's Quick Rag Tricks* (TE p. T191) AND Leveled Theme Paperback: On Level. (TE p. R3) • **Fluency Practice** Reread Phonics Library: *Let's Trim the Track.* (TE pp. T183–T185) AND read Book 31, I Love Reading Books.
Challenge	**Partner or Individual Reading** • Read Phonics Library: *Let's Trim the Track!* (TE pp. T183–T185) • Read Leveled Theme Paperback: On Level. (TE p. R11)	**TEACHER-LED** • Read silently, Anthology: Get Set Story. • Reread aloud to answer Guiding Comprehension. (TE p. T195) • Read Little Big Book *Hilda Hen's Scary Night.* (TE pp. R12–R13) • **Fluency Practice** Read Phonics Library: *Brad's Quick Rag Tricks.* (TE p. T191) ✔
English Language Learners	**TEACHER-LED** • Preview vocabulary; support reading with Vocabulary Reader. • Together, read Phonics Library: *Let's Trim the Track!* (TE pp. T183–T185) • Together, read Book 31, I Love Reading Books.	**TEACHER-LED** • Reread Phonics Library: *Let's Trim the Track!* (TE pp. T183–T185) • Read Phonics Library: *Brad's Quick Rag Tricks.* (TE p. T191) **Partner or Individual Reading** • Read with audio CD of Anthology: Get Set Story.

Independent Activities

• Complete, review **Practice Book** pages (153–165) and **Leveled Readers Practice Blackline Masters** (TE pp. T232–T235).
• Reread familiar selections.
• Read trade book from Leveled Bibliography (TE pp. T6–T7).

✔ Opportunity to informally assess oral reading rate.

DAY 3	**DAY 4**	**DAY 5**
• Daily Routines (TE pp. T198–T199) • Vocabulary, Purpose Setting, Comprehension Strategy and Skill (TE pp. T200–T201) *After Reading at Small Group Time* • Responding (TE p. 211) • Comprehension lesson (TE pp. T212–T213)	• Daily Routines (TE pp. T216–T217) • Science Link (TE pp. T218–T219) • Phonics Review (TE pp. T220–T221)	• Daily Routines (TE pp. T224–T225) • Rereading (TE p. T226)

TEACHER-LED • Read Anthology: Main Story. (TE pp. T200–T210) • **Fluency Practice** Reread Get Set Story (TE pp. T192–T195) AND Phonics Library: *Brad's Quick Rag Tricks.* (TE p. T191) ✔	**TEACHER-LED** • Read the On My Way Practice Reader. (TE p. R10) • **Fluency Practice** Reread Books 31, I Love Reading Books. ✔	**TEACHER-LED** • Read Phonics Library: *Fran Pig's Brick Hut.* (TE pp. T227–T229) • Read Leveled Reader: Below Level (TE p. T232) • **Fluency Practice** Reread the On My Way Practice Reader (TE p. R10) OR Book 31, I Love Reading Books. ✔
TEACHER-LED • Read silently, Anthology: Main Story. • Reread aloud to answer Guiding Comprehension. (TE pp. T195, T200–T210) • **Fluency Practice** Reread Phonics Library: *Brad's Quick Rag Tricks* (TE p. T191) ✔ OR begin Leveled Reader: On Level. (TE p. T233)	**Partner Reading** • **Fluency Practice** Reread Anthology: Main Story (TE pp. T200–T210) OR complete Leveled Reader: On Level. (TE p. T233)	**TEACHER-LED** • Reread Anthology: Link. (TE pp. T218–T219) • Read Phonics Library: *Fran Pig's Brick Hut.* (TE pp. T227–T229) • Respond to Leveled Theme Paperback: On Level. (TE p. R11) • **Fluency Practice** Reread week's Phonics Library books OR Leveled Reader: On Level. (TE p. T233) ✔
Partner or Individual Reading • Read Anthology: Main Story. (TE pp. T200–T210) • **Fluency Practice** Reread Anthology: Main Story OR read Leveled Reader: Above Level. (TE p. T234)	**TEACHER-LED** • Reread silently, Anthology: Link. • Reread aloud to answer Guiding Comprehension. (TE pp. T200–T210, T218–T219) • **Fluency Practice** Reread Little Big Book *Hilda Hen's Scary Night.* (TE pp. R12–R13) ✔	**Individual Reading** • **Fluency Practice** Reread Anthology: Main Story and Link (TE pp. T200–T210, T218–T219) OR Leveled Reader: Above Level. (TE p. T234) • Read Phonics Library: *Fran Pig's Brick Hut.* (TE pp. T227–T229)
TEACHER-LED • Reread Phonics Library: *Brad's Quick Rag Tricks.* (TE p. T191) • Together, reread Anthology: Get Set Story. (TE pp. T192–T195) **Partner or Individual Reading** • Read with audio CD of Anthology: Main Story.	**TEACHER-LED** • Together, reread Anthology: Main Story. (TE pp. T200–T210) • Begin Leveled Reader: Language Support (TE p. T235) OR On My Way Practice Reader. (TE p. R10) **Individual Reading** • **Fluency Practice** Read with audio CD of Anthology: Get Set Story, Main Story.	**TEACHER-LED** • Read Phonics Library: *Fran Pig's Brick Hut.* (TE pp. T227–T229) • Complete Leveled Reader: Language Support (TE p. T235) OR On My Way Practice Reader. (TE p. R10) • **Fluency Practice** Reread Book 31, I Love Reading Books. ✔

Turn the page for more independent activities. ➡

Ready-Made Small Group Activities

 Word Work

 Cross Curricular

Building Vocabulary Center Activity 9
● ▲ ■ *Sink or Swim*

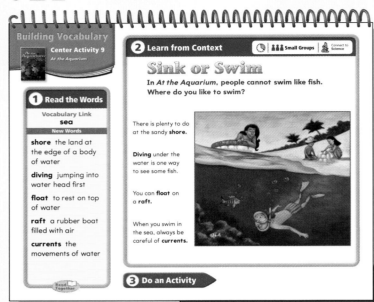

Leveled Activities on side 2

Word Spin
● ▲ ■

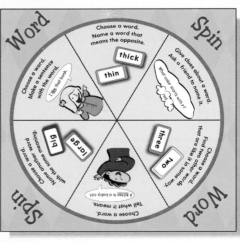

Key Vocabulary Cards 47–53

fish

Spelling Word Cards 13–18

grab

Reading in Social Studies Independent Book
▲ *From the Mountain to the Ocean*

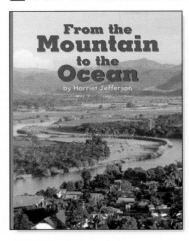

Reading in Social Studies Center Activity 9
● ▲ ■ *Water Animals*

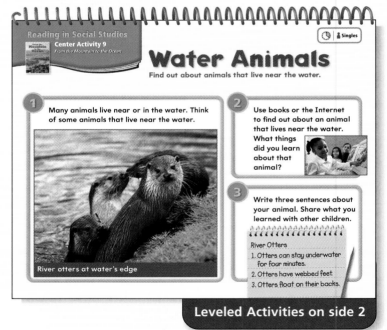

Leveled Activities on side 2

Leveled for ● Below Level, ▲ On Level, ■ Above Level

Reading

Writing

Routine Card 3
● ▲ ■ *Independent Reading*

RC•3

Independent Reading

① Choose a book.

② Read quietly.

Materials
• a book

Show What You Know
Draw and write about the book.
Write the title on your Reading Log.

Grade 1 • Routine Card RC-3 • Side 1

Routine Card 4
● ▲ ■ *Read and Respond*

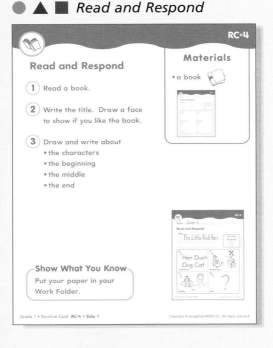

RC•4

Read and Respond

① Read a book.

② Write the title. Draw a face to show if you like the book.

③ Draw and write about
  • the characters
  • the beginning
  • the middle
  • the end

Materials
• a book

Show What You Know
Put your paper in your Work Folder.

Grade 1 • Routine Card RC-4 • Side 1

Routine Card 6
● ▲ ■ *Write in Your Journal*

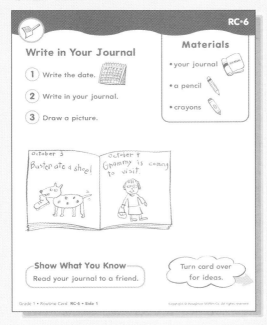

RC•6

Write in Your Journal

① Write the date.

② Write in your journal.

③ Draw a picture.

Materials
• your journal
• a pencil
• crayons

Show What You Know
Read your journal to a friend.

Turn card over for ideas.

Grade 1 • Routine Card RC-6 • Side 1

Challenge Card 3–9
■ *When Tiny Was Tiny*

THEME 3/**Week 3**

1. *When Tiny Was Tiny*

DAY 1

Responding

✏ Write your ideas about the story.

• How were Tiny the dog and Tiny the puppy different?

_____

_____

_____

• How were Tiny the dog and Tiny the puppy the same?

_____

_____

_____

Gr. 1, Challenge Card **3–9**

Multiple Tiers of Intervention

Core Program Intervention

• research-based
• systematic
• assessment-driven
• extra support
• English learner support
• reteaching

Small Group Intervention

Daily lessons and activities for differentiated instruction

Intervention Strategies for Extra Support, pages 98–107

Instructional Activities for Challenge, pages 38-41

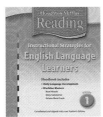

Instructional Strategies for English Learners, pages 102-111

Intensive Intervention

Proven efficacy for struggling readers

Reading Intervention for Early Success

For these materials and more, see **Small Group Independent Activities Kit.**

Day at a Glance
pages T174–T187

Learning to Read

Sharing the Big Book

Phonics Instruction
Clusters with *r*
Contractions with *'s*

Reading Decodable Text
Let's Trim the Track!

• • • • • • • • • • • • • • • •

Leveled Readers, T232–T235
- ● *Let's Grab It!*
- ▲ *Looking for the Birds*
- ■ *On the Beach*
- ◆ *Grab It!*

Word Work

Spelling: Clusters with *r*
Vocabulary: Spelling Patterns
-ick, -ill

Writing & Oral Language

Shared Writing
Viewing

Daily Routines

Daily Message

Review phonics and language skills. Read the message aloud, pointing to each word as it is read. Call on children to answer the question. Then ask individuals to underline action words ending with -*s*. (*shows, sees*) Have children underline all the words they can read.

> Good Morning, Class!
>
> Today's story is about a hen named Hilda. Hilda doesn't think she's very brave. Then one night, she shows just how brave she really is. She sees some scary things, but she does not panic! What do you think she sees?

Model concepts of print. Have children find the sentences that end with an exclamation mark and a question mark. Model how to read the sentences. Then ask children to find words with apostrophes and a comma in one sentence.

Word Wall

KINDERGARTEN REVIEW **High-Frequency Words** Briefly review the words *are, I, said, is, a, here, are, see, the, go,* and *like*. Remind children that they learned these words in kindergarten. Have children chant the spelling of each. Ask individuals to point to and read the words. Tell children they will read these words this week in new stories.

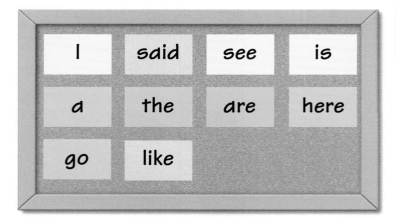

Blackline Masters for these word cards appear in Theme 1 on pp. R39–R41.

Daily Phonemic Awareness

Blending and Segmenting Phonemes: Name That Color

- Display crayons of different colors. Tell children that you are thinking of a color word. Explain that you will say the sounds in the word, and that they should blend the sounds to figure out the word.

- Say these sounds, /r//ĕ//d/. Have children blend the sounds together to say *red* and then point to the matching crayon. Continue with several other colors:

/g//r//ē//n/ (green)   /b//l//ōō/ (blue)
/b//r//ow//n/ (brown)   /g//r//ā/ (gray)

- Next, ask one child to choose a crayon and keep it hidden. As the child says the sounds in that color word, have the class blend the sounds and raise their hands when they know the word.

Daily Language Practice

Grammar Skills: Beginning Sentences with Capital
                    Letters; Punctuation

Have children correct the following sentence:

where do you live

(**W**here do you live?)

Daily Writing Prompt

Ask children to write about something they like to do at night, or have them write on self-selected topics. Encourage them to use what they know about letters and sounds to record their ideas.

Daily Independent Reading

Daily independent exploration and reading of books will increase children's reading fluency. They can read from the following.

- Leveled Bibliography, pages T6–T7

Choose books from this list for children to read, outside class, for at least twenty minutes a day.

- Little Big Book *Hilda Hen's Scary Night*

Sharing the Big Book

Building Background

Read the title and the name of the author/illustrator. Tell children that the story takes place on a farm. Sing "The Barnyard Song" and "My Farm/Mi chacra" with children. (See Teacher's Edition pages R55–R58.)

Fluency Modeling

Tell children you will read a selection about a hen. Explain that you will model how to read with expression.

COMPREHENSION STRATEGY

Question

Teacher Modeling Read aloud the Strategy Focus question on Big Book page 63. Model how to use the Question strategy.

Think Aloud *When I question, I ask myself something about the story. I expect that I will find the answer to my question as I read. For this story, I might ask:* "Why was the night scary?"

Meet the Author and Illustrator

Mary Wormell likes to ride horses on her farm in Scotland. The real Hilda Hen lives there with her. "She is still pecking around the farmyard," says Mary Wormell.

62

HILDA HEN'S SCARY NIGHT

MARY WORMELL

Strategy Focus
What questions do you have during the story?

63

62　　　　　　　　**63**

One sunny afternoon Hilda Hen fell asleep underneath a rosebush.

64

65

64　　　　　　　　**65**

When she woke up it was nighttime.
"Oh dear," clucked Hilda.
"It's so dark. I must get back to the henhouse."

66

It looked very far away. Hilda set off nervously.

67

66　　　　　　　　**67**

"Oh my goodness, there's a snake!" gasped Hilda.
"What shall I do?"

68

She thought for a moment. "I'll just have to tiptoe past as quietly as I can."

69

Hilda tiptoed carefully past the snake. "I didn't know I could be so brave," she clucked proudly.

But just then . . .

70

71

"Oh help, a monster!" squawked Hilda. "What shall I do?"

72

She thought for a moment. "I'll just have to fly past as high as I can."

73

Hilda flapped frantically and flew past the monster. "I didn't know I could fly so high," she clucked proudly.

But just then . . .

74

75

"Oh my word, a lake!" shrieked Hilda. "What shall I do?"

76

She thought for a moment. "I'll just have to swim as best I can."

77

TARGET SKILL

COMPREHENSION SKILL

Categorize and Classify

Tell children that grouping things from the story that are alike in some way can help them understand and remember the story.

Oral Language and Fluency

Read Aloud: Big Book

As you read, ask children to think about how things in the story might be grouped. Pause each time Hilda sees something scary to have children predict what they think the object really is. Ask how the two things are alike.

Concepts of Print

(Big Book, page 63) Point out the apostrophe in the title. Remind children that an apostrophe shows that something belongs to someone. (Big Book, page 66) Explain that quotation marks show the exact words of a speaker.

REACHING ALL LEARNERS

English Language Learners

Develop Vocabulary

Ask children to call out the names of items found on a farm as you hold up pictures and point to them. Help children name those items that may be unfamiliar to them.

Read Aloud

Oral Language: Discussion Options

Retelling Remind children that thinking about how things are alike in this story will help them retell it. Ask these questions:

- *What does Hilda Hen think when she sees a garden hose?* (that it is a snake) *Why?* (because both things are long, round, and coiled up)

- *How are all the things Hilda sees alike?* Hint: *Think about the setting of the story.* (They are all things found on a farm.)

Literature Discussion Circle Quickly review the speaking and listening etiquette in these Discussion Tips:

- Think about what you want to say.
- Raise your hand before talking, and wait your turn.
- Listen politely when other people are talking.

Then discuss the following questions as a class:

- How does Hilda feel when she gets home to the hen house?
- Do you think that Hilda Hen will ever find out what really happened?

THEME 3: Let's Look Around!

Hilda splashed awkwardly across the lake.
"I didn't know I could swim so well," she clucked proudly.

But just then . . .

78

79

"Oh no, a fox," whispered Hilda.
"What shall I do?"

She thought for a moment.
"I'll just have to run as fast as I can."

80

81

Hilda scuttled past the fox.
"I didn't know I could run so fast," she clucked proudly.

But just then . . .

82

83

"Oh dear, I'm under a strange bridge. I must be lost!" cried Hilda.

"What shall I do?"
But before she could think, the bridge moved.

84

85

Hilda got such a fright that she jumped high into the air.

86

"Oh, I can see the henhouse from here. It's a good thing I can jump so high," she clucked proudly.

87

She hurried on to the henhouse and arrived just as everyone was getting up for breakfast.

88

"Oh, I'm so glad I'm back," clucked Hilda. "I've had such a scary night."

89

"There are so many scary things in the farmyard at night," sighed Hilda. "I wonder where they all go during the day?"

90

The other hens looked across the yard, and they all wondered, too.

91

REACHING ALL LEARNERS

Challenge

Write Another Episode

Have children create another episode in which Hilda Hen sees something commonly found around a farm but thinks it is something else. Children can draw and write their story innovations and then share them with classmates.

Extra Support/Intervention

Story Clues

Help children use picture clues to identify what Hilda Hen *really* saw when she saw these things: a snake, a monster, a lake, a fox, and a bridge. Have children explain why Hilda was mistaken about what she saw, and how the things she saw are similar to what she thought she saw.

Read Aloud **T179**

OBJECTIVES

- Associate the clusters *br, cr, dr, fr, gr, pr, tr* with the sounds they represent.

Target Skill Trace

Preteach, Teach	pp. T180–T181
Reteach	p. R26
Review	Theme 4, p. T76
See	*Handbook for English Language Learners,* p. 103; *Extra Support Handbook,* pp. 98, 104.

Materials

- **Picture Cards** *brown, crow, dress, frog, gray, prize, train*
- **Blending Routines Card 1**
- **Large Letter Cards** *a, b, c, d, e, F, g, i, k, l, l, m, n, p, r, s, s, t, u, w*
- **Practice Book** punchout trays and letter cards *a, b, c, d, e, G, g, i, k, l, l, m, n, p. r, s, s, t, u, w*

Practice Book page 153

Clusters with *r*

Name each picture. Circle the letters that stand for the beginning sounds.

[Practice book worksheet with 16 numbered picture items]

TARGET SKILL PHONICS: Clusters with *r*

❶ Phonemic Awareness

Model how to blend and segment phonemes.

- Say /b/ /ĕ/ /d/, *bed.* Have children repeat the sounds and blend to say the word.
- Repeat the procedure with /b/ /r/ /ĕ/ /d/, *bread.*
- Ask what the different sounds are at the beginning of *bed* and *bread.* (/b/ and /b/ /r/)
- Repeat with the following pairs of words: *dip/drip, cab/crab, go/grow, tap/trap, fog/frog, dive/drive.*
- Next, say each of the following words. Have children repeat the word and say its sounds. Model with *crib,* /k/ /r/ /ĭ/ /b/.

  grin (/g/ /r/ /ĭ/ /n/)   *prize* (/p/ /r/ /ī/ /z/)   *trip* (/t/ /r/ /ĭ/ /p/)
  drop (/d/ /r/ /ŏ/ /p/)   *free* (/f/ /r/ /ē/)   *brag* (/b/ /r/ /ā/ /g/)

❷ Teach Phonics

Connect sounds to letters. Tell children that some words begin with two consonants, and that we blend the two sounds together to read the words.

Display **Picture Cards** *gray* and *brown* on the ledge below the board. Above the card for *gray,* write *gr.* Above the card for *brown,* write *br.*

- Have children name each picture, name the letters, and then chant: *grrr, brrr.*
- Repeat for the remaining **Picture Cards.**
- Point out the letter *r* in each cluster. Tell children that all these picture names begin with a consonant + *r.* Have children chant the sounds for each cluster as you point to it.

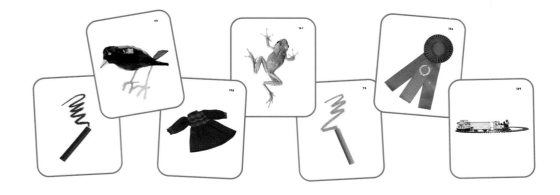

Have children identify initial clusters. Continue to display **Picture Cards** *brown, crow, dress, frog, gray, prize,* and *train.*

- Explain that you are going to say some words and that children should listen carefully to the two beginning sounds of each one.
- After saying each word below, call on a child to name the **Picture Card** that begins with the same two sounds and to tell which letters stand for those sounds.

1. fry	**4.** green	**7.** drill	**10.** print	**13.** grew
2. brush	**5.** crown	**8.** broke	**11.** drum	**14.** truck
3. price	**6.** tree	**9.** fruit	**12.** cream	**15.** drink

Model how to blend words with clusters with *r*. Using **Large Letter Cards** and **Blending Routine 1,** model how to blend *trap.* See Instructional Routines, p. T11. Repeat with *brick.*

Extend. Repeat with *best, class, plants, slug, sand, stand, swim, tank.*

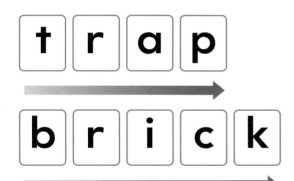

❸ Guided Practice–Word Building

Check understanding. Display **Large Letter Cards** *d, r, i, l,* and *l.* Make *drill* and ask children to blend the sounds as you point to each letter. Have children reread *drill.* Repeat with *grip, crab, trick, brag, Fran, trim, trip, grill, brim.*

Connect sounds to spelling and writing. Distribute punchout trays and letters. Say these words one at a time: *drip, crib, track, grill, Gram, drag, drab, grass, grins.* Have children repeat each word, say its sounds, and build it with letter cards. Then write the word and have children check their work.

Extend. Repeat with *best, class, plants, slug, sand, stand, swim, tank.*

❹ Apply

Have children complete **Practice Book** pages 153–154.

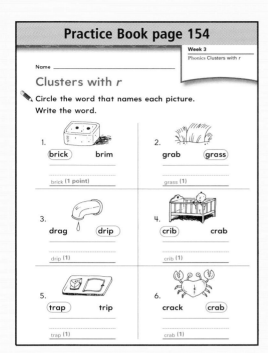

Practice Book page 154

REACHING ALL LEARNERS English Language Learners

Write the following pairs: *dive/drive, tap/trap, cab/crab, fog/frog.* Say each pair several times; have children repeat. Ask how *drive* is different from *dive.* Point to *drive* and circle the *r.* Say, *When we add an* r *after the* d, *we add a new sound and we make a new word.* Say /d/ /r/ several times and have the children repeat. Call children to the board to sound out the remaining word pairs and to circle the *r* in the second word. Ask the children to name more words that begin with *dr, tr, cr,* and *fr.*

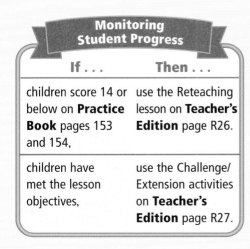

Monitoring Student Progress

If . . .	Then . . .
children score 14 or below on **Practice Book** pages 153 and 154,	use the Reteaching lesson on **Teacher's Edition** page R26.
children have met the lesson objectives,	use the Challenge/ Extension activities on **Teacher's Edition** page R27.

OBJECTIVES

- Blend and segment phonemes.

Target Skill Trace

Preteach, Teach	p. T182
Reteach	p. R28
Review	Theme 4, p. T77
See	*Handbook for English Language Learners*, p. 109; *Extra Support Handbook*, pp. 99, 105.

Materials

- Blending Routines Card 1

Practice Book page 155

Week 3
Phonics Contractions with 's

Name _____

Contractions with 's

Rewrite each sentence. Use a word from the box in place of the underlined words.

Word Bank

He's   It's   What's   Where's   Who's

1. <u>Who is</u> calling you?

Who's calling you? (2 points)

2. <u>He is</u> my dad.

He's my dad. (2)

3. <u>Where is</u> my hat?

Where's my hat? (2)

4. <u>What is</u> in the box?

What's in the box? (2)

5. <u>It is</u> Dad's hat!

It's Dad's hat! (2)

Monitoring Student Progress

If . . .	Then . . .
children score 6 or below on **Practice Book** page 155,	use the Reteaching lesson on **Teacher's Edition** page R28.
children have met the lesson objectives,	use the Challenge/Extension activities on **Teacher's Edition** page R29.

INSTRUCTION

PHONICS: Contractions with 's

❶ Teach Phonics

Connect sounds to letters.
Write the sentences as shown.

> It is a big cat.
> It's a big cat.
> Let us go to the hut.
> Let's go to the hut.

- Have children read the first pair with you. Point out that *It's* is a short way of saying and writing *It is*.
- Explain that the apostrophe in *It's* takes the place of the *i* in *is*.
- Repeat for the sentences with *Let us—Let's*. Explain that *Let's* stands for *Let us* and that the apostrophe takes the place of *u* in *us*.

Model how to blend words with contractions with 's. Point to the word *It's*.

- Using **Blending Routine 1,** model how to blend *It's*. See Instructional Routines, p. T11.

Repeat the routine. Have children blend and read *let's, he's, who's, what's,* and *where's*. Call on children to tell what words the contraction stands for and to use the contraction in a sentence.

❷ Guided Practice

Check understanding. Write these sentences on the board: *Where's Kim? Ben's here. He's in a crib. Let's trick Jan. What's in here? Who's this? She's back. Bill's sick. Let's run.* Have children read each sentence aloud. Call on a child to identify the contraction, name the two words that it stands for, and repeat the sentence using those words.

Connect sounds to spelling and writing.

- Say *let's* and have children write it. Then call on a child to provide the spelling as you write *let's* on the board.
- Have children correct their papers, circling any mistakes and writing the correct spelling.
- Repeat with *it's,* and the sentence *Bill's in his bed*.

❸ Practice/Apply

Have children complete **Practice Book** page 155.

HOUGHTON MIFFLIN

Reading

Decodable Text

Phonics Library

Let's Look Around!

Let's Trim the Track!

by Rafael Lopez
illustrated by Stacey Schuett

Let's trim the grass
at the track.

29

TARGET SKILL

PHONICS LIBRARY

Reading Decodable Text

Have children preview *Let's Trim the Track!* Ask them to tell what the people are doing in the picture on page 29.

Model the Phonics/Decoding Strategy. Read the steps of the strategy on **Poster B** and use the strategy to read the story title.

Think Aloud *I see four words. I think about the sounds for the letters and blend the sounds:* /l//ĕ//t//s/, Let's; /t//r//ĭ//m/, Trim. *The next word is* the. *Then I look at the last word. I see* T, r, a, c, k. *I blend the sounds together:* /t//r//ă//k/, Track. *The title is* Let's Trim the Track!

Apply the Phonics/Decoding Strategy. Have children read *Let's Trim the Track!* If they have difficulty, remind them to look at each letter and sound out the word. If necessary, use prompts such as these:

• *What sound does each letter stand for? Say each sound.*

• *Now say each sound and hold it until you say the next sound. What is the word?*

• *Is that a word you know? Does it make sense in the story?*

> **OBJECTIVES**
>
> • Apply the Phonics/Decoding Strategy to decode clusters with *r*; contractions with *'s.*
> • Reread to build fluency.

> **Word Key**
>
> Decodable words with clusters with *r*; contractions with *'s* ⎯⎯⎯⎯

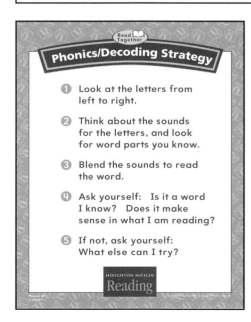

Read Together

Phonics/Decoding Strategy

1. Look at the letters from left to right.
2. Think about the sounds for the letters, and look for word parts you know.
3. Blend the sounds to read the word.
4. Ask yourself: Is it a word I know? Does it make sense in what I am reading?
5. If not, ask yourself: What else can I try?

HOUGHTON MIFFLIN
Reading

Fran can cut the grass.

30

Gran grabs big bags.

31

Oral Language

Discuss these questions with children. Have them speak in complete sentences.

- How does Gran help? (She gets big trash bags.)

- What is Sam's job? (He puts the bags in the van.)

- What is this track for? What clues help you know? (Sample answer: I think the track is for running and sports. One clue is the scoreboard in the pictures.)

Sam can fit the bags
in the big tan van.

32

Build Fluency

Model fluent reading.

- Read aloud pages 29 and 30. Then have children read the pages aloud.

- Have children reread the same pages several times until each child can read them aloud effortlessly.

Home Connection

Hand out the take-home version of *Let's Trim the Track!* Ask children to reread the story with their families. (See the **Phonics Library Blackline Masters.**)

OBJECTIVES

- Identify letters and sounds for consonant clusters with *r*.
- Read words with spelling patterns *-ick*, *-ill*.

Materials

- teacher-made word cards *trick*, *grill*

SPELLING WORDS

Basic

trip*	trap
grab*	drip
crab*	grin

Challenge

crack	brown*

*Forms of these words appear in the literature.

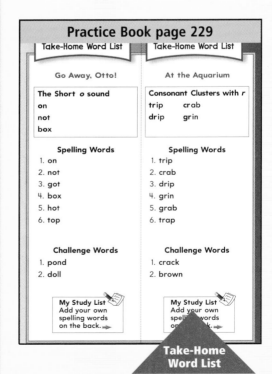

Practice Book page 229

Take-Home Word List	Take-Home Word List
Go Away, Otto!	At the Aquarium
The Short *o* sound	**Consonant Clusters with *r***
on	trip crab
not	drip grin
box	
Spelling Words	**Spelling Words**
1. on	1. trip
2. not	2. crab
3. got	3. drip
4. box	4. grin
5. hot	5. grab
6. top	6. trap
Challenge Words	**Challenge Words**
1. pond	1. crack
2. doll	2. brown
My Study List Add your own spelling words on the back.	My Study List Add your own spelling words on the back.

Take-Home Word List

INSTRUCTION

SPELLING: Clusters with *r*

❶ Teach the Principle

Pretest Say each underlined word, read the sentence, and repeat the word. Have children write only the underlined word.

Basic Words

1. I took a **trip** to the lake.
2. At the beach, I saw a **crab**.
3. Do not let the water **drip**.
4. A happy baby may **grin**.
5. Use your hand to **grab** it.
6. I see a lobster in the **trap**.

Teach Explain that some words begin with two consonant letters: the two sounds blend together when we say the word.

- Explain that each spelling word begins with a consonant followed by *r*. Tell children that *cr*, *dr*, *gr*, and *tr* are clusters with *r*.

❷ Practice/Apply

Identify Consonant Cluster Words Write these pairs of words: *trip/rip, cab/crab, rack/crack, dip/drip, grab/gab, tap/trap*. Ask children to find the word in each pair that begins with a cluster with *r*. Have children read the word and use it an oral sentence.

Practice/Homework Assign **Practice Book** page 229, the Take-Home Word List.

Penmanship Ball-and-stick *and* continuous-stroke penmanship models are available in the **Practice Book** (pp. 216–223) and the **Teacher's Resource Blackline Masters** (pp. 143–194).

INSTRUCTION

VOCABULARY: Spelling Patterns *-ick*, *-ill*

Teach Post *trick* and *grill* on the Word Wall, and have children read them. Say, *These will help you read and spell other words.*

Practice/Apply Make a class chart of words that rhyme with *trick* and *grill*. (*sick, pick, trick, stick, click, slick, brick; hill, pill, grill, drill, frill, spill, skill, will*) Have children identify the word parts that are the same. (*-ick, -ill*)

SHARED WRITING:
A Class Story

Introduce the topic for a class story.

- Tell children that today they will write a story about something scary at night.

Prompt children to contribute to the class story.

- Ask, *What things might be scary at night?* Have children contribute sentences as you write them on chart paper.

- Point out that the story should have a title. Ask, *What would make a good title for this story?* Write the title above the story.

Display the class story.

- Read the story with children.

- Have children illustrate different sentences in the story. Display the story and illustrations in the classroom.

VIEWING:
Main Idea and Details

Display a photograph of a farm scene. Point out that the photo shows a real farm and some of the things on it.

Draw a word web on the board. Write *What I Can See on a Farm* in the center cell and work with children to complete the word web, based upon the photograph.

- Explain that the web shows the main idea of the picture and the details.

- Use the word web to write a paragraph about the photo.

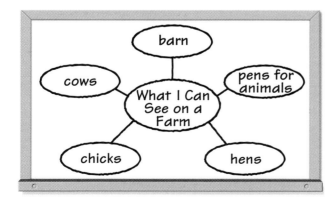

OBJECTIVES

- Contribute sentences for a class story.
- Think of a story title to go with the sentences.
- Note main idea and details in a photograph

Materials

- chart paper
- photograph of a farm

English Language Learners

Review Vocabulary

Before English language learners begin work on the word web, use the picture to review vocabulary relating to animals and farms. Point to different animals and objects in the picture, and have children call out the names. Prompt as necessary. Write the children's responses on the board, and leave them up as a reference.

Day at a Glance
pages T188–T197

Learning to Read

High-Frequency Words
Reading the Get Set Story
The Trip
Reading Decodable Text
Brad's Quick Rag Tricks

• •

Leveled Readers, T232–T235

- ● *Let's Grab It!*
- ▲ *Looking for Birds*
- ■ *On the Beach*
- ◆ *Grab It!*

Word Work

Spelling: Clusters with *r*
Vocabulary: High Frequency Words

Writing & Oral Language

Interactive Writing

Daily Routines

Daily Message

Review skills. Read the message aloud, pointing to each word as it is read. Ask individuals to answer the questions. Record their responses on chart paper. Then call on a few children to find and circle examples of words that begin with clusters with *r*. (*breakfast, fruit, fresh, brown, bread, drink, grape*)

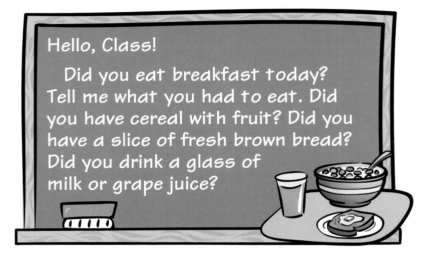

Hello, Class!

Did you eat breakfast today? Tell me what you had to eat. Did you have cereal with fruit? Did you have a slice of fresh brown bread? Did you drink a glass of milk or grape juice?

Word Wall

KINDERGARTEN REVIEW **Pattern Words** Have children find the word *wet* on the Word Wall. Ask children to identify each letter and the sound it stands for. (/w//ĕ//t/) Model blending the sounds. Then, model blending the words *an, at,* and *dig.* Tell children they will work with words that rhyme with these words this week.

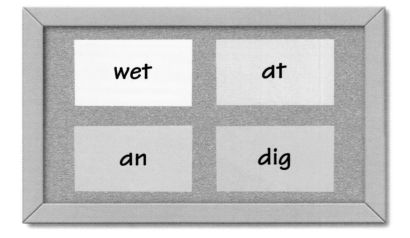

wet   at

an   dig

Blackline Masters for these word cards appear in Theme 1 on pp. R42–R44.

Daily Phonemic Awareness

Blending and Segmenting Phonemes: Word Stretcher

- Provide something stretchy, such as a short length of elastic, a balloon, or a big rubber band. Remind children that it is a word stretcher that can help them stretch words out and put them back together.

- Model how to stretch the band while you stretch a word. Say, *Listen. The sounds are* /l//ĭ//p/. Now release one end of the band as you put the word together. Say, *Together the sounds make* lip.

- Pass the band to a child. Whisper a single-syllable word to that player, such as *trip, sick, hip,* or *mint*. The child stretches the band, says the separate sounds of the word, and asks classmates to signal when they know the word.

- Continue until everyone has had a chance to use the word stretcher.

Daily Language Practice

Grammar Skill: Beginning Sentences with Capital Letters

Spelling Skill: Consonant Clusters with *r*

Have children correct the following sentence:

let's go on a tripe.

(Let's go on a **trip**.)

Daily Writing Prompt

Have children write about what they might eat for breakfast, lunch, or dinner, or have them write on self-selected topics. Before writing, children might look through old magazines to find pictures of different kinds of foods for each meal.

An Activity Master for this writing activity appears on R52.

Daily Independent Reading

Have children read to a partner from the following.

- Leveled Bibliography, pages T6–T7

Choose books from this list for children to read, outside class, for at least twenty minutes a day.

- Reread Phonics Library story *Let's Trim the Track!*

Let's Trim the Track!
by Rafael Lopez
illustrated by Stacey Schuett

Let's trim the grass at the track.

29

OBJECTIVES

- Read and write *also, blue, brown, color, funny, green, like, many, some.*

Target Skill Trace

Teach	pp. T190–T191
Reteach	pp. R34
Review	p. T230
See	*Handbook for English Language Learners,* pp. 105, 107; *Extra Support Handbook,* pp. 102–103.

Materials

- Word Wall Cards and **Practice Book** punchout word cards: *also, blue, brown, color, funny, green, like, many, some*

INSTRUCTION

HIGH-FREQUENCY WORDS

❶ Teach

Reintroduce and review the word *like*. Point to the word *like* in the Kindergarten Review section of the Word Wall.

- Remind children that they have read this word before, and have them read it aloud with you. Point to the letter *l* and have children say the sound for *l*, /l/. Explain that in this word, *i* stands for /ī/, *k* stands for /k/ and the *e* is silent. Blend /l/ /ī/ /k/, *like.*

- Call on children to complete the sentence *I like _____.*

- Lead the class in a cheer to help children remember the word. Clap on each letter as you spell and say the word, *l-i-k-e, like!*

Introduce the new high-frequency words. Display the Word Wall Card *color.*

- Read the word aloud and have children repeat it.

- Post *color* in the New Words section of the Word Wall.

- Have the class clap and spell the word several times: *c-o-l-o-r, color!*

- Repeat the procedure for *green, blue, brown,* and the other high-frequency words.

Chart/Transparency 3–7

Pick a <u>Color</u>.

I <u>like</u> the color <u>green</u>.

My hat is green.

I <u>also</u> like <u>blue</u>.

My rug is blue.

My cat is <u>brown</u>, not tan.

I like my <u>funny</u> cat.

Do you like <u>some</u> colors?

Do you like <u>many</u> colors?

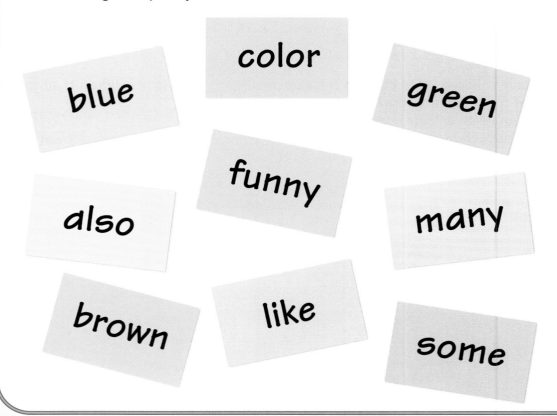

❷ Guided Practice

Have children read the words in context.
Display **Chart/Transparency 3–7.**

• Tell children to follow along as you read the title and the first two sentences. Ask a child to identify the word that names a color.

• Repeat the activity for the next two pairs of sentences.

• Read the two questions and call on children to answer the questions.

• Tell children to read the sentences to themselves.

• Choose children to read the sentences aloud.

❸ Apply

• Have children complete **Practice Book** pages 156 and 157 independently, in pairs, or in small groups.

• Have small groups of children take turns reading their punchout word cards *also, blue, brown, color, funny, green, like, many, some* to one another.

• Have children read the **Phonics Library** story *Brad's Quick Rag Tricks* independently, with partners, or in small groups.

Brad's Quick Rag Tricks

by Diane Patek
illustrated by Lizzy Rockwell

Brad can do quick rag tricks.

33

Practice Book page 156

Week 3
High-Frequency Words

Name _____

Words to Know

Read the story. Color the picture that matches the story.

"Look!" said Kris. "I see many animals!"
"Me, too!" said Brad.
Kris said, "I see some green and brown frogs!"
"Me, too!" said Brad.
Kris said, "I also see a bird as blue as my cap!"
"Me, too," said Brad.
"I like to look at the colors of all the pets," said Kris.
"Me, too!" said the bird.
"Funny bird!" said Brad.

Picture should be colored. (6 points)

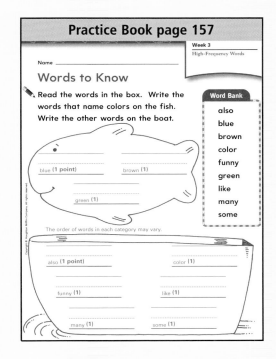

Practice Book page 157

Week 3
High-Frequency Words

Name _____

Words to Know

Read the words in the box. Write the words that name colors on the fish. Write the other words on the boat.

Word Bank
also
blue
brown
color
funny
green
like
many
some

blue (1 point)   brown (1)

green (1)

The order of words in each category may vary.

also (1 point)   color (1)

funny (1)   like (1)

many (1)   some (1)

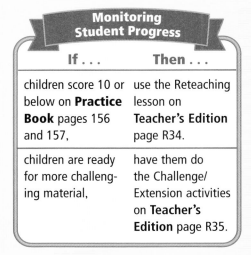

Monitoring Student Progress

If . . .	Then . . .
children score 10 or below on **Practice Book** pages 156 and 157,	use the Reteaching lesson on **Teacher's Edition** page R34.
children are ready for more challenging material,	have them do the Challenge/ Extension activities on **Teacher's Edition** page R35.

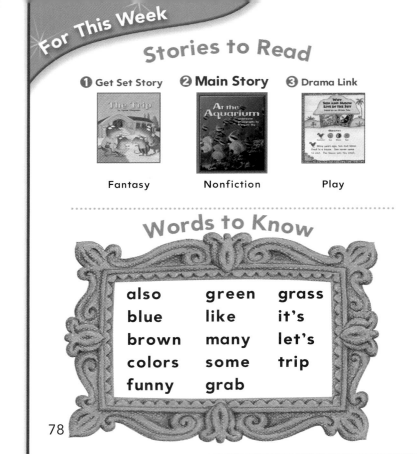

For This Week

Stories to Read

❶ Get Set Story   ❷ **Main Story**   ❸ Drama Link

Fantasy   Nonfiction   Play

Words to Know

also	green	grass
blue	like	it's
brown	many	let's
colors	some	trip
funny	grab	

78

Get Set Story

The Trip
by Lynne Chapman

Museum of Mouse Art

79

Get Set Story

Building Background: Taking a Trip

Tell children that this week they will read stories about visiting places, such as museums and aquariums. Ask them to tell about places they have visited or trips they have taken.

- Have children tell what the mouse family is doing on Anthology page 80. (getting on a city bus) Ask, *Where do you think the mice are going?*

Song Children may wish to sing about a trip to a baseball game with "Take Me Out to the Ball Game" on page R59.

Vocabulary

Have children look at Words to Know on Anthology page 78.

- Read the words with children. Point out that some of the words are on the Word Wall.

- Reread the words *brown, green, grab, grass,* and *trip.* Have children say the sound of each beginning consonant followed by the *r* sound. Reread *it's* and *let's* and remind children that in these contractions, *'s* stands for the /s/ sound.

- Have children read the title of the story on Anthology page 79. Ask how they figured out how to say the words.

THEME 3: Let's Look Around!

Words to Know

High-Frequency Words

also	colors	like
blue	funny	many
brown	green	some

Words with clusters with *r*; contractions with *'s*

grab	let's
grass	trip
it's	

REACHING ALL LEARNERS

English Language Learners

Action Words

Remind children that an action word tells what someone does. Help children demonstrate their understanding of action words from the story. Write *grab, hop, look, yelled,* and *sat* on the board. Read each word aloud with children and help children pantomime its meaning.

Puff and Tip went on a trip.
Dad and Mom went also.
"Grab a bus pass and hop on!"
said Dad.

80

"Look at the big brown cats!"
yelled Tip.
"Let's go in," said Mom.

81

READING STRATEGY

Phonics/Decoding

Clusters with *r*

Teacher/Student Modeling Point out the cluster with *r* in *trip*. Have children say the sounds, /t/, /r/. Help them to blend *trip* sound by sound, /t/ /r/ /ĭ/ /p/, *trip*. Then have children read the first sentence on Anthology page 80.

REACHING ALL LEARNERS **Extra Support/Intervention**

Phonics/Decoding Strategy

If children have trouble decoding clusters, help them blend the *tr* cluster sound by sound before blending the word *trip*. Repeat with *grass*, *grab*, and *brown*.

"I see some cats!" yelled Tip.
"I see many cats," added Puff.

82

"Look at all the colors on the cats!" yelled Tip.
"I like the blue and green cat," added Puff. "It's funny."

83

TARGET SKILL

COMPREHENSION SKILL

Categorize and Classify

Remind children that making groups of things that go together, or categories, can help them remember and make sense of details in stories. Have children look at Anthology pages 82–83 and tell how all the pictures and sculpture in the museum go together. (They all have cats and mice in them.)

Tip and Puff sat on the grass.
"Where is the bus?" said Mom.
"Let's get a cab," said Puff.

84

"Here we are," said Mom.
"What a trip!" added Puff.

85

CRITICAL THINKING
Guiding Comprehension

1 **CATEGORIZE AND CLASSIFY** What types of art do Tip and Puff see in the museum? (Sample answer: paintings on the wall and sculpture/statues)

2 **COMPARE AND CONSTRAST** How are Tip and Puff alike? How are they different? (Tip and Puff are both young mice at the museum; Tip is younger and a boy.)

3 **DRAWING CONCLUSIONS** Why does Puff think the family should take a cab home? (The mice are tired from walking around the museum all day, and the bus has not come yet.)

Extra Support/Intervention

Categorize and Classify

If children have trouble thinking of categories, provide and define some categories for them, such as painting and sculpture, or paintings of mice and cats. Have children page through the story and find examples of things that would fit into each category.

PRACTICE

OBJECTIVES

- Spell the Basic Words.
- Write sentences with high-frequency words.

Materials

- **Practice Book** punchout trays and letters *a, b, c, d, g, i, n, p, r, s, t*

Challenge

Completing Sentences

Have children write a Challenge Word to complete each sentence.

1. This shell has a ___ in it. (*crack*)
2. My new coat is ___. (*brown*)

SPELLING: Clusters with *r*

Review the Principle Remind children that a consonant cluster is two or more consonant letters whose sounds are blended together.

Practice/Apply Have individuals or partners follow the directions below to build words with punchout letters. After children build each word, write the word and have children check their work.

- Build the word *in*.
- Build the word *trap*. Change the vowel letter to build *trip*.
- Change the first letter in *trip* to build *drip*.
- Change the first letter again to build *grip*.
- Now build *crab*. Change the first letter to build *grab*.
- Change the last two letters to build *grin*. Add an *s* to build *grins*.

Penmanship Ball-and-stick *and* continuous-stroke penmanship models are available in the **Practice Book** (pp. 216–223) and the **Teacher's Resource Blackline Masters** (pp. 143–194).

REVIEW

VOCABULARY: High-Frequency Words

Review the Week's Words Point to the new high-frequency words and the Kindergarten Review word *like* on the Word Wall, one at a time. Call on children to read the words.

Practice/Apply Assign a high-frequency word to each child. Have children write sentences with their words. Ask children to share their work in small groups.

INTERACTIVE WRITING: A Class Story

DAY 2

OBJECTIVES
- Contribute sentences for a class story.
- Participate by writing letters, words, and punctuation in a class story.

WRITING

WEEK 3

Model interactive writing.
- Point out that some sounds are loud.
- Model how to write this sentence: *The thunder boomed!* Encourage children to tell you what letters to write.

Introduce the topic for a class story.
- Tell children that now they will write another version of the story *Hilda Hen's Scary Night*. In this version, Hilda hears things that scare her.

Prompt children to contribute to the story.
- Ask, *What sounds might Hilda hear?* You may want to suggest one or two yourself to prompt their thinking. Have children contribute ideas as you record them in a chart.
- Have children dictate sentences for the story, based on the ideas from the chart. As you write the sentences, encourage children to participate by writing familiar letters, words, and punctuation.

Read the story with the class.
- Have children select sentences to copy and illustrate.

What Hilda Hears	What Hilda <u>Thinks</u> She Hears
an owl hooting	a freight train coming
a twig snapping	thunder—a storm coming

DAY 3
week 3

Day at a Glance
pages T198–T215

Learning to Read

Reading the Main Story
At the Aquarium

Responding

Comprehension Instruction
Categorize and Classify

• • • • • • • • • • • • • • • • • • •

Leveled Readers, *T232–T235*

● *Let's Grab It!*
▲ *Looking for Birds*
■ *On the Beach*
◆ *Grab It!*

Word Work

Spelling: Clusters with *r*
Vocabulary: Color Words

Writing & Oral Language

Grammar: Action Part of a Sentence
Writing: Responding

Daily Routines

Daily Message

Review skills. Use the Daily Message for a quick review of phonics and language skills. Read the message aloud, pointing to each word as it is read. Call on individuals to answer the question.

• Ask children to find words with short *i*. Then have them find a short *i* word that ends with *s* to show more than one. (*trips*)

• Ask children to find words that begin with clusters with *r*. (*trips, trip, green, breathe, trick*)

> Good Morning, Class!
>
> I like to take trips. I also like to look at fish. Our story for today is about a class trip to an aquarium. The children see green and blue fish. They learn how fish breathe. They see a fish do a trick. What would you like to see?

Model concepts of print. Ask children to count the sentences in the message. Then ask them to find the *longest* and the *shortest* sentences.

Word Wall

KINDERGARTEN REVIEW **High-Frequency Words** Invite children to point to and read the high-frequency words *and, have,* and *to.* Have children spell the words. Review the Word Wall words from days 1 and 2. Tell children they will work with these words this week.

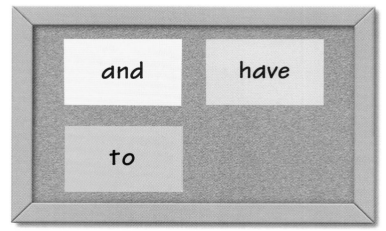

and   have

to

Blackline Masters for these word cards appear in Theme 1 on pp. R39–R40.

 Daily Phonemic Awareness

Blending and Segmenting Phonemes: Blend the Word

Recite the following, saying the phonemes shown. Have children blend the phonemes for each word.

There is one thing I'd like to /h//ă//v/. (have)
It's tiny and can swim. It's a /f//ĭ//sh/. (fish)
I could watch him swim so very /f//ă//s//t/. (fast)
He swims so fast with his /f//ĭ//n//z/. (fins)

Listening for Rhymes:

Say the following:

Fish rhymes with dish. Does fish rhyme with water? (no)
Fin rhymes with tin. Does fin rhyme with skin? (yes)
Which word rhymes with tail: mail or sun? (mail)
Which word rhymes with swim: run or Kim? (Kim)

Daily Language Practice

Grammar Skill: Punctuation

Spelling Skill: Clusters with *r*

Have children correct the following sentence:

Do you see the carb.

(Do you see the **crab?**)

Daily Writing Prompt

Have children write about an animal they would like to be and what they would do for fun, or have them write on self-selected topics. To help organize their thoughts before they write, children might want to draw a picture of their animal.

I would be an elephant and cool off my friends.

Daily Independent Reading

Remind children to practice reading the Word Wall. Children can read from the following.

• Leveled Bibliography, pages T6–T7

Choose books from this list for children to read, outside class, for at least twenty minutes a day.

Brad's Quick Rag Tricks
by Diane Patek
illustrated by Lizzy Rockwell

Brad can do quick rag tricks.
33

• Reread Phonics Library story *Brad's Quick Rag Tricks*.

• Leveled Readers

Main Story

Vocabulary

Review the Words to Know with children.

Words to Know		
New This Week		
also	green	grass
blue	like	it's
brown	many	let's
colors	some	trip
funny	grab	

Use **Chart/Transparency 3–8** to introduce the Story Vocabulary. For practice, assign **Practice Book** page 158.

Vocabulary Preview

The Vocabulary Reader can be used to preteach or reinforce the story vocabulary.

Story Vocabulary		
breathe	otter	sea horse
dolphins	sea	tails
fish		

Purpose Setting

- Invite children to share any experiences they may have had at an aquarium. Ask them to think of questions they might have about an aquarium and to look for answers as they read this story.

Journal ▶ Children can use their journals to draw or write questions they have about the story.

Read Together

Meet the Photographer

Norbert Wu dives into the sea to take pictures of the amazing things that live there. He uses a special camera to take the pictures.

86

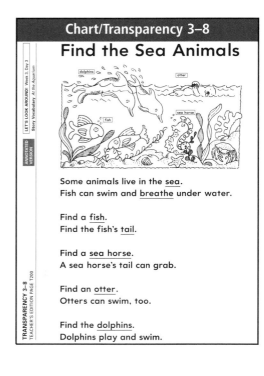

Chart/Transparency 3–8

Find the Sea Animals

Some animals live in the sea.
Fish can swim and breathe under water.

Find a fish.
Find the fish's tail.

Find a sea horse.
A sea horse's tail can grab.

Find an otter.
Otters can swim, too.

Find the dolphins.
Dolphins play and swim.

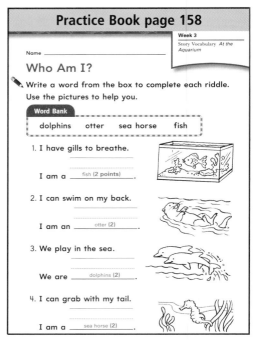

Practice Book page 158

Week 3
Story Vocabulary *At the Aquarium*

Name _____

Who Am I?

✏ Write a word from the box to complete each riddle. Use the pictures to help you.

Word Bank
dolphins   otter   sea horse   fish

1. I have gills to breathe.

   I am a ___fish (2 points)___.

2. I can swim on my back.

   I am an ___otter (2)___.

3. We play in the sea.

   We are ___dolphins (2)___.

4. I can grab with my tail.

   I am a ___sea horse (2)___.

Main Story

At the Aquarium

underwater photographs by Norbert Wu

87

Extra Support/Intervention

Preview the Selection

pages 88–89 Where are the children?

pages 90–99 What kinds of fish do the children see at the aquarium?

pages 100–103 What sea creatures do the children see at the aquarium?

pages 104–105 How does the selection end?

COMPREHENSION STRATEGY

Question

Teacher Modeling Read aloud the story title and author's name. Have children look at the photograph on Anthology pages 88–89. Model how to question.

Think Aloud *When I look at this photograph, I have some questions: "What are the children doing at the aquarium? What will they see there?" I expect to find answers to my questions as I read the story.*

✔ **Test Prep** Explain that thinking of questions and reading to find answers can help children answer test questions more quickly and more accurately.

COMPREHENSION SKILL

Categorize and Classify

Tell children to think about how things fit into groups as they read *At the Aquarium*. Mention that this will help them remember and understand what they read.

Caribbean Reef

Welcome to the Aquarium

We are on a class trip.

88

We will see lots and lots of fish.

89

CRITICAL THINKING

Guiding Comprehension

1 **MAKING PREDICTIONS** What clues could you use to predict what this story is about? (the title, the cover illustration, and/or the photos on the first few pages)

English Language Learners

Language Development

Find out what children know about ocean animals. List their ideas. Then preview the animal names in the selection: *fish, sea horse, crab, sea slug, otter, dolphins.* Name each animal and have children repeat the name. Guide them in pointing to the corresponding picture.

Word Key

Decodable words with clusters with *r;* contractions with *'s* _____

High-Frequency Words _____

Story Vocabulary _____

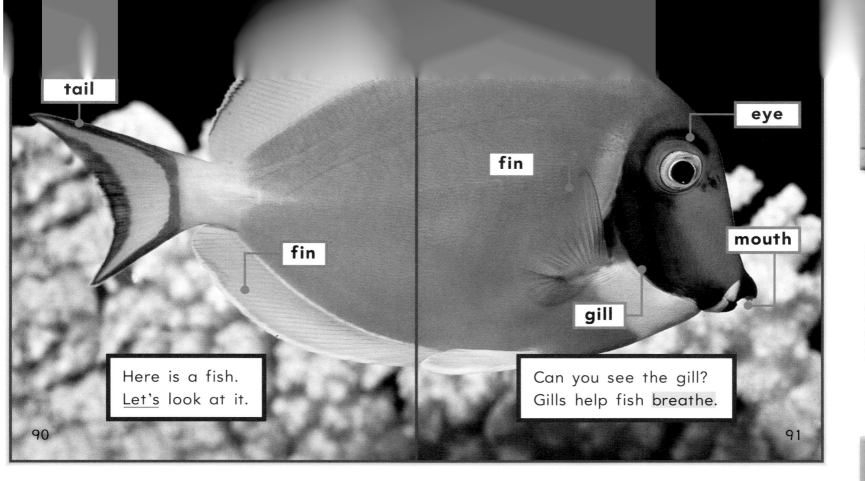

tail

fin

eye

fin

mouth

gill

Here is a fish.
Let's look at it.

Can you see the gill?
Gills help fish breathe.

90

91

CRITICAL THINKING

Guiding Comprehension

2 NOTING DETAILS What part of a fish helps it breathe?
(the gills)

READING STRATEGY

Phonics/Decoding

Blending More Short *i* Words

Teacher/Student Modeling Write *gills* on the board. Underline *i*. Remind children of the short *i* sound, /ĭ/. Have children look carefully at the word, think about the sounds for the letters *g, i, l, l, s,* and blend the word sound by sound. Explain that *gills* are a part of a fish that help it breathe in water. Have children read page 91 to see if *gills* makes sense.

Story Vocabulary

fish an animal with fins and gills that lives in the water

breathe to take air into the lungs and push it back out

REACHING ALL LEARNERS **Extra Support/Intervention**

Reading Diagrams

Have children look at the fish diagram on pages 90–91. Explain that a diagram is a picture that has labels for the names of its parts. Tell children that each label has a line pointing to the part it names. Work with children to read each label and point to the corresponding part.

Let's look at fins and tails.
Fins and tails help fish swim well.

92

Some fins look like fans.

93

CRITICAL THINKING

Guiding Comprehension

❸ NOTING DETAILS What do fish need to swim well? (fins and tails)

COMPREHENSION STRATEGY

Question

Teacher/Student Modeling Ask children to think about what they have learned so far. Ask, *What else would you like to find out? Are there any questions you still have about fish?* If necessary, use the model in the Extra Support/Intervention box on this page.

Story Vocabulary

tail the part of an animal extending from the end of the body opposite the head

tails more than one tail

Extra Support/Intervention

Strategy Modeling: Question

Use this example to model the strategy.

I have learned what the different parts of a fish are called. I know why fish have gills, fins, and tails. Now I have a question: "Do all fish look the same?" I will keep reading to find out the answer.

Fish can have lots of <u>colors</u>.
Look! One is <u>green</u> and <u>blue</u>.
One has a black dot on its fin.

94

We like looking at all the colors.

95

READING STRATEGY

Phonics/Decoding

Clusters with *r*

Teacher/Student Modeling Write *green* on the board. Underline *gr*. Review that some words begin with two consonants, and that the sounds are blended together. Remind children of the sounds for the letters *gr*, /g/ /r/. Have children look carefully at the word, think about the sounds for the letters *g, r, e, e, n,* and blend the word sound by sound. Repeat with other selection words containing clusters with *r*: *trip, breathe, trick, grass, grab, crabs, brown.*

English Language Learners

Color Adjectives

Introduce or review the color adjectives *green, blue, red,* and *brown*. Help children use the adjectives to describe objects pictured in the photographs.

Extra Support/Intervention

Concepts of Print

Exclamation Point Have children note the exclamation point on page 94. Ask how they think the word before the exclamation point should sound when they read it aloud.

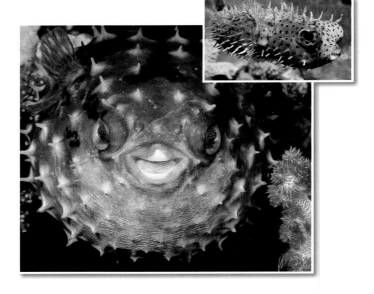

What do fish eat?
Many eat plants.
Some eat fish.

96

Here's a <u>funny</u> fish.
It has a <u>trick</u>.
It can puff up to get a big fish
to go away.

97

CRITICAL THINKING
Guiding Comprehension

4 DRAWING CONCLUSIONS Why does the fish on page 97 want a big fish to go away? (because a big fish might eat the smaller fish)

 READING STRATEGY
Phonics/Decoding

Contractions with 's

Teacher/Student Modeling Write *Here's* on the board. Remind children that *Here's* is a short way of writing *Here is*. Circle the apostrophe and explain that it takes the place of the *i* in *is*. Remind children that the letter *s* can stand for the /z/ sound. Have children look carefully at the word. Remind children that they know the word *Here*. Point to it on the Word Wall. Then have children read *Here's* aloud. Ask them to read the first sentence on page 97 to see if *Here's* makes sense.

THEME 3: Let's Look Around!
(Anthology pp. 96–97)

T206

English Language Learners

Language Development

Children may be unfamiliar with the term *puff up*. To illustrate the term, say, *I will puff up my cheeks.* Then fill your cheeks with air. Have children repeat the sentence and the action.

We see two fish. Can you?
One looks like a rock.
One is in the sea grass.

98

A sea horse can grab on
to a sea plant.

99

CRITICAL THINKING

Guiding Comprehension

5 **DRAWING CONCLUSIONS** Why do the fish in these photos hide in these places? (The fish look a lot like the places they're hiding in, which makes them hard to see.)

Story Vocabulary

sea the ocean

sea horse a small ocean fish with a head that looks like a horse's head

Crabs and sea slugs live
on sand and rocks.
A crab has legs.
It can run fast.

100

A brown otter also lives here.
It can swim on its back.

101

CRITICAL THINKING

Guiding Comprehension

6 **CATEGORIZE AND CLASSIFY** Which photos on pages 98–101 show fish? (the photos on pages 98–99) Which photos show other kinds of sea creatures? (the photos on pages 100–101)

COMPREHENSION STRATEGY

Question

Student Modeling Have children ask a question about the selection. If necessary, ask, *What else do you want to find out about the trip to the aquarium?* If children need more help, use the model in the Extra Support/Intervention box on this page.

Story Vocabulary

otter an animal with thick brown fur that lives in or near water

 Extra Support/Intervention

Strategy Modeling: Question

Use this example to model the strategy.

The class has seen a lot of animals at the aquarium. I'm not sure if their trip is over. I would ask this question: "What else will the children see at the aquarium?"

THEME 3: Let's Look Around!
(Anthology pp. 100–101)

We stop next to a big tank
and see dolphins swim.
It's fun to go on a trip here!

102   103

CRITICAL THINKING
Guiding Comprehension

7 **SEQUENCE OF EVENTS** What is the last thing the children
see at the aquarium? (dolphins in a tank)

Story Vocabulary

dolphins long-nosed sea animals related
to, but smaller than, whales

REACHING ALL LEARNERS

On Level   **Challenge**

Reread a Favorite Part

Have children work in small groups. In turn, ask each
child to read the question on page 104 and choose a
favorite animal. Have the child find and read the page
that describes that animal.

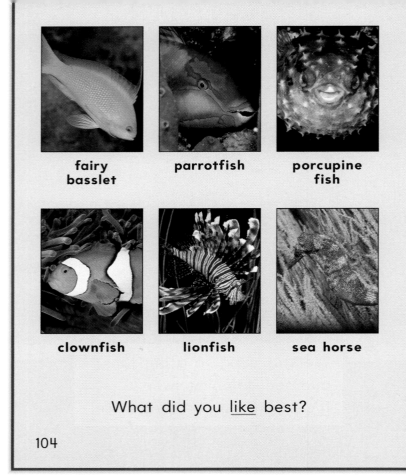

fairy basslet   parrotfish   porcupine fish

clownfish   lionfish   sea horse

What did you <u>like</u> best?

104

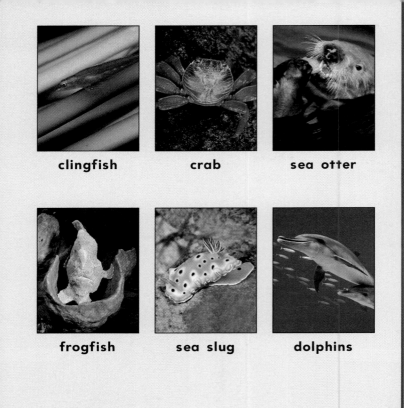

clingfish   crab   sea otter

frogfish   sea slug   dolphins

105

Wrapping Up

Critical Thinking Questions

1. **CATEGORIZE AND CLASSIFY** Do people belong in the group of things that live in the sea? Why? (No, they live on land.)

2. **DRAWING CONCLUSIONS** Do you think the class will want to visit the aquarium again? Why do you think so? (Yes; because they had fun)

Comprehension Check

Assign **Practice Book** page 159 to assess children's understanding of the selection.

Song

As an extension of the story, children may enjoy learning and singing "A Sailor Went to Sea, Sea, Sea." Words and music are on page R60.

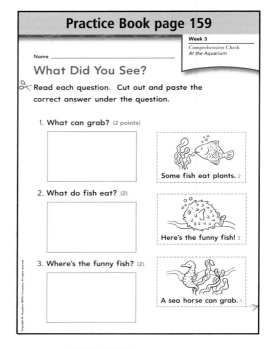

Practice Book page 159

Week 3
Comprehension Check
At the Aquarium

Name _____

What Did You See?

Read each question. Cut out and paste the correct answer under the question.

1. What can grab? (2 points)

Some fish eat plants. 2

2. What do fish eat? (2)

Here's the funny fish! 3

3. Where's the funny fish? (2)

A sea horse can grab. 1

Monitoring Student Progress

If . . .	Then . . .
children have difficulty categorizing and classifying,	have them page through the story and tell which things are fish and which things are other sea creatures.
children have difficulty reading decodable words,	coach them in using the Phonics/Decoding Strategy.

THEME 3: Let's Look Around!
(Anthology pp. 104–105)

Think About the Story

At the Aquarium

1 How are the fish in the story different from each other?

2 Tell two things you learned about fish in this story.

3 Which fish would you like to learn more about? Why?

106

Retell the Story

Pretend you are a guide at the aquarium. Tell classmates what they will see there.

 **Writing** ►

Write a Description

Which fish or animal in the story is your favorite? Write a sentence about it.

I like the porcupine fish because it is funny.

107

Responding

Think About the Story

Discuss the questions on Anthology page 106 and the starred question below. Accept reasonable responses.

1. **CATEGORIZE AND CLASSIFY** Children may suggest that they are different sizes, shapes, and colors.

2. **NOTING DETAILS** Answers will vary but should include details from the story. Possible answers: Gills help a fish breathe. Some fish eat plants. Some fish eat fish.

3. **MAKING JUDGMENTS** Answers will vary but should include reasons.

4. **Connecting/Comparing** Which story did you like better— *Seasons* or *At the Aquarium*? Why? (Answers will vary but should be supported with reasons.)

Retell the Story

Have children refer to the story text and pictures so that they provide accurate information. In small groups children can draw pictures of the fish and sea animals from the story on **Teacher's Resource Blackline Master 44.** They can sequence the pictures and refer to them when they retell the story.

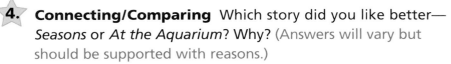

Extra Support/Intervention

Responding: Writing Support

Suggest that children look carefully at the picture that illustrates their favorite fish or animal. They may want to dictate some of their thoughts before writing. Then they can select from the listed words to write their sentences.

English Language Learners

Supporting Comprehension

Beginning/Preproduction Review the story with children and help them name the fish and other sea creatures.

Early Production and Speech Emergence Have children draw make-believe fish. First, brainstorm a list of adjectives and write them on the board as a reference. Help children label their fish with appropriate adjectives.

Intermediate and Advanced Fluency Have children draw make-believe fish. Once they have labeled their fish, children can meet in small groups to tell about their fish.

COMPREHENSION: Categorize and Classify

OBJECTIVES

- Categorize and classify objects in the classroom.
- Categorize and classify objects in *At the Aquarium*.

Target Skill Trace

Preview	p. T177, p. T194
Teach	pp. T212–T213
Reteach	p. R40
Review	p. T226
See	*Extra Support Handbook*, pp. 100–101, 106–107

❶ Teach

Discuss categories. Explain that groups of things that go together are called categories.

- Place a book, a pencil, a magazine, and a pen on the table. Select a child to make one pile of things to read and one pile of things to write with.
- Point out that the book and the magazine are in the category "Things to Read," and the pencil and pen are in the category "Things to Write With."

Explain that putting things in categories can help readers understand what they read.

Modeling Demonstrate how to categorize and classify.

> **Think Aloud** At the Aquarium *tells about different groups, or categories of things. One category is animals. Fish, dolphins, and otters fit in this category. Another category is plants. Sea grass and sea plant fit in the plants category. A third category is nonliving things. Sand and rocks fit into this last category.*

Explain that making categories is one way of remembering and making sense of details in stories.

❷ Guided Practice

Complete Chart/Transparency 3–9 with information from *At the Aquarium*. Have children name objects from the story. Then, using prompts such as the following, help them decide which category each object fits into.

- *Is this object an animal, a plant, or a nonliving thing?*
- *Do nonliving things breath? Can plants move around?*

Review the completed chart. Have children tell what they learned about the categories animals, plants, and nonliving things. Point out that putting things into categories helped them think more about the information in the selection.

Chart/Transparency 3–9

Things at the Aquarium

Animals	Plants	Nonliving Things
fish	sea grass	sand
dolphin	kelp	rocks
otter		
sea horse		
crab		
sea slug		

❸ Apply

Choose one or more activities.

- Have partners put the animals in *At the Aquarium* into categories. Groupings could include animals with tails, animals with stripes, or brightly colored animals. Have children share their categories with the class.

- Assign **Practice Book** page 161.

- Have children apply this skill as they read the Leveled Readers.

✔ **Test Prep** Explain that categorizing and classifying can help children remember information they read for a test. It will also help them remember where to find information in a test passage to answer a question correctly.

Leveled Readers and Leveled Practice

Children at all levels apply the comprehension skill as they read their Leveled Readers. See lessons on pages T232–T235.

● BELOW LEVEL   ▲ ON LEVEL   ■ ABOVE LEVEL   ◆ LANGUAGE SUPPORT

Practice Book page 161

Week 3
Comprehension Categorize and Classify

Name _____

Which Is Which?

🖊 Use the words in the box. List words under **Animals** or **Plants**.

Word Bank

grass	bird	cat	cactus
dog	flower	tree	crab

Animals	Plants
dog (1 point)	grass (1)
bird (1)	flower (1)
cat (1)	tree (1)
crab (1)	cactus (1)

Reading Traits

As children develop the ability to categorize and classify, they are learning to "read beyond the lines" of a selection. This comprehension skill supports the Reading Trait **Integrating for Synthesis.**

Monitoring Student Progress

If . . .	Then . . .
children score 5 or below on **Practice Book** page 161,	use the Reteaching lesson on Teacher's Edition page R40.
children have met the lesson objectives,	have them do the Challenge/Extension activities on Teacher's Edition page R41.

OBJECTIVES

- Sort and read the Basic Words.
- Identify and write color words.

Materials

- index cards with words *brass, brown, brig, crab, crack, drill, drip, grab, gram, grass, grill, grin, track, trap, trick, trill, trip* (set for each group of children)
- color wheel, paints for mixing colors, brushes

Practice Book page 162

Name _____

Week 3
Spelling Clusters with *r*

Clusters with *r*

 Write a word from the box to complete each sentence in the story.

Word Bank

| trip | crab | drip | grin | grab | trap |

1. Dan will go on a __trip (1 point)__ .

2. He will __grab (1)__ his bags.

3. Look at Dad __grin (1)__ !

4. Dad and Dan set the __trap (1)__ .

5. Dad has a big __crab (1)__ .

6. Dan said, "Do not let it __drip (1)__ on me!"

SPELLING:
Clusters with *r*

Sorting Clusters Divide the class into small groups and give each group a set of the index cards.

- Have children sort the words by their beginning cluster and read the words in each group.
- Challenge children to make up a tongue twister with the words from one group.

Practice/Homework Assign **Practice Book** page 162.

Penmanship Ball-and-stick *and* continuous-stroke penmanship models are available in the **Practice Book** (pp. 216–223) and the **Teacher's Resource Blackline Masters** (pp. 143–194).

TARGET SKILL
VOCABULARY:
Color Words

Teach Display a color wheel, and name the colors.

- List the color names on chart paper, using corresponding marker colors.
- Ask children to dictate other color words for the chart.

Practice/Apply Demonstrate how to mix primary colors to get secondary colors (for example, mix red and yellow to get orange).

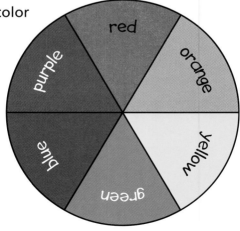

- Have each child choose two colors only and use them, or mixtures of them, to paint a picture.
- Have children write the names of the colors they used.

GRAMMAR:
Action Part of a Sentence

OBJECTIVES

- Identify the action parts of sentences.
- Match naming and action parts to make complete sentences.

Materials

- blank sentence strips
- safety scissors

❶ Teach

Define the action part of a sentence.

- Write the following sentences on the board.

> Kim calls to me.
> Dad and I pick flowers.
> Van fills the pots.
> Bess sells the pots of flowers.

- Read the first sentence with children.

- Explain that a sentence has two parts: a naming part and an action part. Review that the naming part names someone or something. Tell children that the action part tells what someone or something does.

- Draw a vertical line between *Kim* and *calls to me*. Ask which part of the sentence is the action part. (*calls to me*)

- Repeat for the remaining sentences. (Action parts are *pick flowers, fills the pots, sells the pots of flowers*.)

Go over these points:

- Each sentence has a naming part and an action part.

- The action part tells what someone or something does.

❷ Guided Practice

Check children's understanding.

- Have each child copy a sentence from the board onto a blank sentence strip. Have children cut apart their sentences to separate the naming parts from the action parts.

- Challenge children to put the sentences back together. They can refer to the sentences on the board for help.

❸ Apply

Assign Practice Book page 163. Have children write an action part to complete each sentence.

Practice Book page 163

Week 3
Grammar Action Part of a Sentence

Name _____

Make Them Complete!

Write an action part from the box to complete each sentence in the story.

> gets a bass   jump   eat   fix the fish

1. Some fish _jump (2)_ _____ .

2. Mom _gets a bass (2)_ _____ .

3. Dad and the kids _fix the fish (2)_ _____ .

4. Then they _eat (2)_ _____ !

DAY 4 week 3

Day at a Glance
pages T216–T223

Learning to Read

Reading the Drama Link
Why the Sun and the Moon Live in the Sky

Phonics Review
• • • • • • • • • • • • • • • • • •
Leveled Readers, *T232–T235*

- ● *Let's Grab It!*
- ▲ *Looking for Birds*
- ■ *On the Beach*
- ◆ *Grab It!*

Word Work

Spelling: Clusters with *r*
Vocabulary: Words That Show Position

Writing & Oral Language

Independent Writing

Daily Routines

Daily Message

Review phonics and language skills. Read the message aloud, pointing to each word as it is read. Call on children to complete the sentences and answer the question.

- Ask a child to circle words that begin with clusters with *r*.
- Ask individuals to underline the high-frequency word *color*. Then have children point out all the other words they know.

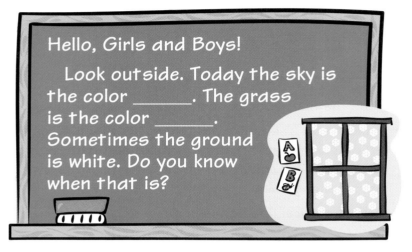

Hello, Girls and Boys!
    Look outside. Today the sky is the color _____. The grass is the color _____. Sometimes the ground is white. Do you know when that is?

Discuss color words. Have children find all of the color words in the message, and find something in the classroom that is each color. Continue with other colors children can name.

Word Wall

KINDERGARTEN REVIEW Write a chart similar to the one shown. Point to and read the word *the*. Ask a child to write the missing letter. Repeat with the other words. Next, read the words together. Finally, have children find each word on the Word Wall.

th_ (the)	hav_ (have)	h_re (here)	d_g (dig)
_s (is)	ar_ (are)	_ee (see)	_n (an)
_nd (and)	_t (at)	w_t (wet)	g_ (go)
li_e (like)			

Daily Phonemic Awareness

Blending and Segmenting Phonemes: Seal's Words

142

- Use the **Picture Card** *seal.* Say, *This is Sam Seal, the talking seal. Sam heard a strange new word today, but he needs your help to figure out the new word. The word is /s//t//ŏ//p/. Blend the sounds together. Raise your hand when you know the word. What is it?* (*stop*)

- Repeat this activity, segmenting the sounds for the words *spun, chip, mast, slip, track,* and *truck.* Have children blend the sounds together and say each word.

- Next, have children work in pairs to think of single-syllable words to solve for Sam. One child can segment the word, and the other child can blend the sounds together to say the word.

Daily Language Practice

Grammar Skill: Capitalize a Name

Spelling Skill: Clusters with *r*

Have children correct the following sentence:

liz will grabb it.

(Liz will **grab** it.)

Daily Writing Prompt

Have children write about how the world outside the window looks today, or have them write on self-selected topics. Encourage children to repeat the assignment each day for several days. Ask how the world outside changes or stays the same.

An Activity Master for this writing activity appears on R53.

Daily Independent Reading

Remind children to practice reading the Word Wall. They can read from the following.

- Leveled Bibliography, pages T6–T7

Choose books from this list for children to read, outside class, for at least twenty minutes a day.

- Leveled Theme Paperbacks

- Reread Anthology story *At the Aquarium.*

The Crab
by Alice E. Lisson
illustrated by Dennis Hockerman

Houghton Mifflin

Drama Link

Read Together

WHY SUN AND MOON LIVE IN THE SKY
based on an African Tale

Characters

Narrator   Sun   Moon   Sea

Many years ago, Sun and Moon lived in a house. Sea never came to visit. The house was too small.

108

So Sun and Moon built a BIG house. Sea and all his sea animals took a trip there.

We are here to visit.

Hello, Sea. Come in!

109

Drama Link

Skill: How to Read a Play

- **Introduce** the play by reading the title and having children look at the text and the illustrations. Discuss how the text looks different from other selections they have read.

- **Explain** that the characters in a play tell a story by talking to one another. Read aloud the list of characters on the page. Explain that a narrator is a special character who gives information about the characters and the story.

- **Point out** the symbols that show who is speaking: the Narrator, Sun, Moon, or Sea.

- **Model** how to read a play. Reread the title and the list of characters. Point out the symbol above each character's name. Remind children that the symbols tell readers which character is speaking. Point to the narrator symbol and read the narrator's lines on page 108. Then, draw boxes to form a sequence chart. Add events to the chart as you read.

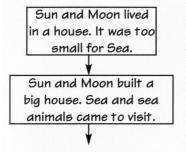

Sun and Moon lived in a house. It was too small for Sea.

↓

Sun and Moon built a big house. Sea and sea animals came to visit.

↓

Vocabulary

Write the Concept Vocabulary on the board and read each word. Tell children that this play is based on a *tale,* or story, from Africa. Ask, *Who are the* characters *in this play? What does the* narrator *do?*

Concept Vocabulary
tale   characters   narrator

Review For children who need a review of phonics and high-frequency words, point out the Words to Know. Remind children that they can use what they've learned to read these words, and coach them to read the sentences in which the words occur.

Words to Know		
blue	some	trip
many	let's	

THEME 3: Let's Look Around!
(Anthology pp. 108–109)

Sea rushed in with fish and other sea animals. Soon Sun and Moon felt water up to their ears.

Can I bring in some more of my sea animals?

Yes!

110

Let's all go in!

Water came up to the roof. Sun and Moon had to go up into the blue sky, and that's where they still live today.

111

Critical Thinking

Guiding Comprehension

1. **CAUSE AND EFFECT** Why didn't Sea ever visit Sun and Moon? (because Sun and Moon's house was too small for Sea)

2. **NOTING DETAILS** What kinds of sea animals did Sea bring to Sun and Moon's new house? (Sample responses: fish, crab, whale, turtles, octopus)

3. **SEQUENCE OF EVENTS** What was the last thing Sun and Moon did at the end of the play? (They moved up into the sky because their whole house filled up with water.)

4. **CONNECTING/COMPARING**
Fantasy and Realism Now you have read *At the Aquarium* and *Why Sun and Moon Live in the Sky*. Which one tells about something that could not happen in real life? (*Why Sun and Moon Live in the Sky*)

Genre

Reading a Play

Teach

Explain that when a play is read aloud, the names of the characters are not spoken; only the characters' lines are read. Then point out that when you are reading a play aloud, it is fun to use a different voice for each character. Model reading the lines on page 109, using different voices for Bird, Sea, Sun, and Moon.

Practice/Apply

Divide the class into groups of four and assign each child a character part. Give children time to practice their lines and experiment with voices to use. Coach children who need help reading their lines, or have them work with partners. Then have each group perform the play together.

Drama Link
(Anthology pp. 110–111) **T219**

OBJECTIVES

- Write and sort words with short *i*.
- Read verbs ending with *-s, -ed, -ing.*
- Read possessives with *'s.*

Review Skill Trace

| Reteach | pp. R20, R22, R24 |
| Review | pp. T220–T221 |

Materials

- **Picture Cards** *dig, kiss, kit, lip, mix, pig, pin, pit, quill, sit, six, wig, zip*
- **Teacher's Resource Blackline Master** 44

PHONICS: More Short *i* Words

❶ Review

Review consonants and short *i*.

- Display the **Picture Cards** along the chalkboard ledge.
- Name each picture with children and ask what all the names have in common. (All have the short *i* sound, /ĭ/.)
- Have children take turns coming to the board, choosing a **Picture Card,** and writing the word that names the picture above the card.
- Once all picture names have been written, have children sort for words that begin the same and words that rhyme.

❷ Guided Practice/Apply

Have children play What's in an Aquarium?

What's in an Aquarium?

- Distribute a copy of **Teacher's Resource Blackline Master** 44 to small groups of children.
- Give children a set time, perhaps five minutes, to write on the aquarium as many short *i* words as they can think of.
- After time has expired, have groups read their words aloud and count them to see which group recorded the most words.

PHONICS:
Verbs Ending with *-s*, *-ed*, *-ing*; Possessives with *'s*

1 Review

Have children read verbs ending with *-s*, *-ed*, and *-ing*.

• Write these words on the board.

look	*looks*	*looked*	*looking*
kick	*kicks*	*kicked*	*kicking*
pull	*pulls*	*pulled*	*pulling*

• Call on a child to read the words in the first column. Together, read aloud the words in the second column. Ask how the words are alike. (All are action words that end with *–s*.)

• Follow a similar procedure for the words in the remaining columns, noting the *-ed* and *-ing* endings.

Have children read possessives with *'s*.

• Write this sentence on the board: *Jim's hat is brown, but Pam's hat is blue*. Have children read the sentence with you.

• Explain that in this sentence, the apostrophe followed by *s* means that something belongs to someone. Ask, *What belongs to Jim?* (a brown hat) *to Pam?* (a blue hat)

2 Guided Practice/Apply

Have children locate verb endings and possessives with *'s*.

Find the Word

• Write on the board: *Jack's dog can jump. She is always jumping! She jumps high. The dog jumped up on Ann's bed.*

• Call on children to go to the board and do the following:

—underline the form of *jump* that ends with *-s*

—underline the form of *jump* that ends with *-ed*

—underline the form of *jump* that ends with *-ing*

—circle a boy's name that ends with an spostrophe and *s*

—circle a girl's name that ends with an spostrophe and *s*

• Ask, *What belongs to Ann?* (a bed) *to Jack?* (a dog)

Practice Book page 164

Name _____

Week 3
Spelling Clusters with *r*

Spelling Spree

✏ Add the missing letter to write each Spelling Word.

Spelling Words
trip
crab
drip
grin
grab
trap

1. t _r_ ap = trap (1 point)

2. d _r_ ip = drip (1)

3. g _r_ ab = grab (1)

✏ Proofread each sentence. Circle each Spelling Word that is wrong, and write it correctly.

4. We go on a (tirp.) ___trip (1)___

5. We get a (krab!) ___crab (1)___

6. We (grinn.) ___grin (1)___

PRACTICE

SPELLING:
Clusters with *r*

Word Pictures Display the list of Basic Words, and have children clap and spell each word.

- Draw a large happy face on the board and write *grin* on the smile line. Point out that by writing *grin* on the smile line, you have shown the word's spelling *and* meaning.
- Brainstorm ways to write the other words and show their meanings, such as writing *c-r-a-b* on claws or *d-r-i-p* in drops of water.
- Have children write and illustrate the spelling words.

Practice/Homework Assign **Practice Book** page 164.

Penmanship Ball-and-stick *and* continuous-stroke penmanship models are available in the **Practice Book** (pp. 216–223) and the **Teacher's Resource Blackline Masters** (pp. 143–194).

INSTRUCTION

VOCABULARY:
Words That Show Position

Teach Write these words: *in, out, on, off, left, right, up, down, here, there.* Explain that these words tell where things are, or in what direction they are going.

Practice/Apply Place a sheet of paper, a pencil, and a box on a desktop. Have children

- put the paper *in* the box, and take it back *out.*
- put the pencil *on* the paper, and take it back *off.*
- stand up and step to the *right*; then step to the *left.*
- point their fingers *up*; then *down.*
- bring the pencil over *here*; put the pencil over *there.*

INDEPENDENT WRITING: Writing About Trips

Provide structured writing practice.

- Discuss field trips.
- Dictate this sentence: *We went to the zoo.*

Ask children to choose a topic.

- Have children name trips they would like to take. List their ideas on the board.
- Tell children to choose one trip to write about.

Trips to Take

a trip to a zoo

a trip to the moon

a trip to a theme park

a trip to visit a friend who has moved

a trip to the seashore

a trip to the mountains

Assign Practice Book page 165.

- Have children think about the beginning of their trip (getting there), the middle (what happens at the place), and the end (getting home).
- Have them write sentences to tell about their trips.
- Remind children to refer to the Word Wall for help with spelling. They should proofread their work to make sure each sentence begins with a capital letter and ends with the correct punctuation mark.

Display children's work. Post the pages on a bulletin board with the title, *What a Trip!*

Practice Book page 165

Week 3
Writing Writing About Trips

Name _____

Plan Your Trip!

Write your ideas about your trip.

Where will you go?

_____
Answers will vary. (2 points)

How will you get there?

_____
Answers will vary. (2)

What will you do there?

_____
Answers will vary. (2)

How will you get home?

_____
Answers will vary. (2)

Day at a Glance
pages T224–T231

Learning to Read

Comprehension: Rereading for Understanding

Rereading for Fluency

Reading Decodable Text
Fran Pig's Brick Hut

• •

Leveled Readers, *T232–T235*

- ● *Let's Grab It!*
- ▲ *Looking for Birds*
- ■ *On the Beach*
- ◆ *Grab It!*

Word Work

Spelling: Clusters with *r*
Vocabulary: Speed Drill

Writing & Oral Language

Grammar Review: Action Part of a Sentence
Independent Writing
Listening

Daily Routines

Daily Message

Strategy Review Remind children of the Phonics/Decoding Strategy. Guide them in applying it to selected words in today's message. Then ask individuals to answer the question.

> Good Morning Boys and Girls!
>
> There are so many good books to read! Most people like some books more than others. I like books about (fill in your reading preferences). What kinds of books do you like to read?

Discuss books to read. Have children name some books they have read and enjoyed during independent reading time. List these books on the board and tell children they may want to read some of these books during the next independent reading period.

Vocabulary

Speed Drill On index cards, write the words *also, blue, brown, color, funny, green, like, many, some, crabs, trick,* and *grass*. Have children take turns holding up the cards for a partner to read. After children have practiced, display the cards. Ask individuals to read them to you as quickly as they can.

also	funny	some
blue	green	many
brown	like	color
trick	crabs	grass

Daily Phonemic Awareness

Blending and Segmenting Phonomes: Number Words

Tell children that you will give them clues to some words for numbers. They should blend the sounds you say to figure out the words: Say, /f//ī//v/ (five);/w//ŭ//n/ (one).

Now have children pretend to be the teacher. Whisper a number word to a child. Have the child say the sounds of the words, and then call on another child to blend the sounds together to say the whole word. Whisper the following sounds:

/th//r//ē/ (three)
/t//oo/ (two)
/f//ôr/ (four)

Daily Language Practice

Grammar Skill: Beginning a Sentence with a Capital
 Letter
Spelling Skill: Clusters with *r*
Have children correct the following sentence:

do not trapp animals.

(**Do** not **trap** animals.)

Daily Writing Prompt

Have children draw and write about a book they would like to recommend to friends, or have them write on self-selected topics.

Daily Independent Reading

Have children read with partners from the following.

• Leveled Bibliography, pages T6–T7

Choose books from this list for children to read, outside class, for at least twenty minutes a day.

• Reread Phonics Library story *Brad's Quick Rag Tricks* or *Fran Pig's Brick Hut*.

OBJECTIVES

- Review categorizing and classifying in the week's selections.

Target Skill Trace

Preview	p. T177
Teach	pp. T212–T213
Reteach	p. R40
▶ Review	p. T226
See	*Extra Support Handbook,* pp. 100–101; pp. 106–107

 TARGET SKILL

COMPREHENSION: Rereading for Understanding

Categorize and Classify

Discuss texts. Briefly review *Hilda Hen's Scary Night, At the Aquarium,* and *The Trip.* Remind children that as they read these selections, they thought about how things fit into groups.

Think Aloud *Hilda Hen's Scary Night takes place on a farm. Thinking about things found on a farm helped me retell the story.* At the Aquarium *takes place at an aquarium. Thinking about things found in the water helped me recall that selection.*

Display Chart/Transparency 3–10. Have children help you list living things found at the farm in the story about Hilda. Have them help you list living things from the selection *At the Aquarium.*

- Next, ask children to review each selection and then suggest some nonliving things mentioned in each story.

- Have children use the chart to compare and contrast things found at farms and at aquariums.

Assign rereading and retelling.

- Have children think about ways to group living and nonliving things as they reread the other selections for the week: **On My Way Practice Reader, On Level/Challenge Theme Paperback, Phonics Library.**

- Have children categorize and classify sea creatures from *At the Aquarium.*

Chart/Transparency 3–10

Where Does It Belong?

At a Farm	At an Aquarium
Living Things	**Living Things**
hens	people
horse	fish
fox	sea grass
snake	plants
	sea slug
	crab
	otter
	dolphins
Nonliving Things	**Nonliving Things**
hen house	pictures
hose	rocks
pool	sand
hat	tank
	building
	signs

 TARGET SKILL

REREADING FOR FLUENCY

Rereading the Selection Have children reread *The Trip* or pages 94–97 of *At the Aquarium* orally in small groups. Model fluent reading, and coach children to read with feeling and expression.

Fran Pig's Brick Hut

by Mark Dempsey
illustrated by Amy Walrod

Fran Pig got some
big, fat bricks.

37

PHONICS LIBRARY

End-of-Week Skills Check

Have children preview Fran Pig's Brick Hut. Ask them to tell what the pig has in the wheelbarrow on page 37.

Observe as children model the Phonics/Decoding Strategy.

- Have children read *Fran Pig's Brick Hut*. As they read, ask individuals to tell how they use the strategy to figure out new words.

- Make note of children who have difficulty applying the strategy, and take oral reading records with these children.

Prompt children in rereading the story. For children who have difficulty, use prompts such as these:

- *Look at the letters from left to right.*

- *Say the sound for each letter and hold it until you say the next sound. What is the word?*

- *Is that a word you know? Does it make sense in the story?*

OBJECTIVES

- Apply the Phonics/Decoding Strategy to decode clusters with *r*; contractions with *'s*.
- Recognize high-frequency words in context.
- Reread to build fluency.

Word Key

Decodable words with clusters with *r*;
contractions with *'s* ———

High-Frequency Words ———

Monitoring Student Progress

Oral Reading Records Take oral reading records of a few children each week as they read the **Phonics Library** book individually or in small groups.

Alternative Assessment Use **Teacher's Resource Blackline Master** 45 to assess individual children's phonics and high-frequency word skills.

Fran Pig also got many pigs
to grab big, fat bricks.

38

The pigs set lots
of big, fat bricks.

39

Oral Language

Discuss these questions with children. Have them speak in complete sentences.

- Why did Fran Pig get lots of bricks? (She wanted to build a big brick hut.)

- Why did Fran Pig get lots of pigs? (She needed help to build the hut.)

It's set!
Fran Pig likes the big brick hut.

40

TARGET SKILL
Build Fluency

Model fluent reading.

- Call attention to the exclamation point on page 40. Explain that this mark means to read with excitement.

- Read page 40 aloud. Have children read it aloud.

- Have children reread pages 39 and 40 several times until each child can read the pages effortlessly.

Home Connection

Hand out the take-home version of *Fran Pig's Brick Hut*. Ask children to reread the story with their families. (See the **Phonics Library Blackline Masters**.)

OBJECTIVES

- Take a test on the Basic Words.
- Review the week's high-frequency words.

SPELLING: Clusters with *r*

Test

Say each underlined word, read the sentence, and then repeat the word. Have children write only the underlined word.

Basic Words

1. I took a **trip** to the lake.
2. At the beach, I saw a **crab**.
3. Do not let the water **drip**.
4. A happy baby may **grin**.
5. Use your hand to **grab** it.
6. I see a lobster in the **trap**.

Penmanship Ball-and-stick *and* continuous-stroke penmanship models are available in the **Practice Book** (pp. 216–223) and the **Teacher's Resource Blackline Masters** (pp. 143–194).

VOCABULARY: High-Frequency Words

Review the Week's Words Review the words in the New Words section and the Kindergarten Review word *like* with "clap and spell." Remove each word as it is reviewed.

- Call on children to move the words to the permanent Word Wall. The class can chant the words as they are moved.

also	blue	brown	color	funny

green	many	some	like

- Review some other words on the Word Wall.

Practice/Apply Have vocabulary speed drills. Assemble the Word Wall Cards for this week's new words, and make cards for words that feature this week's phonics elements.

- At small-group time, have children take turns holding up the cards for a partner to read.
- Then display the cards as a list. Have individuals read them to you as quickly as they can.

GRAMMAR:
Action Part of a Sentence

Review Remind children that the action part of a sentence tells what someone or something does.

Display Chart/Transparency 3–11.

- **Sentences 1–5:** Ask children to draw a line to separate the naming part from the action part of each sentence. Have them underline the action part.

- **Sentences 6–9:** Ask children to suggest the action parts.

Practice/Apply Coach children's writing. Dictate the following sentences for children to write: *A fox jumps. A crab runs fast.* Have children circle the naming part and underline the action part in each sentence.

Independent Writing Have children write a story about what they do after a field trip. Remind them to use naming parts and action parts in their sentences.

- Identify action parts of sentences.
- Write a story independently.
- Gather information from nonfiction sources.

Chart/Transparency 3–11

Action Part of a Sentence

1. Many animals | run.

2. Some animals | jump.

3. The vet | calls to the cat.

4. A green bug | sits on the box.

5. Fish | live in the sea.

Responses will vary.

6. The cat _____ .

7. Ken and Jan _____ .

8. Birds _____ .

9. A whale _____ .

TRANSPARENCY 3–11
TEACHER'S EDITION PAGE T231

LISTENING:
To Gather Information

Start a K-W-L chart.

- Ask children what they know about fish. List their ideas in the first column.

- Ask children what they would like to learn about fish. Record their ideas in the second column.

FISH

K	W	L
What I Know	What I Want to Find Out	What I Learned
Fish live in water		

Read a book about fish. Ask children to listen carefully as you read aloud a nonfiction book about fish, such as *Where's That Fish?* by Barbara Brenner (Scholastic, 1995).

Complete the K-W-L chart.

- Ask children what they learned about fish. Record their responses in the third column.

English Language Learners

Reread the Book

Allow English language learners to listen to the fish book two or three times. During the last reading, pause periodically and ask children if they have learned any new facts about fish. Write their responses in the K-W-L chart.

LEVELED READERS

WEEK 3

● BELOW LEVEL

Building Background and Vocabulary

Read aloud the title and talk about the cover illustration. Explain that this story is about a group of children picking up things left behind on a beach. Invite children to tell their experiences finding things people leave behind at beaches or parks. Then preview the illustrations.

ⓖ Comprehension Skill: Categorize and Classify

Read together the Strategy Focus on the book flap. Remind children to use the strategy and to think, as they read, about how different things in the book could be categorized or classified. (See the Leveled Readers Teacher's Guide for **Vocabulary and Comprehension Practice Masters.**)

Responding

Have partners discuss how to answer the questions on the inside back cover.

Think About What You Have Read   Sample answers:

1. Answers should include: a blue crab and a brown bug.

2. the big fish because it is too quick and gets away

3. Answers will vary.

Making Connections   Answers will vary.

ⓖ Building Fluency

Model   Reread page 2 aloud to children. Then have them read page 3 aloud together. Ask them to compare the two pages to find how the pattern from page 2 is repeated on page 3. (*Look!/Here's a…/Let's grab it!*) Point out that the last line on both pages repeats the book's title.

Practice   Ask children to find the same pattern on other pages in the book and to tell which words are different from the pattern established on pages 2 and 3. Then have them read pages 4 through 8 aloud in unison.

Let's Grab It!

Summary *This story is about a group of children at the beach who find and pick up things there. They grab a pail, a crab, a jug, a bug, and a net. They also try to catch a big fish, but the fish gets away. So the children decide they really don't want to grab it anyway.*

Story Words

Introduce the Story Words, one at a time, providing meaning with objects, pictures, gestures, and/or context sentences. Then ask children to complete the **Vocabulary Practice Master.**

grab (title), *p. 2*

jug *p. 4*

fish *p. 6*

Oops *p. 8*

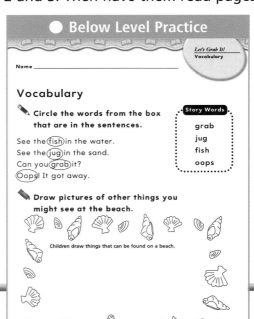

● Below Level Practice

● Below Level Practice

▲ ON LEVEL

Looking for Birds

Summary *In this nonfiction book, readers are introduced to different birds in close-up photographs, as if seen through binoculars. The text tells facts about what each bird looks like, and for some, it tells what they eat or what they do.*

Story Words

Introduce the Story Words, one at a time, providing meaning with objects, pictures, gestures, and/or context sentences. Then ask children to complete the **Vocabulary Practice Master.**

looking (title), *p. 2*

green *p. 3*

flower *p. 4*

blue *p. 5*

brown *p. 7*

found *p. 8*

Building Background and Vocabulary

Invite children to read the title aloud with you. Explain that the photo shows what someone sees through a pair of binoculars. Tell children that the book is about birds. Preview the photos and have children share what they know about real birds and any experiences they've had with binoculars.

Comprehension Skill: Categorize and Classify

Read together the Strategy Focus on the book flap. Remind children to use the strategy and to think, as they read, about how different things in the book could be categorized or classified. (See the Leveled Readers Teacher's Guide for **Vocabulary and Comprehension Practice Masters.**)

Responding

Have partners discuss how to answer the questions on the inside back cover.

Think About What You Have Read Sample answers:

1. different kinds of birds
2. Answers will vary.
3. Answers will vary.

Making Connections Answers will vary.

Building Fluency

Model Ask children to follow along as you reread pages 2 through 4 to them. Then ask them which words tell what each bird looks like and which words tell what it is doing. Write the words they identify on the chalkboard. (*big, green, funny/eating from a flower*)

Practice Have children work in small groups to reread the rest of the book aloud together. Ask them to watch for words to add to the chalkboard lists.

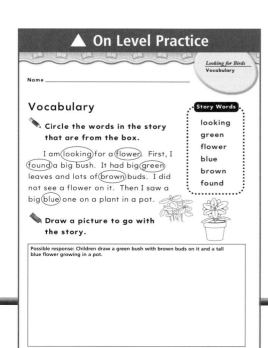

▲ On Level Practice

Looking for Birds
Vocabulary

Name _____

Vocabulary

✎ Circle the words in the story that are from the box.

I am looking for a flower. First, I found a big bush. It had big green leaves and lots of brown buds. I did not see a flower on it. Then I saw a big blue one on a plant in a pot.

Story Words
looking
green
flower
blue
brown
found

✎ Draw a picture to go with the story.

Possible response: Children draw a green bush with brown buds on it and a tall blue flower growing in a pot.

▲ On Level Practice

Looking for Birds
Comprehension Skill
Categorize and Classify

Name _____

Comprehension

✎ Write each word from the box where it belongs under Can Fly or under Can Not Fly.

| cat | jet | crab | bug |
| bird | | bag | pig |

Can Fly	Can Not Fly
jet	cat
bug	crab
bird	pig
	bag

LEVELED READERS

WEEK 3

On the Beach

Summary *In this informational book, children find interesting natural items such as a clamshell, a hermit crab, seaweed, driftwood, and rocks. The text tells facts about their discoveries. When it's time to go home, the children leave their treasures for other people to find and enjoy.*

Story Words

Introduce the Story Words, one at a time, providing meaning with objects, pictures, gestures, and/or context sentences. Then ask children to complete the **Vocabulary Practice Master.**

beach (title), *p. 2*

ocean *p. 2*

smooth *p. 3*

soft *p. 3*

seaweed *p. 5*

drifted *p. 6*

■ ABOVE LEVEL

Building Background and Vocabulary

Explain that this book gives information about some things found on a beach. Preview the illustrations and encourage children to share what they know about things that can be found in or near the ocean.

ⓒ Comprehension Skill: Categorize and Classify

Read together the Strategy Focus on the book flap. Remind children to use the strategy and to think, as they read, about how different things in the book could be categorized or classified. (See the Leveled Readers Teacher's Guide for **Vocabulary and Comprehension Practice Masters.**)

Responding

Have partners discuss how to answer the questions on the inside back cover.

Think About What You Have Read Sample answers:

1. things in the story such as shells, crabs, seaweed, driftwood, and rocks

2. They are hard and help to keep the animals' soft bodies safe.

3. Probable answer: You can try wetting one of two similar rocks and then noticing whether it looks darker and shinier than the dry rock.

Making Connections Answers will vary.

ⓒ Building Fluency

Model Write the word *clam's* on the chalkboard. Tell children the apostrophe here shows that what follows belongs to the clam. Have children reread page 3 and tell what belongs to the clam. (*body*) Repeat for the word *it's* on page 5, telling children that the apostrophe is used here to replace the letter *i* when the words *it* and *is* are put together to make one word.

Practice Ask children to search the book for other words containing apostrophes, to read the sentences those words are in, and to decide the reason the apostrophe is used in each.

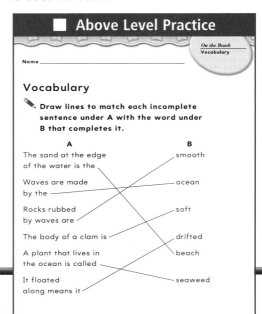

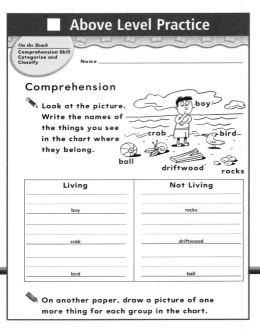

Leveled Readers

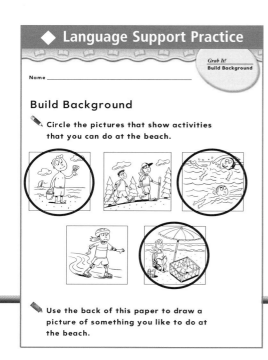

Grab It!

Summary *A group of children are at the beach exploring. In their explorations they grab a blue pail, a big blue crab, a green jug, a funny brown bug, and a net. A child tries to catch a large fish with the net. The fish jumps out of the net as the surprised children look on.*

Story Words

Introduce the Story Words. Then ask children to complete the **Story Words Master.**

here's a (phrase) this is a; to note an object, *p. 2*

grab take hold of quickly; seize, grip, (title), *p. 2*

quick fast; swift, *p. 8*

◆ LANGUAGE SUPPORT

Building Background and Vocabulary

Work with children to develop an understanding of what is found at the seashore. Use pictures of the seashore and point out the water and the beach. Ask: *Have you ever been to the seashore? When did you go to the seashore? Was it in the summer?* Then distribute the **Build Background Practice Master,** read aloud the directions, and have children complete the page. (See the Leveled Readers Teacher's Guide for **Build Background and Story Words Masters.**)

🌀 Reading Strategy: Question

Have children read the Strategy Focus on the book flap. Remind children to use the strategy as they read the book.

Responding

Have partners discuss how to answer the questions on the inside back cover.

Think About What You Have Read Sample answers:

1. Answers should include a blue pail, a blue crab, a green jug, and a brown bug.

2. It's too quick for them; it jumps out of the net.

3. Answers will vary.

Making Connections Answers will vary.

🌀 Building Fluency

Model Read aloud page 2 as children follow along in their books. Point out the exclamation mark at the end of the second sentence. Remind children that sentences with exclamation marks should be read with excitement.

Practice Lead the class in an echo reading of the text. Read each sentence and have them repeat after you. Repeat several times.

◆ Language Support Practice

Grab It!
Build Background

Name _____

Build Background

✏ Circle the pictures that show activities that you can do at the beach.

✏ Use the back of this paper to draw a picture of something you like to do at the beach.

◆ Language Support Practice

Grab It!
Story Words

Name _____

✏ Find the story words hidden in the boxes and circle the letters. Then write each word. Don't forget to write in the ' for here's a!

Story Words
grab
here's a
quick

D	G	B	M	L	H	X	P
G	R	A	Q	U	I	C	K
N	A	H	U	U	B	E	D
W	B	C	Z	T	I	W	B
J	Y	N	T	B	O	C	F
H	E	R	E	S	A	U	K

grab _____

here's a _____

quick _____

T235

Assessing Student Progress

Test Preparation

Throughout the theme, your children have had opportunities to read and think critically and to practice and apply new and reviewed skills and reading strategies.

Monitoring Student Progress

Throughout Theme 3, you monitored your children's progress by using the following program features:

- Guiding Comprehension questions
- Skill lesson applications
- Oral reading records
- Monitoring Student Progress boxes

Your children are now ready for the theme assessments, which allow you to assess each child's progress formally.

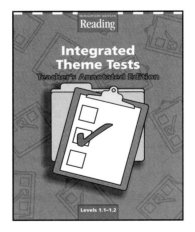

Testing Options

The **Integrated Theme Test** and the **Weekly Skills Test** are formal group assessments used to evaluate children's performance on theme objectives.

Integrated Theme Test

- Assesses children's progress as readers and writers in a format that reflects instruction
- Integrates reading and writing skills: phonics, comprehension strategies and skills, high-frequency words, writing, and listening comprehension
- Uses decodable passages to test children's reading skills in context

Weekly Skills Test

- Assesses children's mastery of discrete reading and language arts skills taught in the week: phonics, comprehension skills, high-frequency words, spelling, and grammar
- Consists of individual skill subtests, which can be administered separately
- **Theme Skills Tests** are also available.

Fluency Assessment

Oral reading fluency is a useful measure of a child's development of rapid automatic word recognition. Children who are on level in mid- to late Grade 1 should be able to read, accurately and with expression, an appropriate level text at the approximate rates shown in the table below. In the early stages of reading development, oral fluency should be observed informally.

Mid-Grade 1	Late Grade 1
23–47 words correct per minute	53–82 words correct per minute

- Consider decoding and comprehension, as well as reading rate, when evaluating children's reading development.
- You can use the **Leveled Reading Passages Assessment Kit** to assess fluency or a **Leveled Reader** from this theme at the appropriate level for each child.
- Check children's oral fluency rate three times during the year. If children are having difficulty learning to read, you might want to check their fluency rate more often.
- For information on how to select appropriate text, administer fluency checks, and interpret results, see the **Teacher's Assessment Handbook,** pp. 25–28.

Spelling Review/Assessment

You may want to review the spelling patterns taught in this theme (pages T42; T114; T186) and test children on selected words from each lesson.

Using Multiple Measures

Children's progress is best evaluated through multiple measures. In addition to the tests mentioned on page T236, multiple measures might include the following:

- **Emerging Literacy Survey** results
- Oral reading records
- Observation Checklist from this theme
- Children's writing from lessons or activities in this theme
- Other writing, other projects, or artwork
- One or more items selected by the child

Multiple measures of assessment can be collected in a portfolio. The portfolio provides a record of children's progress over time and can be useful when conferencing with the child, parents, or other educators.

Turn the page to continue.

Technology

- **Instant Test Results** Use scan-and-score answer sheets for instant test results and diagnosis.
- **Prescriptions** Tailor instructions with prescriptions for differentiated instruction.
- **Reports** Generate detailed reports to track performance standards.
- **Testing Options** Include online delivery and plain-paper scanning.
- **Test Generator** Compatible with Houghton Mifflin's ExamView® Test Generator.

Using Assessment to Plan Instruction

You can use the results of theme assessments to determine an individual child's needs for additional skill instruction and to modify instruction during the next theme. For more detail, see the test manuals or the **Teacher's Assessment Handbook.**

This chart shows Theme 3 resources for differentiating additional instruction. As you look ahead to Theme 4, you can plan to use the corresponding Theme 4 resources.

Differentiating Instruction

Assessment Shows	Use These Resources	
Difficulty with Decoding or Oral Fluency **Emphasize** Phonemic awareness and phonics; rereading for fluency	• Reteaching: Phonics, **Teacher's Edition,** pp. R14, R16, R18, R20, R22, R24; R26, R28 • Reteaching: High-Frequency Words, **Teacher's Edition,** pp. R30; R32; R34 • **Extra Support Handbook,** pp. 78–79, 82–83, 84–85; 88–89, 92–93, 94–95; 98–99, 102–103, 104–105 • **Handbook for English Language Learners,** pp. 82–83, 84–85, 86–87, 88–89, 90; 92–93, 94–95, 96–97, 98–99, 100; 102–103, 104–105, 106–107, 108–109, 110	• **Lexia Phonics CD-ROM Primary Intervention** • Leveled Bibliography, **Teacher's Edition,** pp. T6–T7 • **Phonics Library,** Theme 3 • **I Love Reading Books** • **On My Way Practice Readers** • Below Level **Leveled Readers** • Below Level lessons for **Leveled Readers, Teacher's Edition,** pp. T88; T160; T232
Difficulty with Comprehension **Emphasize** Oral comprehension; strategy development; story comprehension; vocabulary development; Teacher-Supported Reading	• Reteaching: Comprehension, **Teacher's Edition,** pp. R36; R38; R40 • **Phonics Library,** Theme 3 • **Extra Support Handbook,** pp. 80–81, 86–87; 90–91, 96–97; 100–101, 106–107	• Below Level **Leveled Readers** • Below Level lessons for **Leveled Readers, Teacher's Edition,** pp. T88; T160; T232
Overall High Performance **Emphasize** Independent reading and writing; vocabulary development; critical thinking	• Challenge/Extension Activities: Phonics, **Teacher's Edition,** pp. R15, R17, R19; R21, R23, R25; R27, R29 • Challenge/Extension Activities: High-Frequency Words, **Teacher's Edition,** pp. R31; R33; R35 • Challenge/Extension Activities: Comprehension, **Teacher's Edition,** R37; R39; R41	• Above Level **Theme Paperback** • Above Level **Leveled Readers** • Above Level lessons for **Leveled Readers, Teacher's Edition,** pp. T90; T162; T234 • Challenge Activity Masters, **Challenge Handbook,** CH3–1 to CH3–12

Resources for Theme 3

Contents

Lesson Plans for Leveled Theme Paperbacks

Mack **R2**
Barnyard Tracks **R3**
Counting on the Woods **R4**
Apple Picking **R6**
Mud! **R7**
Pearl's First Prize Plant **R8**
The Crab **R10**
When Tiny Was Tiny **R11**
Hilda Hen's Scary Night **R12**

Reteaching Lessons: Phonics

Double Final Consonants **R14**
Blending More Short *a* Words **R16**
Plurals with *-s* **R18**
Verb Endings *-s, -ed, -ing* **R20**
Blending More Short *i* Words **R22**
Possessives with *'s* **R24**
Clusters with *r* **R26**
Contractions with *'s* **R28**

Challenge/Extension Activities: Phonics

Double Final Consonants **R15**
Blending More Short *a* Words **R17**
Plurals with *-s* **R19**
Verb Endings *-s, -ed, -ing* **R21**
Blending More Short *i* Words **R23**
Possessives with *'s* **R25**
Clusters with *r* **R27**
Contractions with *'s* **R29**

**Reteaching Lessons:
High-Frequency Words**

Week 1 . . . . **R30**
Week 2 . . . . **R32**
Week 3 . . . . **R34**

**Challenge/Extension Activities:
High-Frequency Words**

Week 1 . . . . **R31**
Week 2 . . . . **R33**
Week 3 . . . . **R35**

Reteaching Lessons: Comprehension Skills

Topic, Main Idea, Details/Summarizing **R36**
Making Predictions **R38**
Categorize and Classify **R40**

**Challenge/Extension Activities:
Comprehension Skills**

Topic, Main Idea, Details/Summarizing **R37**
Making Predictions **R39**
Categorize and Classify **R41**

Information and Study Skills Lessons

Using the Library **R42**
Alphabetical Order **R43**

Word Wall Cards **R44**

Activity Masters **R48**

Music

"Five Little Pumpkins" **R54**
"Barnyard Song" **R55**
"My Farm"/"Mi chacra" **R56**
"Take Me Out to the Ball Game" **R59**
"A Sailor Went to Sea, Sea, Sea" **R60**

Word Lists **R62**

Technology Resources **R66**

Pronunciation Guide **R67**

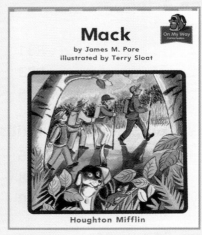

Mack

Summary
Mack the dog and his family enjoy a hike until they run into a skunk!

Building Background

Read aloud the title and the names of the author and the illustrator. Tell children that Mack is a dog who is hiking with his family in the woods. Have children predict what animals they might see in the woods and what might happen.

Supporting the Reading

Introducing the Book Page through the book with children. You may want to point out the following words: *day, hike, ducks, tail, skunk*. The suggestions below can help prepare children to read the story independently.

page 1: *What names have the short* a *sound?* (*Jack, Matt, Nan, Dad*)

page 5: *Find the word that tells what sound a duck makes. The word begins like* quilt. (*quack*)

page 7: *Find the word that has two k's in it.* (*skunk*)

Prompting Strategies Listen to and observe children as they read, and use prompts such as the following to help them apply strategies:

- *Does the word make sense in the sentence?*
- *What can you do if you get stuck on a word?*
- *What does this part of the story mean? Can you tell it in your own words?*

Responding

Ask children to share their thoughts on the story. What did they like about it?

Activity Children can reread the story on their own or with a partner. Spend time with each child or pair of children to assess individual levels of fluency.

English Language Learners

Supporting Comprehension

Model strategies through Think Alouds to allow children to see and hear how a proficient English speaker reaches an understanding of text.

▲ ON LEVEL

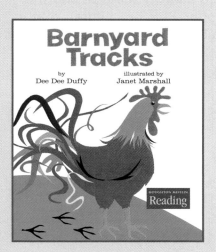

Barnyard Tracks

Summary *The barnyard animals, a fox, and a farmer all leave tracks at the farm.*

Building Background

Read aloud the title and the names of the author and the illustrator. Ask children to predict who might leave tracks in the barnyard.

Supporting the Reading

Introducing the Book Page through the book with children. The suggestions below can help prepare children to read the story independently.

page 2: *The word* tracks *begins with the letters* tr. *Find the word* tracks.

page 3: *The word* listen *begins with the /l/ sound. Find the word* listen.

page 4: *Find the word that is an animal's name and begins with* r. (*rooster*)

page 7: *Find the word that tells the sound pigs make. The word ends with* k. (*oink*)

Prompting Strategies Listen to and observe children as they read, and use prompts such as the following to help them apply strategies:

• *What can you try if a word doesn't sound right?*

• *Did you understand what you just read?*

• *What happens in the story? Can you say it in your own words?*

Responding

Ask children if they enjoyed the story. Were they surprised by any of the tracks? Ask children what other animals might have made tracks at the farm. List their responses. Then have children choose an animal, and draw and label the tracks and the animal.

Activity Children can reread the story, making the animal sounds and acting out the parts of the animals and the farmer.

Little Big Book

THEME PAPERBACKS

WEEK 1

Counting on the Woods

Summary *In this rhyming and counting book, colorful pictures show the different plants and animals that live in the woods.*

Building Background

Display the Little Big Book. Ask a child to identify the title and the names of the author and the photographer. Remind children that you have read aloud the corresponding Big Book. Have children page through the book.

Read aloud the dedication on page 4. Explain that an author often dedicates a book to someone who inspired him or her. Ask why they think this author dedicated her book to the waterfall.

Developing Key Vocabulary

Print the following words on index cards. Display the cards one at a time, say each word, and have children repeat it. Do this several times.

waterfall	rainfall	moss	vines	creek

river	earth	sky

Display the cards again, one at a time. Have children find each word in *Counting on the Woods* and read it from the page.

Reading the Little Big Book

Applying Phonics Skills Before reading, prompt children to use what they know about letters and letter sounds to figure out selected words:

page 4: *Look at the word* waterfall. *It is made from two words. Which of the two words has the /l/ sound?* (*fall*)

page 17: *What two letters stand for the /k/ sound in* tracks? (*ck*)

page 23: *Which word means "more than one shower?"* (*showers*)

Next, have children turn to page 21. Model how to read an unfamiliar word, using this Think Aloud.

Think Aloud *If I didn't know the first word on the page, I would blend sounds for the letters from left to right until I get a word I know that makes sense: /s//ĕ//v//ə//n/, seven. When I reread the sentence, seven makes sense in it.*

Have partners read the book together and help each other identify words.

Rereading the Little Big Book

Building Fluency Ask children to read *Counting on the Woods* independently. Tell them to reread it several times, noticing the rhyming.

Revisiting the Little Big Book

Retelling the Story Ask children to review the book by paging through it. Have volunteers briefly tell what they see in the photographs. Then have each child in turn look at two facing pages, and with eyes closed, think about what they might feel, smell, or hear, and describe the sensation.

On My Way
Practice Readers

Apple Picking

Summary *When a group of children go apple picking, they find the biggest apple they've ever seen!*

Building Background

Read aloud the title and the names of the author and the illustrator. Ask children what they think the book will be about. Have them share any apple picking experiences they may have had.

Supporting the Reading

Introducing the Book Page through the book with children. You may want to point out the following words: *apple, ball, roll, great.* The suggestions below can help prepare children to read the story independently.

page 1: *The word* fall *rhymes with* ball. *Find the words* fall *and* ball.

page 3: *The word* roll *ends with two* l's. *Point to the word* roll.

page 4: *Which two words end with* -ing? (*licking, kicking*)

page 8: *The word* great *begins like* grin. *Point to the word* great.

Prompting Strategies Listen to and observe children as they read, and use prompts such as the following to help them apply strategies:

- *What sound does each letter make?*
- *Blend the sounds. What is the word?*
- *Is there something here you don't understand?*

Responding

Give children an opportunity to express their thoughts about the story.

Activity Ask children to return to the story and find their favorite page or part. They can read aloud their favorite part.

REACHING ALL LEARNERS
English Language Learners

Supporting Comprehension

As children read, have them stop every so often to draw a summary picture of what has happened so far and a prediction picture of what they think will happen next.

▲ ON LEVEL

Mud!

Summary *Three boys enjoy playing in the mud.*

Building Background

Read aloud the title and the name of the author and the photographer. Ask children to predict what they think three boys might do with some mud.

Supporting the Reading

Introducing the Book Page through the book with children. The suggestions below can help prepare children to read the story independently.

page 6: *Notice the letters in* MUD. *They are all capitals. This means that they should be read loudly. Read* MUD *loudly.*

page 12: *The word* stuff *has the same short* u *sound as* mud. *Point to the word* stuff.

page 14: *Which word begins like* play? *Point to the word and read it.* (*plan*)

page 18: *The word* pick *rhymes with* stick. *Find the word* pick.

Prompting Strategies Listen to and observe children as they read, and use prompts such as the following to help them apply strategies:

- *Look at the letters in this word. Blend the sounds.*
- *Why did you stop? Can you try something else?*
- *Try rereading and see if that word is right.*
- *What do you think this part of the story means? Say it in your own words.*

Responding

Have children retell the story in their own words. Discuss how wet weather is good for mud. Brainstorm with children other weather that makes for fun activities. (Sun! Snow! Rain!) Children can write a sequel to *Mud!* by writing about some activities they like to do with friends.

Activity Children can reread the story with a partner. Spend some time with each pair, observing individual strengths and weaknesses.

Little Big Book

THEME PAPERBACKS

WEEK 2

Pearl's First Prize Plant

Summary *Pearl thinks her plant with the little white flower is a first-prize plant—even if it can't compete with the hothouse beauties at the county fair.*

Building Background

Display the Little Big Book. Ask a child to read the title and the name of the author/illustrator. Remind children this story is about a girl who takes her flower to a county fair where people bring their best fruits, vegetables, flowers, and animals. Have children browse through the book.

Ask children to name fresh fruits and vegetables they have seen or eaten. List these on the board. Then ask what color each is, and write the name of the color.

Developing Key Vocabulary

Print the following words on index cards. Display the cards one at a time, say each word, and have children repeat it. Do this several times.

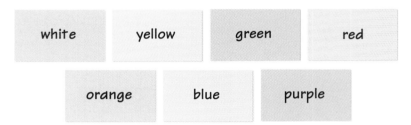

Display the cards again, one at a time. Have children find each word in *Pearl's First Prize Plant* and read it from the page.

Reading the Little Big Book

Applying Phonics Skills Before reading, prompt children to use what they know about letters and letter sounds to figure out selected words:

cover: *Look at the book title,* Pearl's First Prize Plant. *Whose plant is it?* (Pearl's)

page 7: *What letters stand for the ending sound /t/ in* watched? (ed)

page 29: *What letters stand for the ending sound /d/ in* rained? (ed)

Now have children turn to page 30. Model how to read an unfamiliar word (*happy*), using this Think Aloud.

Think Aloud *To figure out this word, I say the sounds I know. First comes* h, */h/. Next is short* a, /ă/, *then* pp, /p/. *So I blend* /h//ă//p/, happ-. *I add the sound* /ē/ *for the ending* y. *Now I'll blend the whole word:* /h//ă//p//ē/, happy. *When I reread the sentence,* happy *makes sense.*

Have partners read the book together and help each other identify words.

Rereading the Little Big Book

Building Fluency Ask children to read the book independently. When they come across an unfamiliar word, remind them to look for letters and word parts they know and then check to see that the word makes sense.

Revisiting the Little Big Book

Retelling the Story Review the main ideas from the Little Big Book. List ideas children suggest on a chart with three parts: Beginning, Middle, End. Review the pictures in the book and help children plan how to act out the story ideas. Have each child copy one idea on a sentence strip. Then do a group retelling, asking children to display and read aloud their strips before performing the actions.

On My Way
Practice Readers

The Crab

Summary *Gram and Brad find a crab at the beach.*

Building Background

Read aloud the title and the author's and the illustrator's names. Ask children to share what they know about crabs.

Supporting the Reading

Introducing the Book Page through the book with children. You may want to point out the word *claws*. The suggestions below can help prepare children to read the story independently.

page 1: *The boy's name begins with* Br. *Point to the name and read it.* (*Brad*)

page 2: *The word* crab *begins with* cr. *Find the word* crab.

page 5: *Which word rhymes with* crab? (*grab*)

page 6: *Find the word that begins with* cl. *What is the word?* (*claws*)

Prompting Strategies Listen to and observe children as they read, and use prompts such as the following to help them apply strategies:

- *Look at the letters from left to right.*
- *Blend the sounds for the letters.*
- *What is the word? Does it make sense in the sentence?*

Responding

Discuss whether children enjoyed the story. What did they learn about crabs that they did not know before?

Activity Have children identify a favorite page or two to read aloud. Use this opportunity to assess individual reading fluency.

English Language Learners

Supporting Comprehension

Graphic organizers, such as story maps and K-W-L charts, can be used before or during reading to help make information more concrete for children.

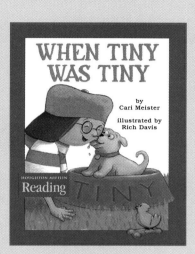

When Tiny Was Tiny

Summary *A boy compares his grown dog, Tiny, to the way he was as a puppy.*

Building Background

Read aloud the title and the author's and the illustrator's names. Ask children what they think the book will be about. Discuss what they know about puppies and dogs.

Supporting the Reading

Introducing the Book Page through the book with children. The suggestions below can help prepare children to read the story independently.

page 3: Tiny *begins with a capital* T *and ends with* y. *Point to* Tiny.

page 5: *The word* pocket *has the letters* ck *in the middle. Point to the word* pocket *and read it.*

page 7: *The word* grew *begins with* gr. *Find the word* grew.

Prompting Strategies Listen to and observe children as they read, and use prompts such as the following to help them apply strategies:

- *What made you hesitate?*
- *Can you try that part again?*
- *Can you explain this section in your own words?*

Responding

Ask children what parts of the book made them laugh. Why is Tiny a funny name for the dog in the story? With children, brainstorm some other funny situations that Tiny might get into because of his large size. Children can write a sentence about their favorite one and illustrate it.

Activity Children can reread the story in pairs, taking turns on every other page. Mention that they should read the story with expression, paying attention to the exclamation points.

Little Big Book

THEME PAPERBACKS

WEEK 3

Hilda Hen's Scary Night

Summary *In this fantasy, a hen named Hilda finds the courage to tiptoe past some scary things—such as a garden-hose snake and a wading-pool lake—as she makes her way back to the hen house one night.*

Building Background

Display the Little Big Book. Have a child read the title and the name of the author/illustrator. Remind children that the story is about a hen that sees scary things in the dark. Have children page through the book.

Ask children if they have had a similar experience in the dark and what the scary thing turned out to be once it was daylight.

Developing Key Vocabulary

Print the following words on index cards. Display the cards one at a time, say each word, and have children repeat it. Do this several times.

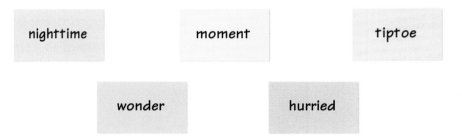

nighttime   moment   tiptoe

wonder   hurried

Display the cards again, one at a time. Have children find each word in *Hilda Hen's Scary Night* and read it from the page.

Reading the Little Big Book

Applying Phonics Skills Before reading, prompt children to use what they know about letters and letter sounds to figure out selected words:

page 8: *What two words does* there's *stand for in* There's a snake? *(there is)*

page 10: *What two letters stand for the /p/ /r/ sounds in* proudly? *(pr)*

page 18: *What letters stand for the /k/ /r/ sounds in the middle of* across? *(cr)*

page 24: *What letters stand for the /b/ /r/ sounds in* bridge? *(br)* *What letters stand for the /j/ sound in* bridge? *(dge)*

Now have children turn to page 14. Model how to read an unfamiliar word, using this Think Aloud.

Think Aloud   *If I didn't know the third word on the page, I would first blend the sounds for* f, r, a, n: /f//r//ă//n/. *That's* fran. *Next is* t, i, c: /t//ĭ//c/. *That's* tic. *So far I have* fran-tic, frantic. *That's a word that means "very excited." The letters* a, l, l, y *form an ending that stands for /l//ē/,* -ly. *Now I'll blend the whole word:* frantic-ly, frantically. *I reread the sentence with* frantically *and think about the meaning.*

Have partners read the book together and help each other identify words.

Rereading the Little Big Book

Building Fluency   Ask children to read the book independently. Have them reread the story several times until they can read it fluently. Then have them team up with a partner and read alternating pages to each other.

Revisiting the Little Big Book

Retelling the Story   Help children review the story by having them page through the book and recall the things Hilda Hen sees and what she thinks she sees on her walk through the farmyard. List their ideas on the board or chart paper. Then discuss what Hilda Hen learned about herself that dark, scary night—that she was brave and could fly high, swim well, run fast, and jump high. Now have children retell the story using the sentence frame, *Hilda learned she could _____ when she saw _____ that she thought was _____.*

Double Final Consonants

OBJECTIVES

- Recognize *ck, s, ll, gg,* and *ss* and the sounds they represent at the end of words.
- Independently read words ending with *ck, s, ll, gg,* and *ss.*

Target Skill Trace

- Final Consonants/Double Final Consonants, p. T36

Materials

- **Large Sound/Spelling Card** *cat*
- **Large Letter Cards** *c, d, e, g, g, i, k, l, l, o, p, r, s, s, u*
- **Blending Routines Card 2**
- **I Love Reading Books,** Books 24–27 and Review Books 24–27

Teach

Ask children to listen for the sound at the end of the word *lock* (/k/). Hold up **Large Sound/Spelling Card** *cat* and point out the _ck on the back. Explain that sometimes two consonant letters together can stand for one sound. In *lock,* the two letters *c* and *k* stand for one sound, /k/. Write *lock* on the board, have a child circle the *ck,* and have the class repeat /k/. Blend the word *lock* with children using **Blending Routine 2.** Have them say the sound for *l,* /l/, then the sound for *o,* /ŏ/, and blend *lllŏŏŏ.* Then have them say the sound for *ck,* /k/, and blend *lllŏŏŏk, lock.*

Tell children that sometimes two of the same consonants can stand for one sound in a word, such as *ll,* /l/, *gg,* /g/, and *ss,* /s/. Have children listen for the ending sound in the words *bell, egg,* and *miss.* Write each word on the board. Have a child circle the double consonant in each word and have the class say the sound. Then help the class blend each word using **Blending Routine 2.**

Practice

Place **Large Letter Cards** in pairs for *ck, ll, gg, ss,* and *s* on the ledge below the board. Write *pi__ __* on the board and say *pick.* Ask a child to say the

sound at the end of *pick* and choose the letters that would complete the word. (*ck*) Then fill in the *ck* and have the class blend, *pĭĭĭk, pick.* Repeat this process for the words *rugs, doll, egg,* and *kiss.*

Apply

Have children look for words that end with *ck, s,* and double consonants in **I Love Reading Books,** Books 24–27. Each time a child finds a word, he or she should blend and read the word aloud as you write it on the board. Have children underline the *ck, s,* or double consonant in each word.

Monitoring Student Progress

If . . .	Then . . .
children need more practice in the sounds for *ck, s, ll, gg,* and *ss* at the end of words,	have children read **I Love Reading Books,** Review Books 24–27.

CHALLENGE/EXTENSION: Double Final Consonants

CHALLENGE

Endings Search

Have children make self-stick notes for *ll, ss,* and *gg.* Then have them look through books in the classroom library for words that end with these letters. Have them attach the notes to the words they have found and then share their discoveries with the class. Help children read any new words.

Word Endings Sorting Game

Make word cards for the following words: *sock, back, block, sack, birds, boys, bags, cars, hill, pill, sell, tell.* Put the cards in a paper bag. Then ask children to empty the bag and to sort the words by the endings *ck, s,* and *ll.* Call on children to read aloud the words in each group.

birds   boys

Blending More Short *a* Words

OBJECTIVES

- Blend phonemes.
- Associate the short *a* sound with the letter *a*.
- Independently read words with short *a*.

Target Skill Trace

- More Short *a* Words, p. T37

Materials

- **Large Sound/Spelling Card** *apple*
- **Picture Cards** *ant, bat, cot, fan, fox, jet, pad, tag*
- **Word Cards** *bat, fan, pad, tag*
- **Blending Routines Card 2**

Teach

Display **Large Sound/Spelling Card** *apple* and remind children that the vowel letter *a* often makes the /ă/ sound. Have them repeat after you, /ă/-/ă/-/ă/. Be sure that children have their mouths in the correct position as they say the sound. Hold up **Picture Card** *ant* and ask children to identify the picture. Have children listen for the short *a* vowel sound in *ant*.

Hold up **Picture Card** *pad* and ask children to identify the picture. Have them listen for the short *a* vowel sound in *pad*. Then hold up **Picture Card** *fox* and ask children to identify the picture. Ask them if they hear the short *a* vowel sound /ă/ in *fox*. Follow the same procedure with **Picture Cards** *bat, cot, fan, jet,* and *tag*.

Display **Word Cards** *bat, fan,* and *tag*. Use **Blending Routine 2** to help children blend *bat*. Have them say the sound for *b*, /b/, then the sound for *a*, /ă/, then blend *bă ă ă*. Finally, have them say the sound for *t*, /t/, and blend *bă ă ă t, bat*. Repeat for *fan* and *tag*.

Practice

Display **Word Card** *pad*. Distribute five self-stick notes with the letters *b, m, h, s,* and *d* written on them. Have children choose a note and place it over the *p* in *pad*. Have them blend the sounds, for example, *bă ă ă d, bad*. List the new words on the board. Distribute self-stick notes with the following letters: *ck, ss, t,* and *n*. Have children cover the *d* in *pad* with one of the new endings to make a different word. Then ask them to blend the word. Have children continue making other new words. List these new words on the board. Have children blend and read all the words.

Apply

Place the **Word Cards** on the ledge below the board. Say the following riddles and have children point to and read the word that answers each riddle.

You can keep cool with this. (fan)

You can hit a ball with this. (bat)

You can tear a piece of paper from this. (pad)

You can find out the price of something by reading this. (tag)

Monitoring Student Progress

If . . .	Then . . .
children need more practice with the short *a* sound,	have children read the **Word Cards** and use the words in oral sentences.

CHALLENGE/EXTENSION:
Blending More Short *a* Words

Independent Activities

CHALLENGE

Rhyming Word Chart

On chart paper, list the following headings: *tag, van, bad, cab*. Have children say as many words as they can that rhyme with each of these words. Ask children to write the words in the correct columns. Then have children choose one of the words to illustrate and attach their picture to the Rhyming Word Chart.

tag	van	bad	cab
bag	tan	sad	nab
wag	man	dad	jab
nag	ran	pad	lab
rag	pan	mad	

CHALLENGE

A Bag of Short *a* Words

Display a large bag at the front of the class. Have children brainstorm a list of short *a* words. As children suggest each word, write the word on a piece of paper and put it into the bag. Then have children pick one word to read, use in a sentence, and then illustrate.

RETEACHING: Phonics Skills

Plurals with -s

OBJECTIVES

- Understand that adding -s to a naming word makes the word mean more than one.
- Independently read plurals with -s.

Target Skill Trace

- Plurals with -s, p. T38

Materials

- **Word Card** cup
- **Large Sound/Spelling Card** zebra
- **Blending Routines Card 2**
- **I Love Reading Books,** Book 23 and Review Book 23

Teach

Display one cup on a table. Place **Word Card** cup next to it and help children read the word cup. Then place three cups on another part of the table. Have children say the word for more than one cup, cups. Have them listen for the sound they hear at the end of cups, /s/. Then write s on a self-stick note and place it on **Word Card** cup so that it now reads cups. Place the card next to the three cups.

Review that cup is a naming word. Naming words name a person, place, or thing. Explain that when a naming word tells about more than one person, place, or thing, it often ends in the letter s, /s/. Point to cups and have children blend cŭpsss, emphasizing the s. Then move the **Word Card** so it is next to the single cup again, remove the self-stick note, and have children read cup.

Display **Word Card** cup and the self-stick note s separately. Explain that the simplest part of a word is called the base word and the letter or letters added to it are called the ending. Point out that the base word in cups is cup. Then stick the s back onto the cup and explain that the -s in cups is the ending.

Hold up **Large Sound/Spelling Card** zebra and point out the _s on the back. Explain that sometimes when an s is at the end of a word it is pronounced /z/. Have children listen for the /z/ sound in cans. Then write cans on the board and have a child circle the s while the whole class says /z/. Help children blend cans using **Blending Routine 2**.

Practice

Draw one large dot on the board and write the word dot underneath it. Have children say the word aloud, helping them to blend if necessary. Ask children how many dots are on the board. (one) Then ask a child to come to the board, draw another dot, and change the word dot to mean more than one. Underline the word dot in dots as you point out that dot is the base word. Then circle the s in dots as you point out that the ending is s and say /s/. Help children blend and read the new word, dŏŏŏtsss, dots. Follow the same procedure with the words mat, jet, and cap.

Apply

Have children look for plurals with -s in **I Love Reading Books,** Book 23. Each time a child finds a plural with -s, he or she should read it aloud and write it in a column on the board. After the search is complete, have children identify the singular base word for each plural and come to the board to circle it.

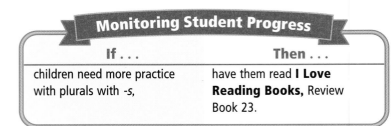

Monitoring Student Progress

If . . .	Then . . .
children need more practice with plurals with -s,	have them read **I Love Reading Books,** Review Book 23.

CHALLENGE/EXTENSION:
Plurals with *-s*

Plurals Picture Dictionary

Write the following words on the board:

    cat   hat   van   pan   map   can

Ask children to write *cat* on a piece of drawing paper. Then ask them to write the word that means more than one cat on the other side of the paper. Have children illustrate *cat* with one cat and *cats* with more than one cat. Ask them to create additional pages using the other words on the board. When they finish, they can combine the pages together to make a Plurals Dictionary. If possible, use a loose-leaf binder so that children can add pages as they learn new words.

CHALLENGE

One or More?

Have children work in pairs to make a card game. One partner makes word cards with any five of the following words: *mat, rat, bat, can, pan, fan, yam, map, cab, rag, cap.* The other partner writes the plural of each word on another set of cards. Mix up the ten cards and place them face-down. In turn, have children pick a card, read aloud the word, and say whether the word tells about one thing or more than one thing. Ask children to use the word in a sentence.

fans   cabs

map   rag

Verb Endings -s, -ed, -ing

OBJECTIVES

- Understand that -s, -ed, and -ing can be added to action words.
- Independently read action words with -s, -ed, and -ing.

Target Skill Trace

- Verbs with -s, -ed, -ing, p. T108

Materials

- **Blending Routines Card 2**
- **I Love Reading Books,** Books 28–30 and Review Books 28–30

Teach

Write the word *lick* on the board and have children say it after you. Remind them that *lick* is an action word that tells what a person or animal does. Then point to the word *lick* and explain that *lick* is a word onto which different endings can be added. Write *licks, licked,* and *licking* under *lick.* Circle the base word *lick* in each word. Explain that this part of a word is called the *base word* and the letter or letters added to it are called the *ending.* Review the sound of each ending: -s, /s/ or /z/; -ing, /ĭng/; -ed, /d/ or /t/.

Write the following sentences on the board:

Jason licks his ice cream cone.

Lindsay and Bob lick their ice cream cones.

Repeat each sentence and ask children to listen carefully for the word *lick* or *licks.* Then underline the *s* in *licks.*

Use **Blending Routine 2** to help children blend *licks.* Have them say the sound for *l,* /l/, then the sound for *i,* /ĭ/, and blend *lllĭĭĭ.* Then have them say the sound for *ck,* /k/, and blend *lllĭĭĭk.* Finally, have them say the sound for *s,* /s/, and blend *lllĭĭĭksss, licks.*

Next, write these sentences on the board:

Today I am licking a strawberry ice cream cone.

Yesterday I licked a chocolate ice cream cone.

Underline the *ed* in *licked* and the *ing* in *licking.* Repeat the two sentences, emphasizing the endings in *licked* and *licking.* Use **Blending Routine 2** to help children blend each word.

Practice

Write the following base words on the board:

  walk   *jump*   *help*

Read each base word aloud, and have children repeat it after you. Call on children to mime the action. Then copy the word three times in a column. Have children come to the board to add -s, -ed, and -ing to the base word, read each new word, and use the word in a sentence.

Apply

Have pairs of children find words with -s, -ed, and -ing in **I Love Reading Books,** Books 28–30. Each time a child finds an -s, -ed, or -ing word, he or she should read it aloud while you write the word on the board. Call on children to come to the board and underline the base word, circle the ending, and tell the class what sound it makes.

Monitoring Student Progress

If . . .	Then . . .
children need more practice with verbs and endings -s, -ed, -ing,	have them read **I Love Reading Books,** Review Books 28–30.

CHALLENGE/EXTENSION:
Verb Endings *-s, -ed, -ing*

Picking Endings!

Write the following words on the board:

pick
lick
kick

Ask children to choose one of the words and write it on two word cards. Then ask them to pick an ending, *-s, -ed,* or *-ing,* and add it to the words so that both words have the same ending. Have children form a group with other children who have written different words on their cards. Ask the group to combine their cards and play a concentration game with all the words.

CHALLENGE

Time for Action!

Have children make individual word cards with the following words on one side of the card: *picks, picked, picking, licks, licked, licking, kicks, kicked, kicking.* Then have them draw a picture on the other side of the card. Place the cards in a pile, picture side up. In turn, children pick a card, read aloud the word, say the base word, and act out the action. Finally, they say the word in a sentence. Remind children that the action for *kick* should only show kicking an object.

Blending More Short *i* Words

OBJECTIVES

- Independently read words with short *i*.
- Associate the short *i* sound with the letter *i*.

Target Skill Trace

- More Short *i* Words, p. T109

Materials

- **Large Sound/Spelling Card** *igloo*
- **Picture Cards** *dig, hat, jam, lip, pig, pin, pit*
- **Word Cards** *dig, lip*

Teach

Display **Large Sound/Spelling Card** *igloo* and remind children that the letter *i* often stands for the /ĭ/ sound. Have them repeat it after you, /ĭ/ - /ĭ/ - /ĭ/. Be sure that children have their mouths in the correct position as they say the sound. Hold up **Picture Card** *dig* and ask children to identify the picture. Have children listen for the short *i* sound as you say *dig*.

Hold up **Picture Card** *pig* and ask children to identify the picture. Ask them which sound they hear in *pig*, /ĭ/ or /ă/. Follow the same procedure with **Picture Cards** *cat, hat, jam, lip, pin,* and *pit*.

Display **Word Card** *dig*. Remind children of the short *i* sound: /ĭ/. Then use **Blending Routine 2** to help children blend and read the word *dig*. Have them say the sound for *d*, /d/, then the sound for *i* /ĭ/, then blend *d* /ĭ//ĭ//ĭ/. Finally, have them say the sound for *g*, /g/, and have them blend *d* /ĭ//ĭ//ĭ/g.

Practice

Display **Word Card** *lip*. Distribute four self-stick notes with the letters *z, r, s,* and *t* written on them. Have children choose a note to place over the *l* in *lip*. Have them blend the sounds, for example, *d* /ĭ//ĭ//ĭ/p, *dip*. List the new words on the board. Distribute self-stick notes with *ck* and *d*. Then have children cover the *p* in *lip* with *ck* and then *d* to make and read new words. Write these words on the board. Finally, have children read each word listed and use it in a sentence.

Apply

Display **Picture Cards** *dig, lip, pig, pin,* and *pit*. Call on children to identify each picture and write the picture name on the board.

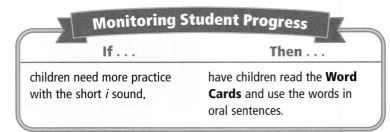

Monitoring Student Progress	
If . . .	**Then . . .**
children need more practice with the short *i* sound,	have children read the **Word Cards** and use the words in oral sentences.

CHALLENGE/EXTENSION:
Blending More Short *i* Words

Short *i* Detectives

Have children listen as you say each group of words and tell which word does not have the short *i* sound.

bat/sit/dig   wig/nap/pick

win/fill/mad   sick/zip/sad

Then say each group of words again, and have children tell which two words have the short *i* sound /ĭ/.

CHALLENGE

Fill the Bin!

Say the words *fill* and *bin* and ask children what sound they hear in those words, /ĭ/ or /ă/. Then place a large bin at the front of the class. Have children brainstorm a list of short *i* words. As children suggest each word, write the word on a strip of paper and place it in the bin. Say, *The bin is filled!* Then have children pick one word out of the bin. Ask children to share the words with classmates by illustrating each word and using it in a sentence.

Possessives with 's

OBJECTIVES

- Understand that possessives are words that show ownership.
- Recognize that 's shows ownership.
- Independently read possessives.

Target Skill Trace

- Possessives ('s), p. T110

Materials

- Blending Routines Card 2

Teach

Ask a child to stand in front of the class with his or her pencil. Then point to the pencil and say, *Whose pencil is this?* When someone says, *It's _____'s pencil*, write on the board, *_____'s pencil*. Circle the possessive noun and remind children that an apostrophe and *s* can show to whom something belongs.

Write the title *Miss Jill's Ice Cream Shop* on the board. Circle the apostrophe and the *s* in the name. Explain that adding an apostrophe and *s* to the name *Miss Jill* tells to whom the ice cream shop belongs. Remind children that another way to say the same thing is to say, *the ice cream shop of Miss Jill*. Write the following on the board:

> the hat of Jim — Jim's hat
>
> the bag of the man — the man's bag
>
> the pen of pam — Pam's pen

Read the phrases in each pair aloud and point out that they mean the same thing. Both phrases show to whom something belongs. Use **Blending Routine 2** to help children blend *Jim's*. Say the sound for *j*, /j/, then the sound for *i*, /ĭ/, and blend *j*/ĭ//ĭ//ĭ/. Then have them say the sound for *m*, /m/, and blend *j*/ĭ//ĭ//ĭ/mmm. Finally, have them say the sound for 's, /z/, and blend *j*/ĭ//ĭ//ĭ/mmmzzz, *Jim's*. Repeat this routine with *man's* and *Pam's*.

Practice

Write the following on the board:

the pig's wig	Sam's ham
the cat's hat	Dan's van

Read each phrase aloud and ask to whom each item belongs. Then have children come to the board to circle the 's in each phrase and blend the possessive word. Have partners work together to write each phrase in a sentence.

Apply

Write these phrases on the board:

> the pet of Jen
> the box of Tim

Have children read the phrases and then write the possessive noun for each one. (Jen's pet, Tim's box)

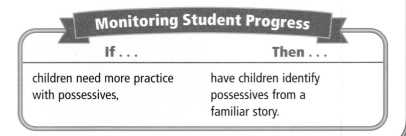

Monitoring Student Progress

If . . .	Then . . .
children need more practice with possessives,	have children identify possessives from a familiar story.

CHALLENGE/EXTENSION:
Possessives with 's

Independent Activities

Favorite Things

Have children draw a picture of their favorite possession and label their pictures to show to whom the item belongs. Staple all the pictures together into a class book titled *Our Favorite Things*.

Nat's hat

CHALLENGE

Whose Is It?

Pass out pictures cut from old magazines that show people or animals with something that belongs to them such as a child on a bike or an animal with its baby. Have children work in pairs to make up a sentence about the picture that includes a possessive noun. For example, a child looking at a boy on a bike might say: *The boy's bike is big*. Ask, *Whose bike is it?* Write each possessive noun on the board as children say it and then call on children to circle each 's.

The boy's bike is big.

CHALLENGE / EXTENSION

Clusters with *r*

OBJECTIVES

- Independently read words beginning with consonant clusters with *r*.
- Associate the letters *br, cr, dr, fr, gr, pr,* and *tr* with the sounds they represent.

Target Skill Trace

- Consonant Clusters with *r*, pp. T180–T181

Materials

- **Large Letter Cards** *b, c, d, f, g, p, r, t*
- **Blending Routines Card 2**
- **I Love Reading Books,** Book 31 and Review Book 31

Teach

Display **Large Letter Card** *f* and remind children of the sound for the letter *f*. Have them repeat the sound after you, /f/-/f/-/f/. Be sure children have their mouths in the correct position as they say the sound. Repeat the procedure with **Large Letter Card** *r*.

Write the word *frog* and ask children to read it with you. Remind them that when a consonant and an *r* are side by side, such as *fr* in *frog,* the sounds for the consonant and *r* are so close together they almost seem to be one sound.

Use **Large Letter Cards** *f* and *r* to model how to blend the sounds /f//r/. Hold the cards apart, and as you say *fffrrr,* move the cards together until they touch. Have children repeat *fffrrr* as you move the cards next to each other a few times. Follow the same procedure for *tr, br, gr, dr, cr,* and *pr*.

Blend *frog* aloud using **Blending Routine 2** as you run your finger under each letter. Have children say the sound for *f,* /f/, then the sound for *r,* /r/, then blend *fffrrr.* Then have them say the sound for *o,* /ŏ/, and blend *fffrrrŏŏŏ*. Finally, have them say the sound for *g,* /g/, and blend *fffrrrŏŏŏg, frog.* Underline the *fr* as you remind children that *r* often

appears with other consonants in the beginning of words. Then write on the board other words with *r* clusters, such as *dress, crack, brick, grin, frill, press,* and *trim.* Underline the consonant cluster in each word. Have children blend the word with you.

Practice

Write *br, cr, dr, fr, gr, pr,* and *tr* in a column on the board. Next to the column, write _ _ab. Tell children that you have written part of the word *crab.* Have them repeat *crab,* listening carefully to the beginning consonant sounds. Then have a child come to the board and draw a circle around the consonant cluster that begins the word *crab.* Have everyone say /k//r/, *crab* as the child fills in the blank spaces with the letters *cr.* Repeat this process with the words *brim, drip, from, grab, prim,* and *trip.*

Apply

Have partners work together to find words with clusters with *r* in **I Love Reading Books,** Book 31. Each time a child finds a word, he or she should say the sound of the consonant cluster, read the word aloud, and have his or her partner read the sentence that contains the word.

Monitoring Student Progress

If . . .	Then . . .
children need more practice with blending consonant clusters with *r,*	have them read **I Love Reading Books,** Review Book 31.

CHALLENGE/EXTENSION:
Clusters with *r*

Cluster Bags

Place **Picture Cards** for *braid, brown, crow, dress, frog, gray, prize, tray,* and *train* on a tray. Then give children seven empty plastic sandwich bags labeled *br, cr, dr, fr, gr, pr,* or *tr.* Have them put each **Picture Card** in the correct bag. Ask them to create their own picture card for a word beginning with a consonant cluster with *r* and place that card in the correct bag.

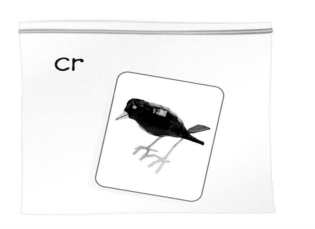

CHALLENGE

Tongue Twisters

Have children form groups to brainstorm a list of words with one of the consonant clusters with *r.* Then help them write tongue twisters using the words they have listed. Have children take turns presenting their tongue twisters to the class.

Creepy crabs can cross the creek.

CHALLENGE / EXTENSION

RETEACHING: Phonics Skills

Contractions with 's

Teach

Write the words *she* and *is* on the board. Then write the contraction *she's* and remind children that the words *she* and *is* are joined to form the contraction *she's*. Circle the word *she* in the contraction *she's*. Then point to the apostrophe and remind children that it takes the place of the letter *i* in the word *is*. Say *she's* aloud and have children repeat it after you.

Write the following sentence on the board: *He's sad.* Then write *he is* above the contraction. Remind children that the words *he is* have the same meaning as *he's*. Then point to the apostrophe and ask children what the apostrophe takes the place of. (the missing letter *i*)

Repeat for the contraction *it's*.

Practice

Write the following sentences on the board:

> It is big.   He is a man.
>
> She is big.   It is a ham.

Read the sentences aloud and point to the underlined words. Have children say the contraction that can be formed by each pair of words, and write that contraction above each pair. Have partners work together to make up other sentences using each of the contractions on the board.

Apply

Write the following contractions and words on word cards: *he's, she's, it's, that's, he is, she is, it is, that is.* Distribute the word cards and have children match the contraction and the two words that form the contraction. Ask pairs to read their words to the group.

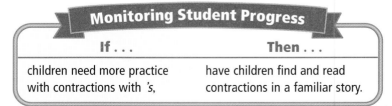

Monitoring Student Progress	
If . . .	Then . . .
children need more practice with contractions with 's,	have children find and read contractions in a familiar story.

CHALLENGE/EXTENSION:
Contractions with *'s*

Name That Contraction!

Write the following contractions on separate index cards: *she's, he's,* and *it's.* On the reverse side of each card, write the two words that form the contraction. Place the cards, contraction-side down, on a table. Have children pick a card, read the words, and say the contraction. If a child cannot name the contraction, have him or her turn over the card and read the two words. Then call on children to use each contraction in a sentence.

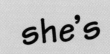

CHALLENGE

Match It!

Make a set of playing cards for the following matching game. On one set of cards write the following sentences: *He is big. She is a cat. It is jam. He is mad. She is sad. It is a trick. He is sick. She is a kid.* On another set of cards write the following: *He's big. She's a cat. It's jam. He's mad. She's sad. It's a trick. He's sick. She's a kid.* Place the cards face down on a table. Have the first player choose two cards. If one card has a sentence with a contraction and the other card has the same sentence with the two words that form the contraction, the two cards are a match and the player keeps the pair. The game continues until all the cards are matched.

He's sick.

He is sick.

RETEACHING: High-Frequency Words

Words for Week 1

Teach

Write the words *animal, bird, cold, fall, flower, full, look, of,* and *see* on the board. Read the words aloud, pointing to each as you go. Then have children read the words along with you.

Display the **Letter Cards** on the ledge below the board. Ask the group, *How many letters are in the word* animal?

Draw six squares on the board.

Ask two children to come up. Ask one child to find the letters *a, n,* and *i,* and the other to find the letters *m, a,* and *l.* Ask the children to help you spell *animal.*

> *Show me the letter I should write in the first box.* Continue the process with the second box, and so on.
>
> *How many different letters did I write?*
>
> *How many times did I write the letter a?*
>
> *How many times did I write the letter i?*

Tell the children to put the letters back with the other cards. Have them help lead the cheer to remember the word. Tap your right index finger in your left palm for each letter and syllable as you spell and say the word: *a-n-i-m-a-l, an-i-mal!*

Repeat the lesson procedure with the other words in the list. Remind children to use what they know about letters and sounds to help them remember the words.

Practice

On the board, write the sentence, *I see a big animal.* Ask children if they can find the word *see* in the sentence. Point to each word and ask them if it is *see.* Tell children to slap their knees and say the word with you when you read the word *see.* Next, have children find the word *animal.*

Repeat the procedure with each of these sentences: *It can be cold in the fall. Look at the bird. I have a flower. The vat is full of soup.*

Apply

Have children work in pairs. Give each pair nine large index cards and have them write the new words on them. Then have them go back to the story *Seasons* and find each of the words. When children match a word, have them read the sentence in the story that contains the word. Have them continue in this way until they have matched all of the words and read all the corresponding sentences.

Monitoring Student Progress

If . . .	Then . . .
children need more practice with the high-frequency words,	have them match high-frequency word cards to corresponding words on the Word Wall.

CHALLENGE/EXTENSION:
High-Frequency Words

Rebuild Sentences

Have children work in small groups. Give each group two of these sentence starters on sentence strips. Ask them to draw a picture or write the words to complete the sentence.

In the fall I see _____.

One big animal is a _____.

My flower is _____.

The vat is full of _____.

When finished, have children cut up the sentence strips, exchange their strips with others, and rebuild the sentences. Then ask groups to share their completed sentences to see how many different endings they have.

In the fall I see

red and yellow

CHALLENGE

Seasons Book

Have children write and illustrate a story about the seasons. Children might want to develop the story idea into a little book. Encourage them to use as many new words in their story as they can. When finished, display their seasons books in the reading corner for others to read.

RETEACHING: High-Frequency Words

Words for Week 2

OBJECTIVE

- Read and write new high-frequency words *all, call, eat, every, first, never, paper, shall, why.*

Target Skill Trace

- High-Frequency Words Lesson, pp. T118–T119

Materials

- **Letter Cards** *a, c, e, e, f, h, i, l, l, n, p, p, r, s, t, v, w, y*
- **Anthology 1.2,** pages 56–77

Teach

Write the words *all, call, eat, every, first, never, paper, shall,* and *why* on the board. Read the words aloud, pointing to each as you go.

Display the **Letter Cards** on the ledge below the board. Ask the group, *How many letters are in the word* all?

Draw three squares on the board.

Ask two children to come up. Ask one child to find the letter *a,* and the other to find the letter *l.* Ask the children to help you spell *all.* You might say, for example, *Show me the letter I should write in the first box (in the second box, and so on).* Once you have written the word, ask children to read it along with you.

Tell the children to put the letters back with the other cards. Have them help lead the cheer to remember the word. Tap your right index finger in your left palm for each letter and syllable as you spell and say the word: *a-l-l, all!*

Repeat the lesson procedure with the other words in the list.

Practice

On the board, write the sentence, *We shall eat.* Ask children if they can find the word *shall* in the sentence. Point to each word and ask them if it is *shall.* Tell children to tap their finger and say the word with you when you read the word *shall.* Read the sentence. Next have them find the word *eat.*

Repeat the procedure with each of these sentences: *Why did Jack eat mint ice cream first? Why do all of you call for the paper every day? I never get the paper.*

Apply

Have children work in pairs. Give each pair nine large index cards and have them write the new words on them. Then have them go back to *Miss Jill's Ice Cream Shop* and find each of the words. When children match the word, have them read the sentence in the story that contains the word. Have them continue in this way until they have matched all of the words and read all the corresponding sentences.

Monitoring Student Progress

If . . .	Then . . .
children need more practice with the high-frequency words,	have them match high-frequency word cards to corresponding words on the Word Wall.

CHALLENGE/EXTENSION:
High-Frequency Words

Independent Activities

Build a Sentence!

Have children work in small groups. Give each group two of these sentence starters on sentence strips. Ask them to draw a picture or write a word on an index card to complete each one.

Then have children show how they completed each sentence. Ask the groups to read their sentences to each other. You might want to have children cut up their sentences and exchange them with classmates so that the children can rebuild the sentences.

> I shall eat all of the _____.

> Why is _____?

> His mom and dad said, "Never _____."

> Every piece of paper is _____!

CHALLENGE

Ice Cream Shop Menu

Have children write a complete menu for *Miss Jill's Ice Cream Shop*. Remind children to look at the Word Wall. Children might also want to make a list of eating rules for the shop.

Words for Week 3

OBJECTIVE

- Read and write new high-frequency words *also, blue, brown, color, funny, green, like, many, some.*

Target Skill Trace

- High-Frequency Words Lesson, pp. T190–T191

Materials

- **Letter Cards** *a, b, c, e, e, f, g, i, k, l, m, n, n, o, o, r, s, u, w, y*

Teach

Write the words *also, blue, brown, color, funny, green, like, many,* and *some* on the board. Read the words aloud, pointing to each as you go.

Display the **Letter Cards** on the ledge below the board. Ask the group, *How many letters are in the word* also?

Draw four squares on the board.

Ask four children to come up and find each letter in the word *also.* Ask the children to help you spell *also* as you write the word in the four squares.

Tell the children to put the letters back with the other cards. Have them help lead the cheer to remember the word. Tap your left foot for each letter and then each syllable as you spell and say the word: *a-l-s-o, al-so!*

Repeat the lesson procedure with the other words in the list.

Practice

On the board, write the sentence, *This fish is also blue.* Ask the children to help you read the sentence. Tell them you want them to read the word *also* altogether when it occurs in the sentence. Point to each word in the sentence as you read. Pause before the word *also* and resume reading after the group has supplied the word.

Repeat this activity for each high-frequency word.

Apply

Have children work in pairs. Give each pair nine large index cards and have them write the new words on them. Then have them go back to *At the Aquarium* and find each of the words. When children match the word, have them read the sentence in the story that contains the word. Have them continue in this way until they have matched all of the words and read all the corresponding sentences.

Monitoring Student Progress

If . . .	Then . . .
children need more practice with the high-frequency words,	have them match high-frequency word cards to corresponding words on the Word Wall.

CHALLENGE/EXTENSION:
High-Frequency Words

Complete the Sentences

Provide sentence starters and ask children to complete each sentence with a word or picture. If children draw pictures, ask them to tell about their pictures while you record their responses.

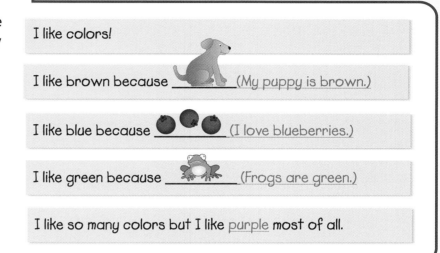

I like colors!

I like brown because _____ (My puppy is brown.)

I like blue because _____ (I love blueberries.)

I like green because _____ (Frogs are green.)

I like so many colors but I like <u>purple</u> most of all.

CHALLENGE

Picture Glossary

Have children develop a picture glossary of fish that live in the sea. Children can use labels to indicate color, size, and kind of fish. Some children might want to use reference materials to help them with their glossary.

RETEACHING: Comprehension Skills

Topic, Main Idea, Details/Summarizing

OBJECTIVES

- Identify the topic, main idea, and details of a story.
- Use the topic, main idea, details/summarizing to understand a text structure.

Target Skill Trace

- Topic, Main Idea, Details/Summarizing, pp. T68–T69

Teach

Begin a discussion of the story *Seasons* by asking children what the story is mostly about. (seasons) Explain that the title of a story often tells the topic. Ask children to name the four seasons.

Then ask, *What is the main idea of the story?* (The seasons change.) To guide children who have difficulty identifying the main idea, ask, *What happens to the animals and plants in each season?* (They change.) *Why do they change?* (because the weather changes) Explain that the main idea tells the most important idea about the topic *Seasons*.

Next, ask children to describe the weather and what happens to the animals and plants in different seasons. Tell them that these story details explain the main idea, *The seasons change*.

Finally, tell children that the topic, main idea, and details make up the summary of the story.

Practice

Draw the following graphic organizer. Ask children to help you complete the graphic organizer for the story *Seasons*.

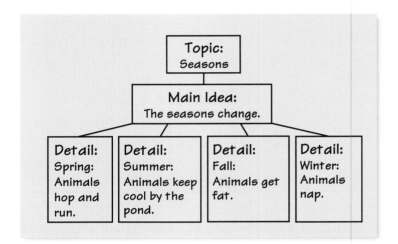

Apply

Complete a graphic organizer such as the one in the Practice activity for another nonfiction story children know, such as one about animals, holidays, or weather.

Monitoring Student Progress

If . . .	Then . . .
children need more practice with topic, main idea, details/summarizing,	have them repeat the Practice activity.

CHALLENGE/EXTENSION: Topic, Main Idea, Details/Summarizing

Independent Activities

Seasons Posters

Small Group Activity Have children make posters depicting weather conditions and activities that are typically done in each of the four seasons where they live. Children can name their posters *The Four Seasons*. Ask them to write a main idea sentence at the bottom of the poster to identify what the illustrations represent. Invite children to present their posters to classmates, pointing out the picture details that support the main idea.

Reading Nonfiction

Small Group Activity Select a nonfiction library book on a topic of choice. Provide each group with a copy of a Topic/Main Idea/Details/Summarizing graphic organizer. Have children work together to identify and then record (in pictures or words) the selection's topic, main idea, and details in the graphic organizer. Compile the work from different groups and use those as models to reinforce instruction.

CHALLENGE

Seasons Mural

Small Group Activity Have children work together to make a mural entitled *Seasons*. Provide small groups with mural paper. Have each child draw and write about one of the seasons. Encourage the groups to plan their mural to determine how they will illustrate each season. Display the murals for others to enjoy.

RETEACHING: Comprehension Skills

Making Predictions

OBJECTIVES

- Make predictions based on prior knowledge.
- Apply what has been learned to make new predictions.

Target Skill Trace

- Making Predictions, pp. T140–T141

Teach

Ask, *How do you know when it is lunchtime*? Encourage children to answer based on their experience. (It is the same time every day, or We eat lunch after _____.) Then ask,

> *What other things do you predict will happen today?*

> *What will happen tomorrow? Will you come to school? Why? or Why not?*

Practice

Discuss the story *Miss Jill's Ice Cream Shop* with children. Ask, *What did Bill predict when he saw Jack's big ice cream cone?* (He predicted that Jack would never eat all the ice cream.) *Why did Bill predict that?* (because there was too much ice cream) Guide children to understand that we make predictions based on what we know and what we read.

Apply

Point out that Jack learned a lesson in the story—he learned not to be greedy. Ask children to predict what Jack might do the next time he goes to Miss Jill's shop. Have them draw a picture to show what they think would happen.

Monitoring Student Progress

If . . .	Then . . .
children need more practice with making predictions,	have them repeat the Practice activity with another story they know.

COMPREHENSION

CHALLENGE/EXTENSION:
Making Predictions

What Will the Weather Be?

Paired Activity Explain to children that we can often make predictions about the weather because of what we have experienced when living through the four seasons. Have partners make a chart showing the different kinds of weather that occur in each of the four seasons. Tell children to draw pictures or cut out magazine pictures to show the different kinds of weather. Have children share their predictions about the kinds of weather that will happen in each of the seasons.

A Story Sequel

Small Group Activity Provide several familiar fairy tales and fables. Have children identify a character from one of the stories. Have them talk about what the characters are like, noting things that the characters say and do. Based on what children say, have them make predictions about how the character might behave in a similar situation or when placed in a different setting. Have children create a sequel to the story, making sure that the character behaves in ways true to his or her character traits. Ask children to give reasons for their predictions.

CHALLENGE

Patterns

Paired Activity Explain to children that we make predictions in math as well as in reading. Tell children that when we see a pattern in math, we can often predict how that pattern will continue. Have children work with blocks and create patterns with colors, shapes, and sizes. Once they have established a pattern, for example, three blue blocks, three red blocks, two blue blocks, etc., have their partner predict how to continue the pattern.

Categorize and Classify

OBJECTIVES

- Categorize and classify information.
- Identify information in stories by category.

Target Skill Trace

- Classify and Categorize, pp. T212–T213

Teach

Gather a variety of writing tools (including pencils, crayons, markers) and three small boxes or bins for sorting the items. Explain that all of the tools can be used to write or draw. Then hold up a pencil, a crayon, and a marker, and ask, *How are these items different?* Prompt children with questions such as these:

Which one is the shortest?

Which one has a top?

Which one has an eraser?

After children name the differences, ask them to help you sort the tools into the containers. Ask children to justify their sorting methods.

Practice

Make a T chart with the headings *Animals that live on land* and *Animals that live in water*. Explain that a chart can help us see what belongs in each category. Ask children to name animals for each category.

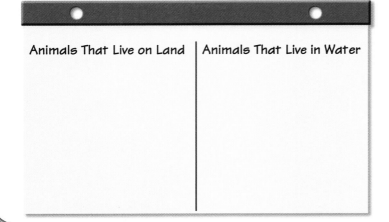

Animals That Live on Land	Animals That Live in Water

Write the animal names on the chart.

Apply

Draw a new T chart with the headings *Things that live on land* and *Things that live in water*. Explain the new chart headings. Tell children that as you read *At the Aquarium*, you want them to name things from the story that can fit in each category.

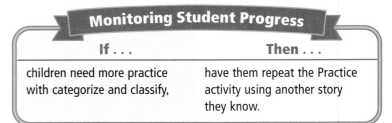

Monitoring Student Progress

If . . .	Then . . .
children need more practice with categorize and classify,	have them repeat the Practice activity using another story they know.

CHALLENGE/EXTENSION:
Categorize and Classify

Comparison Chart

Small Group Activity Give each group a T chart with the headings *Ways to Get Around Using Cars* and *Ways to Get Around Without Using Cars*. Have children use pictures or words to fill in each side of the chart. Tell them to count the items in each column when they are finished and to write that number at the bottom of the list. Have them compare their totals with those of other groups.

CHALLENGE

Sort It!

Paired Activity Give each pair a small pile of different materials such as colored squares, colored beads, and colored markers. Tell them to sort the materials in as many ways as they can, for example, by color, by name, or by shape. Have them draw a picture or write words to show how they classified the objects.

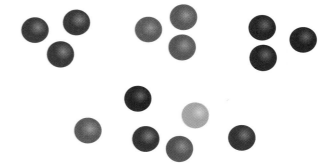

What Can I Wear?

Small Group Activity Show children how to draw a four-column chart. Have them label the columns *summer, fall, winter, spring*. Tell them to draw pictures or write the names of the clothing for each season in the appropriate columns. Have them work with a partner to ask one another, *What Can I Wear?*

STUDY SKILL:
Using the Library

OBJECTIVES

- Distinguish between nonfiction and fiction materials.
- Learn how to use the card catalog or computer database.

Teach

Introduce the purpose of libraries. Tell children that a library is a place that has books, encyclopedias, magazines, newspapers, and other resources. People can borrow or use the materials at the library, as long as they return them. Ask children who have been to a library to tell what they saw and did there.

Display **Chart/Transparency 3–12.** Tell children that the diagram shows how a library might be arranged. Explain that materials in a library are organized so people can find them easily. Point to and read the chart/transparency labels. Then explain the following:

- A librarian can help you if you have questions about a library or its resources.
- Card catalogs or computer databases can be used to find specific resources and information.
- It is a good idea to use the card catalog or computer database to find out if the library has the book and where it is located.
- Fiction books are made-up stories. Fiction books are organized on shelves, alphabetically by the author's last name.
- Nonfiction gives facts about real people, places, and things. Nonfiction books are organized by subject matter.

Practice

Have children answer questions about the chart/transparency. Have individual children tell and show on the chart/transparency where they can find answers to questions such as the following:

- *Where would I find a book of fairy tales?* (fiction shelves)

- *Where would I find a book about whales?* (nonfiction shelves)
- *If I'm looking for a book called* Guess Whose Shadow?, *what should I do?* (use the card catalog or computer database to see if the library has the book and to find out where it is)
- *Where would I find the magazines?* (in the racks of magazines)

Apply

Have partners complete the assignable activity below.

Can You Find It?

- Individually, search the classroom to find one book, magazine, or other reading resource that is fiction and one that is nonfiction.
- With your partner, compare the reading materials you each found.
- Tell how you knew which was fiction and which was nonfiction.

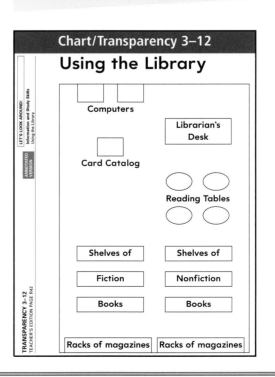

Chart/Transparency 3–12

Using the Library

Computers

Librarian's Desk

Card Catalog

Reading Tables

Shelves of Fiction Books	Shelves of Nonfiction Books

| Racks of magazines | Racks of magazines |

STUDY SKILL:
Alphabetical Order

OBJECTIVES

- Identify alphabetical order.
- Arrange words in alphabetical order.

Teach

Introduce the concept of alphabetical order.
Write the alphabet and recite it with children. Explain that the letters of the alphabet are in *alphabetical order*. For example, *b* always comes before *c* and after *a*. Tell children that they will learn how to put *words* in alphabetical order.

Model how to alphabetize. Print the following words on the board, and have children read them aloud: *down, and, cat, big*. Underline the first letter in each word, and then model.

Think Aloud *I want to put the words* down, and, cat, *and* big *in alphabetical order. First, I look at the beginning letter in each word:* d, a, c, *and* b. *Next, I ask myself which of these letters comes first in the alphabet. Since* a *is first, I'll write* and *at the top of my alphabetical word list. I see that* big *begins with the second letter of the alphabet,* b, *so I will write* big *second on my list.*

Practice

Have children practice alphabetizing. Continue the alphabetical list, calling on individual children to tell which word (*down* or *cat*) comes next. Then print *have, eat, jump,* and *go* on the board. Call on children to read them aloud and underline each initial letter. Ask children which of the underlined letters comes before the others in the alphabet, and which word should come next on the alphabetical list. (*e, eat*)

Tell children that since no word among the words you are putting in order begins with *f,* they should look for a word that begins with the next letter of the alphabet, *g.* (*g, go*) Continue with the words *have* and *jump*.

Apply

Have small groups complete the assignable activity below. Assign groups so that the names of children within each group begin with different letters.

ABC for You and Me!

- Write your names on one piece of paper.
- Circle the first letter in everyone's name.
- Decide which of the circled letters comes first in the alphabet.
- Write that name at the top of a list.
- Work together to put all the names in alphabetical order.

flower

full

look

of

animal

bird

cold

fall

every

first

never

paper

see

all

call

eat

Use for Theme 3, Weeks 1 and 2.

brown

color

funny

green

shall

why

also

blue

Use for Theme 3, Weeks 2 and 3.

like

many

some

Use for Theme 3, Week 3.

Name _____

I See . . .

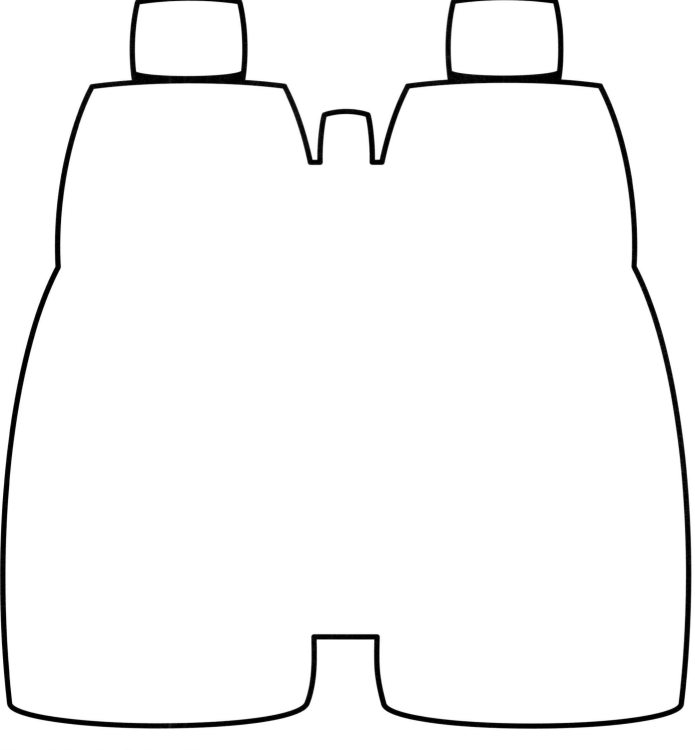

Theme 3: **Let's Look Around!**

Name _____

My Favorite Season

Theme 3: **Let's Look Around!**

Name _____

The Prize

Theme 3: **Let's Look Around!**

Name _____

A Good Book

Theme 3: **Let's Look Around!**

Name _____

I Like to Eat . . .

Theme 3: **Let's Look Around!**

Name _____

What I See

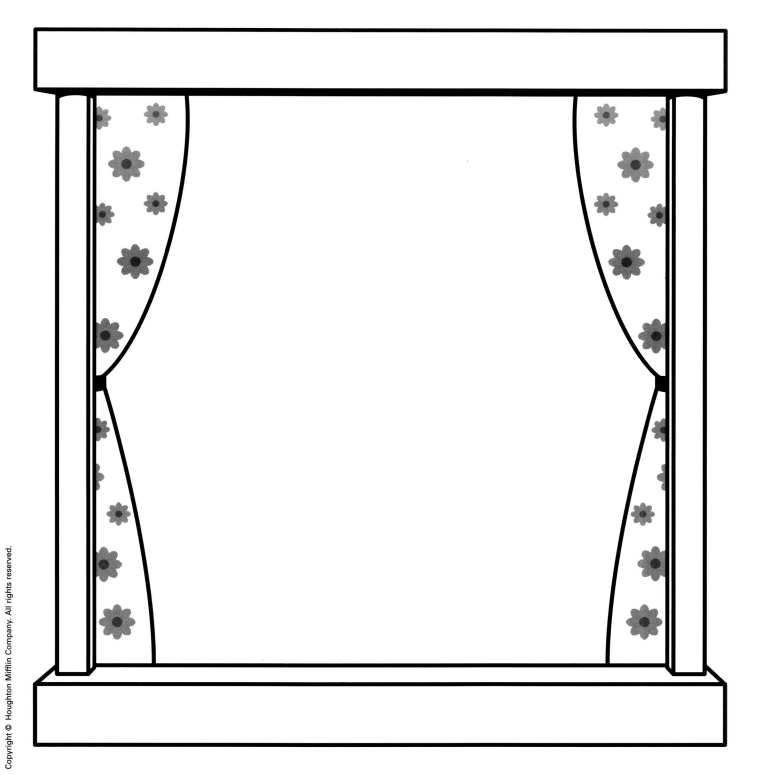

Theme 3: **Let's Look Around!**

Five Little Pumpkins

Traditional

Five lit-tle pump-kins sit-ting on a gate. First one said, "Oh

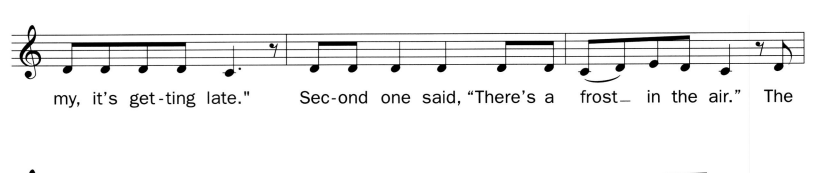

my, it's get-ting late." Sec-ond one said, "There's a frost— in the air." The

third one said, "But we don't care." The fourth one said, "Let's run and run and run." The

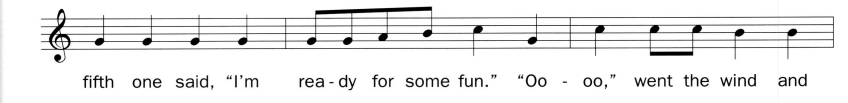

fifth one said, "I'm rea-dy for some fun." "Oo - oo," went the wind and

out went the light, And the five lit-tle pump-kins rolled out of sight.

Barnyard Song

or, I Had a Cat

Traditional

1. I had a cat and the cat pleased me, Fed my cat un-der

1 (first verse)

yon-der tree; Cat went "Fid-dle-i-fee, fid-dle-i-fee." 2. I

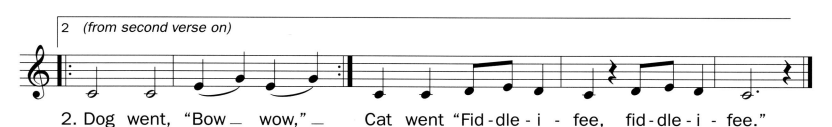

2 (from second verse on)

2. Dog went, "Bow— wow,"— Cat went "Fid-dle-i-fee, fid-dle-i-fee."

2. I had a dog and the dog pleased me.
Fed my dog under yonder tree.
Dog went, "Bowwow,"
Cat went, "Fiddle-i-fee, fiddle-i-fee."

3. I had a hen and the hen pleased me.
Fed my hen under yonder tree.
Hen went, "Ka-ka,"
Dog went, "Bowwow,"
Cat went, "Fiddle-i-fee, fiddle-i-fee."

4. I had a duck and the duck pleased me.
Fed my duck under yonder tree.
Duck went, "Quack, quack,"
Hen went, "Ka-ka," etc.

5. I had a goose and the goose pleased me.
Fed my goose under yonder tree.
Goose went, "Swishy, swashy,"
Duck went, "Quack, quack," etc.

6. I had a sheep and the sheep pleased me.
Fed my sheep under yonder tree.
Sheep went, "Baa, baa,"
Goose went, "Swishy, swashy," etc.

7. I had a cow and the cow pleased me.
Fed my cow under yonder tree.
Cow went, "Moo, moo,"
Sheep went, "Baa, baa," etc.

8. I had a horse and the horse pleased me.
Fed my horse under yonder tree.
Horse went, "Neigh, neigh,"
Cow went, "Moo, moo," etc.

My Farm

Folk song from Argentina
Translated by Olcutt and Phyllis Sanders

Come, come and see my farm for it is love - ly.

Come, come and see my farm for it is love - - - ly

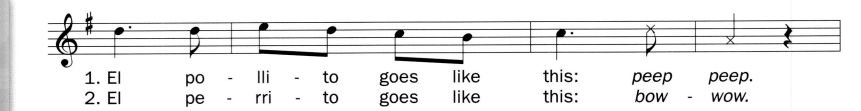

1. El po - lli - to goes like this: *peep peep.*
2. El pe - rri - to goes like this: *bow - wow.*

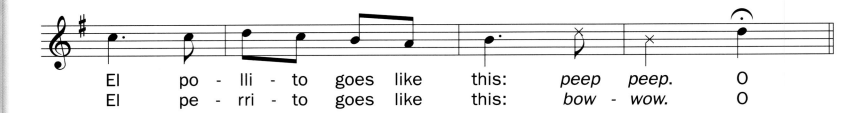

El po - lli - to goes like this: *peep peep.* O
El pe - rri - to goes like this: *bow - wow.* O

vas ca - ma - ra - da, vas ca - ma - ra - da, vas, O vas, O vas, O

vas ca - ma - ra - da, vas ca - ma - ra - da, vas, O vas, O vas.

MUSIC

1. El pollito goes like this: peep peep.

2. El perrito goes like this: bow-wow.

3. El gatito goes like this: mee-ow.

4. El burrito goes like this: hee-haw.

5. El patito goes like this: quack quack.

6. El chanchito goes like this: oink oink.

1. El pollito hace así: pipi-ri.

2. El perrito hace así: guau-guau.

3. El gatito hace así: mi-au.

4. El burrito hace así: ji-jo.

5. El patito hace así: cua cua.

6. El chanchito hace así: oinc oinc.

Mi chacra

Folk song from Argentina
Translated by Olcutt and Phyllis Sanders

Ven - gan a ver mi cha - cra que es her - mo - sa.

Ven - gan a ver mi cha - cra que es her - mo - sa.

1. El po - lli - to hace a - sí: *pi - pi - ri.*
2. El pe - rri - to hace a - sí: *guau - guau.*

El po - lli - to hace a - sí: *pi - pi - ri.* O
El pe - rri - to hace a - sí: *guau - guau.* O

vas ca-ma-ra - da, vas ca-ma-ra - da, vas, O vas, O vas. O

vas ca-ma-ra - da, vas ca-ma-ra - da, vas, O vas, O vas.

MUSIC

Take Me Out to the Ball Game

Music by Albert von Tilzer
Words by Jack Norworth

A Sailor Went to Sea, Sea, Sea

Traditional

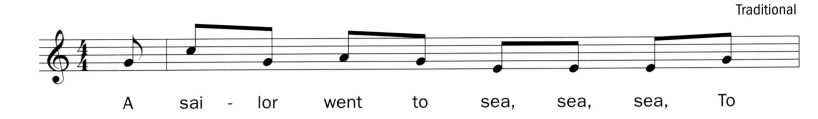

A sai - lor went to sea, sea, sea, To

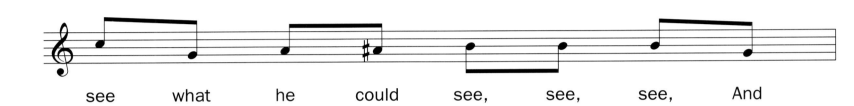

see what he could see, see, see, And

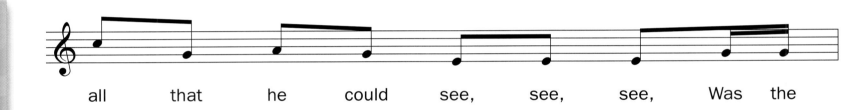

all that he could see, see, see, Was the

deep dark bot - tom of the sea, sea, sea.

WORD LIST

THEME 3, WEEK 1

Phonics Skills:
Double final consonants; Final Consonants *ck*, *s* as /z/; Plurals with -*s*; Short *a*

High-Frequency Words:
animal, bird, cold, fall, flower, look, of, see

Day 1

Phonics Library: *Cabs, Cabs, Cabs*

Phonics Practice Words: cab, cabs, can, has, Mack, pass, tack, tan, *big, hit, quit*

High-Frequency Words: *a,* the, to, two

Day 2

Phonics Library: *Fall Naps*

Phonics Practice Words: an, **and,** bugs, can, Dad, dens, Jack, nap, naps, pass, Sam, tap, *get, it, set*

High-Frequency Words: animal, birds, cold, fall, *to*

Anthology: *Animals in the Cold*

Phonics Practice Words: **and,** buds, can, **is,** lots, pick, pups, will, *big, cub, den, dig, dip, fox, get, hot,* **in,** *it, its,* **not,** *sun, up, wet*

High-Frequency Words: animal, animals, birds, cold, fall, flowers, full, look, of, see, *a, are, do, here, for, go, live, the, they*

This list includes all words in Phonics Library and Anthology selections for Theme 3. Words in regular type apply skills for the week; words in italics apply previously taught skills; words in boldface type indicate high-frequency words that are now decodable. High-Frequency Words are practiced in Phonics Library and Anthology selections and in Practice Book and Word Wall activities; each is practiced at least six times in the week it is taught. Challenge words include some known phonics elements and some that are unfamiliar.

Day 3

Anthology: *Seasons*

Phonics Practice Words: and, at, buck, buds, buzz, can, ducks, eggs, fat, grass, has, **is,** kick, lots, nap, nest, nests, nuts, pass, pick, pups, quack, will, *big, den, end, fox, get, hop, hot,* **in,** *it,* **jump,** *mud,* **not,** *pond, red, run, set, sip, sun, up, wet*

High-Frequency Words: animal, animals, birds, cold, flower, flowers, fall, full, look, of, see, *a, are, do, for, go, here, the, they, three, to, too, two, where, who*

Kindergarten High-Frequency Words: play

Story Vocabulary: bear, insects, leaves, rain, south, spring, summer, trees, winter

Day 5

Phonics Library: *Pam Can Pack*

Phonics Practice Words: at, can, has, jugs, pack, Pam, sack, tan, *big, get, ten*

High-Frequency Words: flowers, full, look, of, *a, the*

THEME 3, WEEK 2

Phonics Skills:
Verb Endings -*s*, -*ed*, -*ing*; Possessives ('*s*); Short *i*

High-Frequency Words:
all, call, eat, every, first, never, paper, shall, why

Day 1

Phonics Library: *Lots of Picking*

Phonics Practice Words: big, bins, filled, gets, **is,** Kim, Kim's, picking, picks, *can, Dad, get, lots*

High-Frequency Words: *of, they, too*

Day 2

Phonics Library: *Bill Bird*

Phonics Practice Words: big, Bill, figs, gets, **is,** Jill's, picked, picking, six, quit, will, **and,** *can, lots,* **not,** *nuts*

High-Frequency Words: eat, first, *bird, of*

Anthology: *Ham and Eggs*

Phonics Practice Words: bit, fixed, his, **is,** it, Jack's, licked, lips, will, yelled, **and,** *at, can, Dad, eggs, fun, had, ham, Jack, let,* **not,** *pen, Ted, up, us, yum*

High-Frequency Words: all, called, eat, eating, every, first, never, paper, shall, why, *a, go, have, here,* **I,** *of, said, to, we, what, you*

Day 3

Anthology: *Miss Jill's Ice Cream Shop*

Phonics Practice Words: added, asked, big, Bill, Bill's, bumped, dumped, filled, fixed, his, in, **is,** it, Jack, Jack's, Jill, Jill's, lick, licked, lips, mint, Miss, will, yelled, **and,** *at, can, fell, get, had, help, lots, mess,* **not,** *nuts,* **on,** *plum, ran, run, top, up, went, yes, yum*

High-Frequency Words: all, call, eat, eating, every, first, never, paper, shall, why, *a, animals, do, falling, for, go, have, he, here,* **I,** *likes, look, of, said, the, to, too, what, you*

Kindergarten High-Frequency Words: she

Story Vocabulary: cone, dish, green, kind, ice cream, napkins, shop, try, wish

Day 5

Phonics Library: *Tim's Cat*

Phonics Practice Words: his, Hiss, hissed, hissing, **is,** Miss, Tim, Tim's, *at, but, cat, has*

High-Frequency Words: called, never, paper, why, *look, the*

THEME 3, WEEK 3

Phonics Skills:
Consonant Clusters with *r*; Contractions with -'*s*

High-Frequency Words:
also, blue, brown, color, funny, green, like, many, some

Day 1

Phonics Library: *Let's Trim the Track!*

Phonics Practice Words: Fran, grabs, Gran, grass, let's, track, trim, *at, bags, big, can, cut, fit,* **in,** *Sam, tan, van*

High-Frequency Words: *the*

WORD LIST

Day 2

Phonics Library: *Brad's Quick Rag Tricks*

Phonics Practice Words: Brad, Brad's, Gran, Let's, rag's, trick, tricks, *big, can, did, get, picks, quick, rag*

High-Frequency Words: brown, green, ***a,*** *do, look, the*

Anthology: *The Trip*

Phonics Practice Words: grab, grass, it's, let's, trip, *added,* ***and,*** *at, big, bus, cab, cat, cats, Dad, get, hop,* ***in, is,*** *Mom,* ***on,*** *pass, Puff, sat, Tip, went, yelled*

High-Frequency Words: also, blue, brown, colors, funny, green, like, many, some, ***a,*** *all, are, go, here,* ***I,*** *look, said, see, the, we, what, where*

Day 3

Anthology: *At the Aquarium*

Phonics Practice Words: crab, crabs, grab, grass, it's, let's, trick, trip, ***and,*** *at, back, best, big, black, can, class, did, dot, fans, fast, fin, fins, fun, get, gill, gills, has, help,* ***in, is,*** *it, legs, lots, next,* ***on,*** *plant, plants, puff, rock, run, sand, slug, stop, swim, tank, up, well, will*

High-Frequency Words: also, blue, brown, colors, funny, green, like, many, some, ***a,*** *all, are, away, do, eat, go, have, here, here's, live, look, looking, looks, of, one, see, the, to, two, we, what, you*

Story Vocabulary: breathe, dolphins, fish, otter, sea, sea horse, tails

Day 5

Phonics Library: *Fran Pig's Brick Hut*

Phonics Practice Words: brick, bricks, Fran, grab, it's, *big, fat, got, hut, lots, Pig, pigs, Pig's, set*

High-Frequency Words: also, likes, many, some, *of, the, to*

HIGH-FREQUENCY WORDS

Word	Taught as High-Frequency Word THEME/WEEK	Decodable THEME/WEEK
a	1/3	1/1
*able	10/3	n/a
about	8/1	n/a
*above	10/2	n/a
*afraid	7/2	n/a
after	9/2	10/1
again	7/1	n/a
*against	10/2	n/a
all	3/2	n/a
*already	10/2	n/a
*also	3/3	n/a
always	8/2	n/a
and	1/2	5/2
*animal	3/1	n/a
any	7/2	n/a
are	2/3	n/a
*arms	8/2	10/2
around	9/1	n/a
away	2/3	n/a
*baby	9/3	n/a
*bear	7/2	n/a
because	8/1	n/a
been	6/3	n/a
before	9/2	n/a
*began	10/1	n/a
*begin	10/2	n/a
*bird	3/1	10/1
blue	3/3	7/3
*body	8/2	n/a
both	7/1	n/a
*break	10/1	n/a
brown	3/3	8/2
*build	7/3	n/a
*butter	8/3	10/1
buy	9/2	n/a
by	6/1	9/1
call	3/2	n/a
*car	4/3	10/2
carry	8/3	9/1
*caught	10/2	n/a
*children	4/1	n/a
*climb	6/1	n/a
cold	3/1	n/a
*color	3/3	n/a
come	4/1	n/a
could	5/2	n/a
*cow	6/2	8/2
*dance	9/1	n/a
*divide	10/1	n/a
do	2/2	n/a
does	2/3	n/a
done	9/2	n/a
*door	6/2	n/a
down	4/3	8/2
draw	8/1	9/3
eat	3/2	6/2
*edge	9/3	n/a
eight	8/2	n/a
*else	9/1	n/a
*enough	9/3	n/a
*evening	6/3	n/a
*ever	9/1	10/1
every	3/2	n/a
*eye	10/3	n/a
fall	3/1	n/a
*family	4/1	n/a
far	6/3	10/2
*father	4/1	n/a
find	1/3	n/a
first	3/2	10/1
five	2/1	5/3
*flower	3/1	10/1
fly	5/3	9/1
*follow	7/2	8/2
for	2/2	10/1
*forest	6/3	10/1
found	6/1	8/2
four	2/1	n/a
*friend	4/2	n/a
full	3/1	n/a
funny	3/3	9/1
*garden	9/3	10/2
*girl	4/2	10/1
give	5/3	n/a
go	1/1	6/1
goes	6/3	n/a
*gone	7/1	n/a
good	5/3	7/2
green	3/3	6/2
grow	5/1	7/1
*happy	8/1	9/1
*hard	7/1	10/2
have	1/3	n/a
he	2/3	6/2
*head	10/1	n/a
*hear	4/3	n/a
her	5/3	10/1
here	1/2	n/a
hold	4/3	n/a
*horse	6/2	10/1
*house	5/2	8/2
how	5/2	8/2
*hungry	6/3	n/a
hurt	4/3	10/1
I	2/2	2/2
*idea	7/2	n/a
in	2/1	1/3
is	2/2	1/3
jump	1/2	4/3
kind	8/3	n/a
know	4/2	7/1
laugh	10/1	n/a
*learn	4/3	n/a
light	5/1	7/3
like	3/3	5/3
little	5/3	n/a
live	2/3	n/a
long	5/1	5/2
look	3/1	7/2
*love	4/1	n/a
many	3/3	n/a
me	2/2	6/2
*minute	10/2	n/a

Word	Taught as High-Frequency Word THEME/WEEK	Decodable THEME/WEEK	Word	Taught as High-Frequency Word THEME/WEEK	Decodable THEME/WEEK	Word	Taught as High-Frequency Word THEME/WEEK	Decodable THEME/WEEK
*more	5/1	10/1	*school	9/2	n/a	walk	4/3	n/a
*morning	6/1	10/1	*second	10/1	n/a	*wall	6/2	n/a
*most	7/2	n/a	see	3/1	6/2	want	7/1	n/a
*mother	4/1	n/a	seven	8/2	n/a	warm	8/2	n/a
my	2/2	9/1	shall	3/2	5/1	was	5/3	n/a
*near	6/3	n/a	*sharp	9/3	10/2	wash	9/2	n/a
never	3/2	n/a	she	4/2	6/2	*watched	9/3	n/a
not	1/2	2/1	*shoe[s]	7/3	n/a	*water	7/2	n/a
now	6/2	8/2	*shout	6/1	8/2	we	1/2	6/2
*ocean	9/1	n/a	show	6/1	7/1	*wear	7/3	n/a
of	3/1	n/a	sing	4/2	5/2	were	8/3	n/a
off	9/2	n/a	small	5/1	n/a	what	2/1	n/a
old	7/3	n/a	so	5/2	6/1	where	2/3	n/a
on	1/1	2/1	some	3/3	n/a	who	1/3	n/a
once	2/1	n/a	soon	6/3	7/3	why	3/2	9/1
one	1/3	n/a	start	7/3	10/2	work	8/3	n/a
only	9/3	n/a	*sure	10/1	n/a	*world	5/2	n/a
open	9/1	n/a	*table	6/2	n/a	would	4/3	n/a
or	7/1	10/1	*talk	9/1	n/a	write	4/2	5/3
*other	5/1	n/a	*tall	7/2	n/a	you	2/2	7/3
our	5/3	8/2	*teacher	8/1	10/1	your	4/1	n/a
out	6/1	8/2	the	1/1	6/2			
over	5/2	n/a	their	4/3	n/a			
own	5/2	7/1	there	6/2	n/a			
*paper	3/2	n/a	these	5/1	6/2			
*part	8/1	10/2	they	2/3	n/a			
*people	4/1	n/a	*though	9/1	n/a			
*person	8/3	n/a	*thoughts	10/3	n/a			
*picture	4/1	n/a	three	2/1	6/2			
*piece	7/3	n/a	*through	6/2	n/a			
play	4/2	6/3	*tiny	8/1	n/a			
*present	10/3	n/a	to	1/3	n/a			
pretty	9/2	n/a	today	4/2	n/a			
pull	2/3	n/a	together	9/3	n/a			
put	8/3	n/a	too	1/2	7/3			
read	4/2	6/2	try	5/3	9/1			
*ready	8/2	n/a	*turn	7/1	10/1			
right	5/1	7/3	two	2/1	n/a			
*room	5/1	7/3	under	7/3	10/1			
said	2/2	n/a	upon	2/1	n/a			
saw	8/3	9/3	very	7/3	n/a			

* Words from the 800 Base Words of Highest Frequency of Occurrence in the American Heritage Computerized Study of the Vocabulary of Published Materials Used in Public Schools. Words without asterisks are from the Dolch list.

TECHNOLOGY RESOURCES

American Melody
P.O. Box 270
Guilford, CT 06437
800-220-5557
www.americanmelody.com

Audio Bookshelf
174 Prescott Hill Road
Northport, ME 04849
800-234-1713
www.audiobookshelf.com

Baker & Taylor
100 Business Center Drive
Pittsburgh, PA 15205
800-775-2600
www.btal.com

BDD Audio/Random House
400 Hohn Road
Westminster, MD 21157
800-733-3000

Big Kids Productions
1606 Dywer Ave.
Austin, TX 78704
800-477-7811
www.bigkidsvideo.com

Books on Tape
P.O. Box 25122
Santa Ana, CA 92799
800-541-5525
www.booksontape.com

Broderbund Company
1 Martha's Way
Hiawatha, IA 52233
www.broderbund.com

Filmic Archives
The Cinema Center
Botsford, CT 06404
800-366-1920
www.filmicarchives.com

Great White Dog Picture Company
10 Toon Lane
Lee, NH 03824
800-397-7641
www.greatwhitedog.com

HarperAudio
10 E. 53rd St.
New York, NY 10022
800-242-7737
www.harperaudio.com

Houghton Mifflin Company
222 Berkeley St.
Boston, MA 02116
800-225-3362

Informed Democracy
P.O. Box 67
Santa Cruz, CA 95063
800-827-0949

JEF Films
143 Hickory Hill Circle
Osterville, MA 02655
508-428-7198

Kimbo Educational
P.O. Box 477
Long Branch, NJ 07740
800-631-2187
www.kimboed.com

Library Video Co.
P.O. Box 580
Wynnewood, PA 19096
800-843-3620
www.libraryvideo.com

Listening Library
P.O. Box 25122
Santa Ana, CA 92799
800-541-5525
www.listeninglibrary.com

Live Oak Media
P.O. Box 652
Pine Plains, NY 12567
800-788-1121
www.liveoakmedia.com

Media Basics
Lighthouse Square
P.O. Box 449
Guilford, CT 06437
800-542-2505
www.mediabasicsvideo.com

Microsoft Corp.
One Microsoft Way
Redmond, WA 98052
800-426-9400
www.microsoft.com

National Geographic School Publishing
P.O. Box 10597
Des Moines, IA 50340
800-368-2728
www.nationalgeographic.com

New Kid Home Video
P.O. Box 10443
Beverly Hills, CA 90213
800-309-2392
www.NewKidhomevideo.com

Puffin Books
345 Hudson Street
New York, NY 10014
800-233-7364

Rainbow Educational Media
4540 Preslyn Drive
Raleigh, NC 27616
800-331-4047
www.rainbowedumedia.com

Recorded Books
270 Skipjack Road
Prince Frederick, MD 20678
800-638-1304
www.recordedbooks.com

Sony Wonder
Dist. by Professional Media Service
19122 S. Vermont Ave.
Gardena, CA 90248
800-223-7672
www.sonywonder.com

Spoken Arts
195 South White Rock Road
Holmes, NY 12531
800-326-4090
www.spokenartsmedia.com

SRA Media
220 E. Danieldale Rd.
DeSoto, TX 75115
800-843-8855
www.sra4kids.com

Sunburst Technology
1550 Executive Drive
Elgin, IL 60123
800-321-7511
www.sunburst.com

SVE & Churchill Media
6677 North Northwest Highway
Chicago, IL 60631
800-829-1900
www.svemedia.com

Tom Snyder Productions
80 Coolidge Hill Road
Watertown, MA 02472
800-342-0236
www.tomsnyder.com

Troll Communications
100 Corporate Drive
Mahwah, NJ 07430
800-526-5289
www.troll.com

Weston Woods
143 Main St.
Norwalk, CT 06851-1318
800-243-5020
www.scholastic.com/westonwood

PRONUNCIATION GUIDE

In this book some unfamiliar or hard-to-pronounce words are followed by respellings to help you say the words correctly. Use the key below to find examples of various sounds and their respellings. Note that in the respelled word, the syllable in capital letters is the one receiving the most stress.

Dictionary letter or mark		Respelled as	Example	Respelled word
ă	(pat)	a	basket	BAS-kiht
ā	(pay)	ay	came	kaym
âr	(care)	air	share	shair
ä	(father)	ah	barter	BAHR-tur
ch	(church)	ch	channel	CHAN-uhl
ĕ	(pet)	eh	test	tehst
ē	(bee)	ee	heap	heep
g	(gag)	g	goulash	GOO-lahsh
ĭ	(pit)	ih	liver	LIHV-ur
ī	(pie, by)	y	alive	uh-LYV
		eye	island	EYE-luhnd
îr	(hear)	eer	year	yeer
j	(judge)	j	germ	jurm
k	(kick, cat, pique)	k	liquid	LIHK-wihd
ŏ	(pot)	ah	otter	AHT-ur
ō	(toe)	oh	solo	SOH-loh
ô	(caught, paw)	aw	always	AWL-wayz
ôr	(for)	or	normal	NOR-muhl
oi	(noise)	oy	boiling	BOYL-ihng
ŏŏ	(took)	u	pull, wool	pul, wul
ōō	(boot)	oo	bruise	brooz
ou	(out)	ow	pound	pownd
s	(sauce)	s	center	SEHN-tur
sh	(ship, dish)	sh	chagrin	shuh-GRIHN
ŭ	(cut)	uh	flood	fluhd
ûr	(urge, term, firm, word, heard)	ur	earth	urth
			bird	burd
z	(zebra, xylem)	z	cows	kowz
zh	(vision, pleasure, garage)	zh	decision	dih-SIHZH-uhn
ə	(about)	uh	around	uh-ROWND
	(item)	uh	broken	BROH-kuhn
	(edible)	uh	pencil	PEHN-suhl
	(gallop)	uh	connect	kuh-NEHKT
	(circus)	uh	focus	FOH-kuhs
ər	(butter)	ur	liter	LEE-tur

Acknowledgments

Index

Boldface page references indicate formal strategy and skill instruction.

Acquiring English, students. *See* English Language Learners; Reaching All Learners.

Activating prior knowledge. *See* Background, building.

Alphabetic principle
alphabetical order, *R43*
letter and sound match, *T36, T38, T108, T109, T110, T180, T182*

Art activities. *See* Cross-curricular activities.

Assessment
Assessing Student Progress, *T236–T238*
Comprehension Check, *T66, T137, T210*
Formal Assessment, *T14*
Informal Assessment, *T14*
Monitoring Student Progress, *T36, T37, T38, T47, T69, T83, T108, T109, T110, T119, T137, T141, T155, T181, T182, T191, T210, T213, R14, R16, R18, R20, R22, R24, R26, R28, R30, R32, R34, R36, R38, R40*
planning for, *T14–T15*
See also Teacher's Assessment Handbook; Teacher's Resource Blackline Masters.

Authors of Anthology selections
Shaw, Nancy, *T56*
Wolff, Ashley, *T128*

Automatic recognition of words. *See* High-frequency words; Spelling; Vocabulary, selection.

Background, building
for the week's stories, *T48, T120, T192*
in a teacher read aloud, *T32, T104, T176*
previewing. *See* Previewing.
prior knowledge, *T32, T104, T176*

Bibliography, Leveled, *T6–T7*

Big Book selections
fantasy
Hilda Hen's Scary Night by Mary Wormell, *T176–T179*
fiction
Pearl's First Prize Plant, by A. Delaney, *T104–T107*
nonfiction
Counting on the Woods by George Ella Lyon,

photographs by Ann W. Olson, *T32–T35*

Blending. See Decoding skills, phonics/decoding strategy; Phonemic awareness; Phonics.

Books for independent reading. *See* Independent and recreational reading; Leveled Bibliography; Leveled Readers; Leveled Theme Paperbacks.

Brainstorming, *T29, T70, T148, T151, T222, T230, R17, R23, R27*

Categorizing and classifying. *See* Comprehension skills.

Cause-effect relationships. *See* Comprehension skills.

CD-ROM diskettes, *T91, T163, T235*

Center activities, *T12–T13, T28–T29, T100–T101, T172–T173*

Challenge. *See* Reaching All Learners.

Classroom management
groups, *T28, T37, T38, T76, T82, T101, T108, T109, T110, T114, T119, T142, T148, T154, T155, T158, T172, T181, T182, T191, T209, T211, T226, R37, R39, R41*
individuals, *T28, T29, T37, T38, T100, T101, T108, T109, T110, T119, T155, T172, T173, T181, T182, T191*
partners, *T29, T37, T38, T67, T69, T86, T88, T89, T90, T91, T100, T108, T109, T110, T119, T141, T160, T161, T162, T163, T173, T181, T182, T191, T213, T230, T232, T233, T234, T235, R19, R20, R26, R30, R32, R34, R39, R41*
Ready-Made Small Group Activities, *T28–T29, T100–T101, T172–T173*
whole class, *T30–T31, T32–T35, T36–T38, T44–T45, T46–T47, T48, T54–T55, T56–T57, T64–T65, T67, T68–T69, T72–T73, T74–T75, T76–T77, T80–T81, T102–T103, T104–T107, T108–T110, T116–T117, T118–T119, T120, T126–T127, T128–T129, T138–T139, T140–T141, T144–T145, T146–T147, T148–T149, T152–T153, T154, T174–T175, T176–T179, T180–T182, T188–T189, T190–T191, T192, T198–T199, T200–T201, T211, T212–T213, T216–T217, T218–T219, T220–T221, T224–T225, T226*

Coherence in narrative text. *See* Comprehension, story structure.

Combination classroom, *T16*

Communication activities. *See* Listening; Speaking; Viewing.

Compare/contrast. *See* Comprehension skills.

Comparing. *See* Connections.

Comprehension skills
categorize and classify, ***T177, T194,*** *T195,* ***T201,*** *T208, T210, T211,* ***T212–T213,*** *T226, R40–R41*
cause and effect, *T139, T147, T219*
compare and contrast, *T62, T66, T75, T134, T139, T195, T211, T219*
conclusions, drawing, *T66, T67, T75, T123, T133, T137, T195, T206, T207, T210*
details, noting, *T61, T67, T75, T136, T139, T147, T203, T204, T211, T219*
fact and opinion, *T87*
fantasy and realism, *T51, T59, T75, T219*
inferences. *See* Inferences, making.
judgments, making, *T211*
making predictions, *T63,* ***T105, T121,*** *T123,* ***T129, T135,*** *T137, T139,* ***T140–T141,*** *T154, T160–T163, T202, R38–R39*
sequence of events, *T209, T211, T218, T219*
story structure, *T65, T131, T159*
topic, main idea, details/summarizing, *T33,* ***T50,*** *T51, T58, T60, T64, T67,* ***T68–T69,*** *T82, T88–T90, T147, T187, R36–R37*
See also Critical thinking; Strategies, reading.

Comprehension strategies. *See* Strategies, reading.

Concepts of print
capitalization
first word of a sentence, *T30, T45, T73, T103, T117, T145, T175, T189, T223*
names, *T31, T127, T153*
headings, *T62*
punctuation
apostrophe, *T116, T174, T177*
commas, *T126, T174*
end of sentence, *T116, T174, T223*
exclamation point, *T116, T174, T205*
period, *T80, T81, T116, T174*
question mark, *T44, T55, T72, T80, T116, T152, T174, T199*
quotation marks, *T120, T177*

tracking print, *T105, T144*
See also Mechanics, language.

Connections
between selections, *T66, T137, T210, T219*
between spelling and writing, *T36, T37, T38, T108, T109, T181, T182*
between strategies and skills, *T49*
connecting/comparing, *T67, T75, T138, T146, T211, T219*
home. *See* Home connections.

Constructing meaning from text. *See* Comprehension skills; Concepts of print; Decoding skills; Phonics; Strategies, reading.

Content areas, reading in the
drama, *T218–T219*
language arts, *T74–T75*
social studies, *T146–T147*

Context clues. *See* Decoding skills.

Conventions of language. *See* Grammar and usage; Mechanics, language.

Cooperative reading. *See* Reading modes.

Creative dramatics
role-play, *T116*

Creative response. *See* Responding to literature, options for.

Creative thinking, *T67, T138, T139, T211*

Critical thinking, *T51, T58, T59, T60, T61, T63, T64, T65, T66, T67, T75, T123, T131, T133, T134, T135, T136, T137, T139, T147, T195, T202, T203, T204, T206, T207, T208, T209, T211, T219*

Cross-curricular activities
math, *R39*
science, *R37, R39, R41*
social studies, *R37, R41*
See also, Ready-Made Small Group Activities.

Cue systems. *See* Decoding skills; Phonics; Structural analysis.

Daily Language Practice, *T31, T45, T55, T73, T81, T103, T117, T127, T145, T153, T175, T189, T199, T217, T225*

Decodable text, *T39–T41, T47, T83–T85, T111–T113, T119, T155–T157, T183–T185, T191, T227–T229, R14, R18, R20, R26*

Decoding skills
context clues, *T39, T49, T58, T59, T60, T63, T66, T80, T83, T111, T122, T130, T131, T132, T135, T137, T152, T155, T183, T191, T193, T203, T205, T206, T210, T224, T227*
nonverbal cues, *T115*

phonics/decoding strategy, *T39, T49, T58, T59, T60, T63, T66, T80, T83, T111, T122, T130, T131, T132, T135, T137, T152, T155, T183, T191, T193, T203, T205, T206, T210, T224, T227*
story clues, *T115*
See also Decodable text; Phonics; Structural analysis; Vocabulary, selection.

Details, noting important. *See* Comprehension skills.

Diagrams. *See* Graphic information, interpreting.

Diaries and journals. *See* Journals.

Drama. *See* Creative dramatics.

Drawing conclusions. *See* Comprehension skills.

English Language Learners
beginning/preproduction, *T67, T138, T211*
building background, *T35, T43*
early production and speech emergence, *T67, T138, T211*
intermediate and advanced fluency, *T67, T138, T211*
language development, *T53, T60, T61, T79, T115, T133, T179, T181, T70, T187, T202, T205, T206*
supporting comprehension, *T58, T67, T87, T107, T138, T211, T231, R2, R6, R10*

Evaluating literature. *See* Literature, evaluating.

Evaluation. *See* Assessment.

Expanding literacy. *See* Skills links.

Experience story. *See* Writing modes, shared writing.

Expository text, *T56–T67, T74–T75, T146–T147, T200–T209*

Extra Support/Intervention. *See* Reaching All Learners.

Fact and opinion. *See* Comprehension skills.

Fantasy and realism. *See* Comprehension skills.

Fiction. *See* Selections in Anthology.

Fluency
assessing, *T82, T154, T226*
modeling, *T32, T41, T83, T88, T89, T90, T91, T104, T111, T113, T157, T160, T161, T162, T163, T176, T185, T229, T232, T233, T234, T235*
leveled activities for, *T22, T94, T166*

practice for, *T41, T47, T82, T85, T89–T91, T113, T119, T154, T157, T160–T163, T185, T191, T226, T229, T232–T235, R5, R9, R13*
rereading for, *T82, T154, T226*
See also Lesson plans; Leveled Bibliography; Leveled Readers; Leveled Theme Paperbacks; Managing Flexible Groups.

Genre. *See* Selections in Anthology.

Grammar and usage
sentence, parts of a
action part, **T215,** *T231*
naming part, **T143,** *T159*
sentences, types of
what is a, **T71,** *T87*
spelling connection. *See* Lessons, specific, grammar.
See also Daily Language Practice.

Graphic information, interpreting
captions, *T33*
diagrams, *T203*
webs, *T70, T187*

Graphic organizers
categorize/classify chart, *T212*
rhyming words chart, *R17*
class story chart, *T197*
K-W-L chart, *T231*
sequence chart, *T218*
story structure chart, *T159*
T-chart, *R40*
topic/main idea/details chart, *T51, T68, T82*
word web, *T70, T187*

Graphophonemic/graphophonic cues. *See* Phonics.

Handwriting. *See* Penmanship.

High-frequency words
a, T126
all, **T118–T119,** *T120, T128, T144, T146, T152, T158, R32–R33*
also, **T190–T191,** *T192, T224, T230, R34–R35*
an, T44, T116, T188
and, T126, T144, T198, T216
animal, **T46–T47,** *T56, T80, T86, R30–R31*
are, T30, T72, T216
at, T72, T188
bird, **T46–T47,** *T56, T80, T86, R30–R31*
blue, **T190–T191,** *T192, T224, T230, R34–R35*
brown, **T190–T191,** *T192, T224, T230, R34–R35*
call, **T118–T119,** *T120, T128, T144, T152, T158, R32–R33*

can, T80

chanting, T30, T44, T54, T72, T80, T102, T116, T126, T144, T152, T174, T188, T198, T216, T224

cold, **T46–T47,** T56, T72, T80, T86, R30–R31

color, **T190–T191,** T192, T216, T224, T230, R34–R35

do, T72

eat, **T118–T119,** T120, 126, T128, T146, T152, T158, R32–R33

every, **T118–T119,** T120, T128, T144, T152, T158, R32–R33

fall, **T46–T47,** T56, T72, T80, T86, R30–R31

first, **T118–T119,** T120, T128, T152, T158, R32–R33

flower, **T46–T47,** T56, T72, T80, T86, R30–R31

for, T144

full, **T46–T47,** T56, T80, T86, R30–R31

funny, **T190–T191,** T192, T224, T230, R34–R35

go, T72, T102, T144, T174, T216

green, **T190–T191,** T192, T224, T230, R34–R35

grow, T102

have, T144, T198

he, T144

here, T72, T102, T144, T174, T216

I, T174

in, T72

is, T30, T56, T72, T126, T174, T216

it, T44, T72, T116, T144

like, T126, T174, **T190–T191,** T192, T216, T224, T230, R34–R35

look, **T46–T47,** T56, T80, T86, R30–R31

many, **T190–T191,** T192, T224, T230, R34–R35

never, **T118–T119,** T120, T128, T152, T158, R32–R33

of, **T46–T47,** T56, T80, T86, R30–R31

paper, **T118–T119,** T120, T128, T152, T158, R32–R33

play, T72

recognizing, T30, T44, **T46–T47,** T52, T54, T72, T80, T102, T116, **T118–T119, T124,** T126, T144, T152, T174, T188, **T190–T191,** T196, T198, T216, T224

see, T30, **T46–T47,** T56, T72, T80, T86, T102, T174, T216, R30–R31

she, T144

shall, **T118–T119,** T120, T128, T144, T152, T158, R32–R33

spelling, T30, T44, T54, T72, T80, T102, T116, T126, T144, T152, T174, T188, T198, T216, T224

some, **T190–T191,** T192, T224, T230, R34–R35

the, T72, T144, T174

there, T30

to, T126, T198

today, T102

too, T126

what, T72

why, **T118–T119,** T120, T128, T152, T158, R32–R33

you, T72, T126

Home-Community Connection. *See* Home-Community Connections book.

Home Connection, T41, T85, T113, T157, T185, T229

Home-School Connection. *See* Home-Community Connections book.

Illustrators of Anthology selections
Apple, Margot, T128
Wolff, Ashley, T56

Inclusion strategies. *See* Reaching All Learners.

Independent and recreational reading
bibliography, leveled, T6–T7
daily, T6–T7, T31, T45, T55, T73, T81, T87, T88–T91, T103, T117, T127, T145, T153, T158, T160–T163, T175, T189, T199, T217, T225, T232–T235
See also Reading modes; Ready-Made Small Group Activities.

Independent writing
daily, T31, T45, T55, T73, T81, T103, T117, T127, T145, T153, T175, T189, T191, T199, T217, T225, T231
suggestions for, **T79, T151, T223**

Individual needs, meeting. *See* Reaching All Learners.

Inferences, making
about characters' actions and feelings, T123
from illustrations, T115
See also Comprehension skills: cause and effect.

Information skills. *See* Reference and study skills.

Journals, T56, T128, T200

Knowledge, activating prior. *See* Background, building.

Language concepts and skills
idioms, T206
primary language activities. *See* English Language Learners.
word play: jokes, puns, riddles, tongue twisters, **T74–T75, T173,** T214, R27

See also Links, content area; Vocabulary, building.

Language games, T76, T77, T148, T149, T221

Language mechanics. *See* Mechanics, language.

Learning styles, activities employing alternate modalities to meet individual, T67, T138, T139, T211. *See also* Reaching All Learners.

Lesson plans
daily, T24–T25, T96–T97, T168–T169
Managing Flexible Groups, T26–T27, T98–T99, T170–T171

Lessons, specific
comprehension, **T68–T69, T140–T141, T212–T213**
decoding, **T39–T41, T83–T85, T111–T113, T155–T157, T183–T185, T227–T229**
grammar, **T71, T143, T215**
high-frequency words, **T46–T47, T190–T191**
listening, speaking, **T87, T231**
literary genre, **T219**
phonics, **T36–T38, T108–T110, T180–182T**
spelling, **T42, T114**
structural analysis, **T38, T108, T110, T182**
viewing, **T115, T187**
visual literacy, **T147**
vocabulary, **T42, T70, T78, T222**
writing, **T43, T115, T197**

Leveled Bibliography. T6–T7

Leveled Books. *See* Leveled Bibliography; Leveled Readers; Leveled Theme Paperbacks.

Leveled independent activities. *See* Ready-Made Small Group Activities.

Leveled Readers
Fall Leaves, T69, T90
Fun in the Snow, T69, T89
Grab It!, T213, T235
Lazy Fox, T141, T163
Let's Grab It!, T213, T232
Looking for Birds, T213, T233
Mama and Kit Go Away, T141, T161
On the Beach, T213, T234
Summer, T69, T91
Summer Day, A, T69, T88
Tim's Pig, T141, T160
Tim's Pig Eats, T141, T164

Leveled Theme Paperbacks
Apple Picking, R6–R7
Barnyard Tracks, R3
Counting on the Woods, R4–R5
Crab, The, R10
Hilda Hen's Scary Night, R12
Mack, R2
Mud!, R7
Pearl's First Plant Prize, R8
When Tiny Was Tiny, R11

Library, using. *See* Reference and study skills.

Limited English proficient students. *See* English Language Learners; Reaching All Learners.

Linking literature. *See* Connections; Cross-curricular activities.

Links, content area
drama, *T218–T219*
language, *T74–T75*
social studies, *T146–T147*

Listening
assessing, *T34, T106, T178*
for information, *T146–T147*
for pleasure/enjoyment, *T74–T75, T218–T219*
guidelines
for demonstrating appropriate listening behaviors, *T34, T106, T178*
for listening politely, *T34, T106, T178*
personal response to, *T34, T106, T178*
prior knowledge for, *T32, T104, T176*
purpose
to identify facts and opinions, **T87**
to gather information, **T231**
to retell a story, **T159**
to think aloud. *See* Modeling, Think Aloud.
to a play, *T218–T219*
to a read aloud. *See* Reading modes.
to creative dramatics. *See* Creative dramatics.
to directions, *T146–T147*
to literature discussion. *See* Responding to literature, options for.
to oral reading. *See* Reading modes, oral reading; Rereading.
to riddles, *T74–T75*

Listening comprehension
categorize and classify, **T176–T179**
making predictions, **T104–T107**
topic/main idea/details/summarizing, **T33–T35**

Literary genres, characteristics of
drama, **T218–T219**
See also Selections in Anthology.

Literature
comparing. *See* Connections.
discussion. *See* Responding to literature, options for.
evaluating, *T32, T57, T62, T65*
responding to. *See* Responding to literature.
See also Leveled Bibliography; Leveled Readers; Leveled Theme Paperbacks; Selections in Anthology; Teacher Read Alouds.

Little Big Books, *R4–R5, R8–R9, R12–R13*

Locating information. *See* Information skills.

Main idea and supporting details, identifying. *See* Comprehension skills, topic, main idea, supporting details.

Managing
assessment. *See* Assessment, planning for.
instruction. *See* Classroom management.
program materials. *See* Teaching and management.
small groups, *See* Ready-Made Small Group Activities.

Managing Flexible Groups, *T26–T27, T98–T99, T170–T171*

Mathematics activities. *See* Cross-curricular activities.

Meaning, constructing from text. *See* Comprehension skills; Concepts of print; Decoding skills; Language concepts and skills; Phonics; Strategies, reading.

Mechanics, language
capitalization
first word of sentence, *T45, T73, T103, T117, T145, T175, T189, T225*
names of people, *T31, T127, T153, T217*
punctuation
apostrophe in contractions, *T182, R28*
apostrophe in possessives, *T110, T221, R24*
end marks, *T55, T81, T199*
period, *T81*
question mark, *T55, T199*
See also Concepts of print.

Metacognition. *See* Comprehension skills; Modeling, Think Aloud; Strategies, reading.

Modeling
student, *T49, T58, T59, T60, T62, T63, T64, T83, T122, T129, T130, T131, T132, T134, T135, T136, T155, T193, T203, T204, T205, T206, T208, T227*
teacher, *T32, T36, T37, T38, T39, T43, T49, T53, T57, T58, T59, T60, T62, T63, T64, T68, T74, T82, T104, T109, T111, T113, T122, T125, T129, T130, T131, T132, T134, T135, T140, T146, T154, T159, T176, T180, T181, T182, T183, T185, T193, T201, T203, T204, T205, T206, T208, T212, T218, T226, T229, T232, T233, T234, T235*
Think Aloud, *T32, T39, T57, T68, T82, T104, T111, T140, T154, T176, T183, T201, T212, T226*

Narrative text, *T129–T139, T218–T219*

Newsletters. *See* Home-Community Connections book.

Nonfiction. *See* Selections in Anthology.

On My Way Practice Readers
Apple Picking, R6
Crab, The, R10
Mack, R2

Onset and rime. *See* Phonemic awareness.

Oral composition. *See* Speaking.

Oral language
Phonics Library, *T40, T84, T112, T156, T184, T191, T228*
retelling, *T34, T106, T178*
See also Listening; Speaking.

Oral presentations. *See* Speaking activities.

Oral reading. *See* Fluency; Reading modes; Rereading.

Paired learning. *See* Reading modes, partner reading.

Parent involvement. *See* Home-Community Connections book.

Penmanship, *T42, T70, T86, T142, T150, T186, T196, T222, T230*

Personal response. *See* Responding to literature, options for.

Phonemic awareness
blending and segmenting phonemes, *T31, T36, T45, T55, T73, T81, T87, T103, T117, T127, T145, T153, T180, T175, T189, T199, T217, T225*
rhyming words, *R17*

Phonics
blending
more short *a* words, **T37,** *T39, T59, T183, R16, R17*
more short *i* words, **T109,** *T111, T131, T183, T203, R22, R23*
consonant clusters
with *r,* **T172, T180,** *T188, T189, T192, T198, T199, T205, T216, R26*
consonants, double
ff, **T36,** *T149*
ll, **T36,** *T149*
ss, **T36, T60,** *T149*
zz, **T60,** *T149*

consonants, final
   -*ck*, ***T36****,* *T63*, *T149*
   -*s*, ***T38****,* *T174*
consonants, final/double final, ***T36, T60****,* *T149*,
   R14–R15
vowel(s)
   short *a*, *T28*, *T37*, *T59*, *T148*, *R16–R17*
   short *i*, ***T101, T109****,* *T131*, *T198*, *T203*,
      R22–R23
   short *u*, *T76–T77*
   See also Decoding skills; Spelling.

Phonics Library
   Bill Bird, *T119*
   Brad's Quick Rag Tricks, *T191*
   Cabs, Cabs, Cabs, *T39–T41*
   Fall Naps, *T47*
   Fran Pig's Brick Hut, *T227–T229*
   Let's Trim the Track!, *T183–T185*
   Lots of Picking, *T111–T113*
   Pam Can Pack, *T83–T85*
   Tim's Cat, *T155–T157*

Phonological awareness. *See* Phonemic
awareness.

Photographers of Anthology selections
   Wu, Norbert, *T200*

Possessives. *See* Structural analysis.

Predicting outcomes. *See* Comprehension
skills.

Predictions, making and checking
   from previewing, *T39*, *T83*, *T111*, *T155*
   review, ***T140–T141***

Previewing
   extra support for, *T57*, *T121*, *T129*, *T201*
   captions, *T33*
   illustrations/pictures, *T32*, *T104*, ***T140–T141****,*
      T176, *T183*, *T192*, *T227*
   text, *T57*, *T121*, *T129*, *T201*, *T227*

Prewriting. *See* Writing skills, prewriting.

Print awareness. *See* Concepts of print.

Process writing. *See* Writing skills.

Proofreading. *See* Writing skills, proofreading.

Publishing. *See* Writing skills, publishing.

Punctuation. *See* Concepts of print; Mechanics,
language.

Purpose setting for reading, *T56*, *T128*, *T200*

Questions, formulating, *T176*, *T201*,
T204, *T207*

Reaching All Learners
   Challenge, *T35*, *T52*, *T63*, *T107*, *T124*, *T177*,
      T196, *T209*
   Challenge/Extension, *R15*, *R17*, *R19*, *R21*, *R23*,
      R25, *R27*, *R29*, *R31*, *R33*, *R35*, *R37*, *R39*, *R41*
   English Language Learners, *T35*, *T43*, *T53*, *T58*,
      T60, *T61*, *T79*, *T87*, *T107*, *T115*, *T130*, *T133*,
      T138, *T177*, *T181*, *T187*, *T202*, *T205*, *T206*,
      T211, *T231*, *R2*, *R6*, *R10*
   Extra Support/Intervention, *T48*, *T49*, *T57*, *T62*,
      T64, *T65*, *T105*, *T120*, *T121*, *T122*, *T129*, *T134*,
      T136, *T138*, *T177*, *T193*, *T195*, *T201*, *T203*,
      T204, *T205*, *T208*, *T211*
   On-Level, *T209*

Read Alouds. *See* Teacher Read Alouds.

Reading across the curriculum. *See* Cross-
Curricular Activities; Links, content area.

Reading fluency. *See* Fluency.

Reading log. *See* Journals.

Reading modes
   cooperative reading, *T218–T219*
   guiding comprehension. *See* Critical thinking.
   independent reading, *R2*, *R3*, *R4–R5*, *R6*, *R7*,
      R8–R9, *R10*, *R11*, *R12–R13*
   oral reading, *T40*, *T82*, *T83*, *T111*, *T146*, *T154*,
      T156, *T218–T219*, *T226*, *T227*, *T231*
   partner reading, *T31*, *T45*, *T55*, *T73*, *T81*, *T103*,
      T117, *T127*, *T145*, *T153*, *T175*, *T189*, *T191*,
      T199, *T217*, *T225*
   teacher read aloud, *T32–T35*, *T104–T107*,
      T176–T179
   See also Independent and recreational reading;
      Rereading.

Reading strategies. *See* Strategies, reading.

Reading traits
   Establishing Comprehension, *T69*
   Integrating for Synthesis, *T213*
   Realizing Context, *T141*

Ready-Made Small Group Activities
   cross curricular, *T28*, *T100*, *T172*
   reading, *T29*, *T101*, *T173*
   word work, *T28*, *T100*, *T172*
   writing, *T29*, *T101*, *T173*

Reference and study skills
   alphabetical order, *R43*
   graphic sources. *See* Graphic information,
      interpreting; Graphic organizers.
   library, using, *R42*

Rereading
   for comprehension, *T67*, *T82*, *T137*, *T154*, *T226*
   for dramatic role-play, *T218–T219*
   for fluency, *T82*, *T154*, *T226*
   orally, *T39*, *T74*, *T82*, *T83*, *T111*, *T154*, *T155*,
      T226, *T227*

   with feeling and expression, *T82*, *T83*, *T111*,
      T154, *T185*, *T229*

Responding to literature, options for
   discussion, *T34*, *T88*, *T89*, *T90*, *T91*, *T106*, *T107*,
      T138, *T139*, *T160*, *T161*, *T162*, *T163*, *T178*,
      T211, *T232*, *T233*, *T234*, *T235*, *R2*, *R3*, *R4*, *R6*,
      R7, *R8*, *R10*, *R11*, *R12*
   writing, *T67*, *T138*, *T211*

Reteaching, *R14*, *R16*, *R18*, *R20*, *R22*, *R24*, *R26*,
R28, *R30*, *R32*, *R34*, *R36*, *R38*, *R40*, *R42–R43*

Retelling, *T67*, *T82*, *T106*, *T139*, *T154*, ***T159****,*
T178, *T226*, *T210*, *T211*, *T226*

Revising. *See* Writing skills.

Rhyme. *See* Phonemic awareness.

Routines
   Daily Routines, *T30–T31*, *T44–T45*, *T54–T55*,
      T72–T73, *T80–T81*, *T102–T103*, *T116–T117*,
      T126–T127, *T144–T145*, *T152–T153*,
      T174–T175, *T188–T189*, *T198–T199*,
      T216–T217, *T224–T225*
   Daily Message, *T30*, *T44*, *T54*, *T72*, *T80*, *T102*,
      T116, *T126*, *T144*, *T152*, *T174*, *T188*, *T198*,
      T216, *T224*
   Instructional, *T11*
   Management, *T10*

Science activities. *See* Cross-curricular activities.

Selecting books. *See* Independent and
recreational reading.

Selections in Anthology
   fantasy
      Miss Jill's Ice Cream Shop, written by Nancy
         Shaw and illustrated by Margot Apple,
         T128–T139
      The Trip, *T192–T195*
   nonfiction
      Animals in the Cold, *T48–T51*
      At the Aquarium, underwater photographs by
         Norbert Wu, *T200–T209*
      Seasons, written and illustrated by Ashley
         Wolff, *T56–T67*
      "Ha! Ha! Ha!," *T74–T75*
      "Making Ice Cream," *T146–T147*
   play
      "Why Sun and Moon Live in the Sky,"
         T218–T219
   realistic fiction
      Ham and Eggs, *T120–T123*
      See also Teacher Read Alouds.

Semantic cues. *See* Decoding skills, context
clues; Vocabulary skills.

Sentences. *See* Grammar and usage.

Sequence of events, noting. *See* Comprehension skills.

Shared writing. *See* Writing modes, shared writing.

Sight words. *See* High-frequency words.

Singing
"A Sailor Went to Sea, Sea, Sea," *T210*, **R60**
"Barnyard Song," *T176*, **R55**
"Five Little Pumpkins," *T82*, **R54**
"My Farm," *T176*, **R56–R57**
"Mi chacra," *T176*, **R58**
"Season's Song," *T74*
"Take Me Out to the Ball Game," *T192*, **R59**

Skills links
play, how to read, *T218–T219*
jokes and lyrics, how to read, *T74–T75*
social studies article, how to read, *T146–T147*

Small Group Activities. *See* Ready-Made Small Group Activities.

Social studies activities. *See* Cross-curricular activities.

Songs. *See* Singing.

Sounding out words. *See* Phonemic awareness; Phonics.

Sound-spelling patterns. *See* Phonics; Spelling.

Speaking
discussion, *T40, T84, T105, T106, T112, T138, T139, T156, T178, T184, T228*
dictate sentences, *T53*
dramatics. *See* Creative dramatics.
guidelines for
discussion tips, *T34, T106*
raising your hand before talking, *T34, T106, T178*
thinking before speaking, *T106, T178*
literature discussion. *See* Responding to literature, options for, discussion.
retelling. *See* Retelling.
role-play. *See* Creative dramatics.
singing, *T74*
tongue twisters, **T173**, *R27*
See also Creative dramatics; Reading modes; Rereading.

Spelling
assessment, *T86, T158, T230*
consonant clusters with *r*, **T172, T186**, *T188, T189, T196, T198, T199, T214, T216, T222, T230, R26*
consonants, final, **T36, T38**
integrating grammar and spelling, *T31, T45, T55, T73, T81, T103, T117, T127, T145, T153, T175, T189, T199, T217, T225*
vowel(s)
short *a*, **T42**, *T45, T52, T55, T70, T73, T78, T81, T86*

short *i*, **T114**, *T117, T124, T127, T142, T145, T150, T153, T158*
See also Decoding skills.

Story elements. *See* Comprehension skills, story structure.

Storytelling. *See* Retelling; Creative dramatics.

Strategies, reading
Evaluate, *T32, T57, T62, T65*
Phonics/Decoding, *T39, T49, T58, T59, T60, T63, T66, T80, T83, T111, T122, T130, T131, T132, T135, T137, T152, T155, T183, T191, T193, T203, T205, T206, T210, T224, T227*
Predict/Infer, *T104, T129, T134, T136*
Question, *T176, T201, T204, T207*
Summarize, *T69*

Structural analysis
contractions with *'s*, **T182**, *T192, T206, R28–R29*
plurals with *-s*, **T38**, *T54, T120, R18–R19*
possessives (*'s*), *T105*, **T110**, *T177, R24–R25*
verb endings (*-s, -ed, -ing*), **T108**, *T120, T132, T135, T144, T221, R20–R21*
See also Decoding skills; Vocabulary, building.

Study skills. *See* Reference and study skills.

Study strategies. *See* Test Prep.

Summarizing
oral summaries, *T69*
strategy for. *See* Strategies, reading.

Syntactic cues. *See* Structural analysis.

Teacher Read Alouds
fantasy
Hilda Hen's Scary Night by Mary Wormell, *T176–T179*
fiction
Pearl's First Prize Plant by A. Delaney, *T104–T107*
nonfiction
Counting on the Woods by George Ella Lyon, photographs by Ann W. Olson, *T32–T35*

Teaching across the curriculum. *See* Content areas, reading in the; Cross-curricular activities.

Teaching and management
instructional routines, *T11*
management routines, *T10*
managing assessment, *T14–T15*
managing instruction, *T8–T9*
special needs of students, meeting. *See* Reaching All Learners.

Technology resources
address list, *R63*

Test Prep, *T57, T69, T129, T141, T201, T213*

Theme
Let's Look Around!, *T16–T240*

Theme, Launching the, *T16–T19*

Theme paperbacks. *See* Leveled Theme Paperbacks.

Theme Resources, *R1–R67*

Theme Skills Overview, *T8–T9*

Think Aloud. *See* Modeling.

Thinking
creatively. *See* Creative thinking.
critically. *See* Critical thinking.

Topic, main idea, and supporting details. *See* Comprehension skills.

Topics, selecting. *See* Writing skills, prewriting.

Usage. *See* Grammar and usage.

Viewing
nonverbal cues, **T115**
photographs, **T187**
purpose
to gather information, **T43**
to identify main idea, supporting details, **T187**
to recognize/respond to visual messages, **T115**

Vocabulary, building
adjectives, *T60, T205*
action words, *T192*
animal words, *T187, T202*
color words, *T205*, **T214**
context, using. *See* Decoding skills.
fact/opinion language, *T87*
farm words, *T187*
favorite foods, *T120, T151*
months of the year, **T78**
position words, **T222**
seasons of year, *T43, T48*, **T70**, *T79*
size words, **T150**
spelling patterns
-ack, -ap, **T42**
-ick, -ill, **T186**
-ip, -in, **T114**
See also Language concepts and skills, Ready-Made Small Group Activities, word work.

Vocabulary Readers
At the Ice Cream Shop, T128
Sea Animals, T200
Seasons, T56

Vocabulary, selection
concept vocabulary, *T74, T146, T218*
high-frequency words. *See* High-frequency
words.
story vocabulary, *T48, T56, T59, T60, T62, T63,
T64, T65, T88, T89, T90, T91, T120, T128,
T131, T132, T135, T136, T160, T161, T162,
T163, T200, T203, T204, T207, T208, T209,
T232, T233, T234, T235*
See also Decoding skills.

Vocabulary skills
possessives, *T105,* **T110,** *T142, T176*
See also Vocabulary, building; Vocabulary,
selection.

Vowels. *See* Decoding skills; Spelling.

Word analysis. *See* Structural analysis;
Vocabulary, building; Vocabulary, selection.

Word Wall, *T30, T44, T46–T47, T52, T54, T72,
T80, T102, T116, T118–T119, T124, T126, T144,
T152, T174, T188, T190–T191, T196, T198, T216,
T224*

Word Work activities. *See* Ready-Made Small
Group Activities, word work.

Writer's log. *See* Journals.

Writing activities and types
about favorite foods, **T151**
about meals, *T189*
about seasons, **T79**
about trips, *T223*
book report, **T145**
cooperative writing. *See* Writing modes, shared
writing.
descriptions, **T31, T43, T45, T53, T55, T73,
T79, T81, T103, T127, T151, T175, T199,
T223**
draw and name a pet, **T153**
independent. *See* Independent writing.
journal entry, *T56, T128, T200*
letters and cards, **T29**
menu, ice-cream shop, *R33*
persuasive writing, **T115, T125**
posters for a fair, *T101*
Plurals Picture Dictionary, *R19*
Seasons Book, *R25, R37*
sentences, *T64,* **T87, T117, T142, T151**
story, *T179,* **T187, T197,** *R31*
story sequel, *R39*
words and word play, *T77*
See also Ready-Made Small Group Activities,
writing.

Writing modes
coached writing, *T87*

descriptive, *T31, T43, T45, T53, T55, T73, T79,
T81, T103, T127, T151, T175, T199, T223*
independent writing, *T79, T87, T151, T159,
T223, T231*
interactive writing, **T53, T125, T197**
narrative, *T179, T187, T197, R31*
persuasive, *T125*
shared writing, **T43,** *T53,* **T115,** *T125,* **T187,**
T197

Writing skills
drafting
persuasive letter
writing date, **T125**
writing greeting, **T125**
writing topic sentence, **T125**
sequence of events, *T223*
formats. *See* Writing activities and types.
prewriting skills
choosing a story title, *T187*
choosing a topic, *T53, T151*
collecting magazine pictures, *T151*
proofreading
capital letters, *T223*
punctuation, *T223*
publishing and sharing
class book, *R25*
matching pictures with descriptions, *T151*
read own writing, *T115*